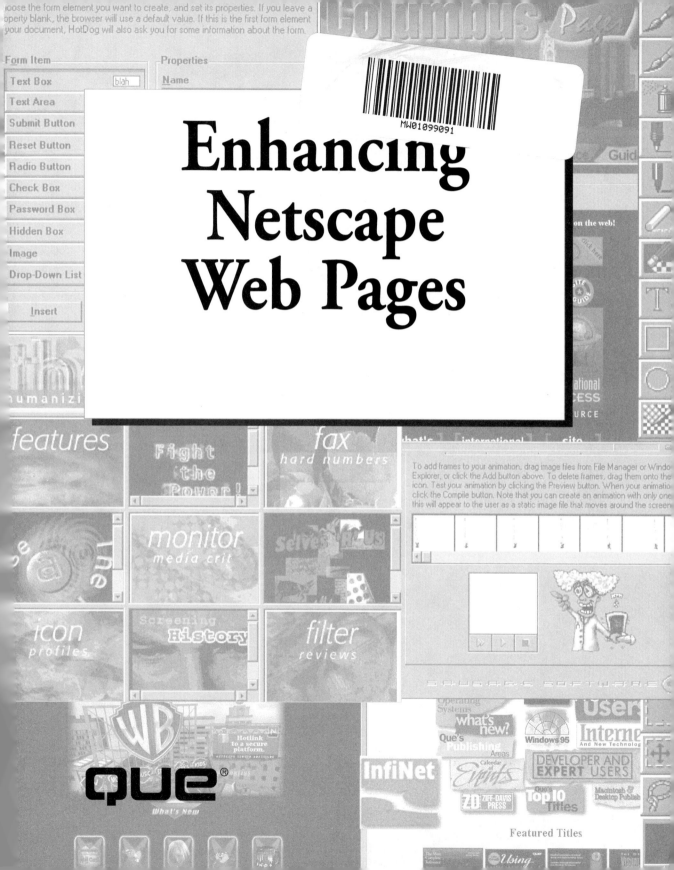

Enhancing Netscape Web Pages

MW01099091

QUE®

Enhancing Netscape Web Pages

Written by
Andy Shafran

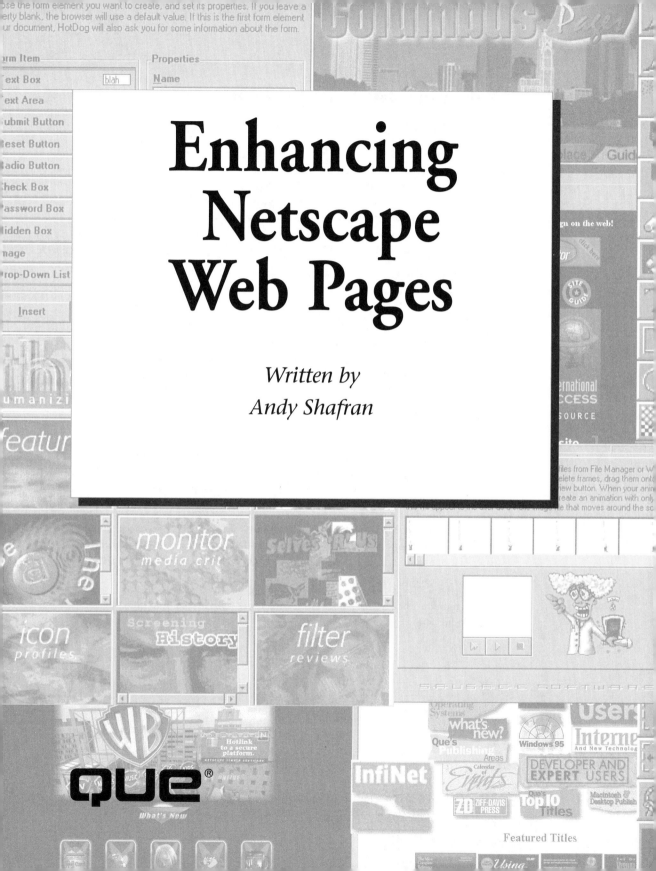

QUE®

Enhancing Netscape Web Pages

Copyright© 1996 by Que® Corporation

Library of Congress Catalog No.: 96-68039

ISBN: 0-7897-0790-x

98 97 96   6 5 4 3 2 1

Interpretation of the printing code: the rightmost double-digit number is the year of the book's printing; the rightmost single-digit number, the number of the book's printing. For example, a printing code of 96-1 shows that the first printing of the book occurred in 1996.

Screen reproductions in this book were created using Collage Plus from Inner Media, Inc., Hollis, NH.

Composed in *Stone Serif* and *MCPdigital* by Que Corporation

Credits

About the Author

Andy Shafran has been writing computer books for several years. He enjoys working with the Internet, World Wide Web, and related information technologies such as Lotus Notes. Born in Columbus, Ohio, Andy recently graduated from Ohio State University with a degree in Computer Science Engineering. He has written several other computer books for Que including *Creating Your Own Netscape Web Pages*, *The Complete Idiot's Guide to CompuServe*, and *Easy Lotus Notes (R3)*.

When he's not writing, Andy enjoys live theater, particularly Broadway shows. He also loves traveling abroad and is constantly making excuses to buy yet another plane ticket to a foreign country. You can talk to Andy via e-mail at **andy@shafran.com** or visit his WWW page at **http://www.shafran.com**.

Acknowledgments

Although I wrote this book, many, many people put in significant effort to making this book a reality. Most importantly, I'd like to acknowledge Liz Muska, for abandoning me for another couple of months while I worked on this project.

As with any book, it takes an entire team of people to go through the whole writing and publishing process. There are many people who really helped me along the way, and I'd like to thank a few of them individually. Jan Miller, whose JavaScript insights proved useful. Matt Wright and Matt Kruse for their great CGI scripts. Bill Gerrard for letting me profile his personal Web page. Scott Lanes for hosting my new Web page at his site. Lisa Swayne who helped me negotiate through some rough spots. Steve Hawley and Sherry Northrop for valuable information of their company and product. Chris Skinner, Stephen Wassell, and Tory Smith for their examples and samples.

I'd also like to thank the hundreds of people who've sent me e-mail on my first Netscape book and during the process of writing this one. They really helped me focus this book to the right audience and put together a cohesive, usable, and entertaining book on enhanced Web pages.

Additionally, there are several individuals at Que who I'd like to thank individually. Jim Minatel helped me create this book from scratch, and through his experience helped me put together a solid publication. Stephanie Gould and Debbie Abshier were excellent acquisitions editors and successfully put up with my constant challenges to the imposed deadlines. Oran Sands put together the CD-ROM that accompanies this book. Maureen Schneeberger was an insightful editor whose poignant comments helped improve the text. Marty Wyatt served as a solid technical editor. Patty Brooks and Andrea Duvall also helped significantly by quickly sending me books and software so I could meet my ludicrous deadlines. The entire team at Que has been fantastic to work with. In exchange for getting such a good team, I had to promise never again to fly overseas the day the book gets finished.

We'd Like To Hear from You!

As part of our continuing effort to produce books of the highest possible quality, Que would like to hear your comments. To stay competitive, we *really* want you, as a computer book reader and user, to let us know what you like or dislike most about this book or other Que products.

You can mail comments, ideas, or suggestions for improving future editions to the address below, or send us a fax at (317) 581-4663. For the online in-clined, Macmillan Computer Publishing has a forum on CompuServe (type **GO QUEBOOKS** at any prompt) through which our staff and authors are available for questions and comments. The address of our Internet site is **http://www.mcp.com** (World Wide Web).

In addition to exploring our forum, please feel free to contact me personally to discuss your opinions of this book: I'm **jminatel@que.mcp.com** on the Internet.

Thanks in advance—your comments will help us to continue publishing the best books available on computer topics in today's market.

Jim Minatel
Product Development Specialist
Que Corporation
201 W. 103rd Street
Indianapolis, Indiana 46290
USA

Contents at a Glance

Contents

2 Getting Familiar with HotDog   31

3 Additional Design Suggestions for Web Sites   47

4 Important Details for Enhanced Sites   65

II Livening Up Your Web Page   85

5 The New Generation of HTML Tags   87

6 Framing Your Work   105

III **Multimedia**   **175**

Appendixes   **295**

A References Used in This Book   **297**

B How To Register Your Own Domain Name   **305**

Introduction

In the movie business, sequels are almost never as good as the originals. The same story line can only be reworked a finite number of times before the audience gets bored and watches something else. This book exists to show you that the same rule doesn't apply to computer books. In many ways, *Enhancing Netscape Web Pages* picks up right where *Creating Your Own Netscape Web Pages* left off—and is thus a sequel. But it's much more than that. This book talks about the newest and most useful features that let you create cool and enhanced Web pages.

Within the covers of this book, I'll lead you through many different ways of modifying and updating your Web pages so that they are on the cutting edge, are put together well, and, most importantly, look great. You'll work with emerging technologies and limited scripting and programming languages, and learn some of the hottest professional WWW design tips.

Before you start learning though, start off by flipping through this introduction. In it, you'll learn a lot of the important assumptions and conventions that are prevalent throughout the whole book. I'll go over who this book is intended for, what you'll learn, and even summarize each chapter for quick reference. You'll learn why this book is vital to your WWW library and it will teach you how to have the most stunning Web pages out there.

Continue reading and I hope you enjoy *Enhancing Netscape Web Pages*.

What You'll Learn in This Book

As you start reading this book, you'll learn a lot of new information that can help enhance your Web page. Whether it's understanding a new technology or incorporating important design considerations, I've carefully written this book to bring you through the entire process of enhancing your existing Web pages.

Specifically, in this book, you'll learn how to do the following:

- Work with important new Netscape features and tags
- Use HotDog and HotDog Pro to build and update your Web pages interactively
- Redesign your Web pages using Netscape frames
- Build a new level of interaction using client-side image maps
- Learn how to build your own cool graphics from scratch
- Add animation and special effects to your pages
- Enhance your page's multimedia capabilities with the new Netscape plug-ins
- Feature forms on your home page
- Build simple CGI scripts, JavaScript applets, and Java worlds
- Make your Web page sizzle with professional-looking design tips and considerations
- Maintain larger Web sites filled with many different pages and media clips
- Register your own unique Internet domain name

Practicality is Its Own Virtue

This book is written from a very specific point of view—trying to answer "how can I enhance my Web page?". In a practical and easy-to-understand manner, I'll answer that question thoroughly, so that by the end of this book, you'll have a solid handle on all the changes the Web is presenting and use them to your advantage.

With that goal in mind, this book is organized into practical and usable blocks of text. Each chapter is relatively concise and to the point. I don't waste your time (or mine) teaching you how to use some farfetched HTML tag, or adding an obscure new element to your home page. Instead, I focus on how to make your changes quickly and easily. You'll find that I mix real life Web pages with contrived examples to show how different features can be used when enhancing Web pages. I'll give you the URL of every page I discuss so that you can see that site for yourself.

Who is This Book For?

Everyone who has used the World Wide Web and has made an attempt at creating their own Web page will find this book useful. Combined with

Creating Your Own Netscape Web Pages, this book guides you through the whole process of creating, enhancing, and livening up pages on the Web.

I've tried to gear the topics so that even the absolute beginner will find this book useful. But in general, individuals who have seen and used the Web to build Web pages will get the most value out of the next 13 chapters.

Following are some assumptions that I've made about you while writing, organizing, and putting together this book. By always keeping these assumptions in mind, you'll find that this book is geared for someone who has a Web page already, likes to use Netscape, and doesn't want to learn every detail there is to know about Web pages:

- **You use the Web**—This book helps you enhance your pages and incorporate some of the neat innovations that you've probably seen on the Web. I assume that you already have your own Internet connection of some type and know your way through the WWW. Terms like *bookmarks*, *URLs*, and *HTML* should sound familiar to you.

- **You have a Web page**—To enhance your Web page, you've got to start from somewhere. This book shows you how to build on your existing page to add innovative features to it. You won't find much of an introduction to HTML or an explanation of how to use lists and tables—I assume you already know that stuff, or have another book (like *Creating Your Own Netscape Web Pages*) to show you.

- **You use Netscape 2.0**—Probably the biggest and most important assumption, much of the information contained in this book will only work if you're using Netscape Navigator 2.0—the world's most popular WWW browser. Later in this introduction, I'll show you where to pick up the latest version of Netscape, and throughout the book, I'll remind you when you are using a Netscape 2.0 only feature.

What This Book Isn't

No book can be everything. Technology is constantly changing, books don't often have 2,500 pages, and you, the reader, don't need to worry about every detail about the Web that exists.

I've tried to include the information that you would find most valuable when trying to enhance your Netscape Web pages. While I try to cover new technology, the World Wide Web is an evolving project and new enhancements are constantly being introduced. In this book, you'll find some of the most popular and useful enhancements that exist. But you won't find a comprehensive list of the HTML tags such as images and URLs.

Also be aware that topics such as CGI scripting, JavaScript, and Java can require advanced programming knowledge to take full advantage of their possibilities. Instead of teaching you how to be a great programmer, I focus on introducing you to these new technologies and show you how to use them with several examples.

How This Book Helps Enhance Your Web Page

This book is split up and organized to be read in logical order of the degree of difficulty. Divided into four different sections and 13 chapters, I've covered a lot of material that can enhance the presentation of your Web page significantly.

Although meant to be read in order, you'll probably find that each chapter is structured so that you can read it individually. Each chapter is more or less self-contained and dissects an issue thoroughly and completely in byte-size readable chunks. So, if you want to skip straight to Chapter 10 and learn all about Netscape plug-ins, you aren't required to read Chapters 1 through 9 first, but they may help.

This section breaks down each part of the book and explains what information you can expect to learn on a chapter-by-chapter basis.

Part I: Taking Advantage of Netscape Only

In this initial part of the book, you'll learn about many new features and tags that are built into Netscape 2.0. Chapter 1, "Understanding the WWW Evolution and Netscape's Revolution," talks about the exploding proliferation of the WWW and how Netscape is dominating the browser market. I'll also introduce you to many of the new features in Netscape 2.0 and spend a few pages reviewing some of the important basic HTML tags you should be familiar with already.

Building on the first chapter, Chapter 2, "Getting Familiar with HotDog," discusses the HotDog Web page editor and how to use it as an interactive tool to build and enhance your Web pages. A widely-used product, HotDog lets you modify your pages and easily lets you incorporate many of the features discussed in this book.

The next two chapters help tie all of your Web knowledge together by focusing on important issues that Web developers should be aware of when creating attractive and enhanced Web pages. Chapter 3, "Additional Design Suggestions for Web Sites," brings several useful design suggestions to the table and talks about important issues to keep in mind when using some of the new Netscape enhancements.

Meanwhile, Chapter 4, "Important Details for Enhanced Sites," talks about development and maintenance issues that experienced Web users and Web page creators may want to use and keep in mind. You'll learn ways to maintain large Web sites and about legal issues to keep in mind when working with the Internet and WWW.

Part II: Livening Up Your Web Page

After working through many new general Netscape features, this part shows you how to liven up your Web page and add a new level of attractive graphics and interaction. Chapter 5, "The New Generation of HTML Tags," discusses the new and advanced HTML tags that can be used. You'll learn all about HTML 3, some advanced color and imaging tags that only Netscape supports, and how to include special characters and math equations on your Web pages. I'll even spend some time talking about some non-Netscape features—such as the Microsoft extensions—to explain other evolving Web technology.

Chapter 6, "Framing Your Work," brings you up to speed with Netscape frames. Serving as powerful navigational and user interface tools, frames let you organize and split up your Web page logically and graphically. I'll show you what they are, where to include them, and how to use them correctly.

Chapter 7, "Advanced Graphics Issues," describes many advanced techniques that you may find useful when including images on your Web pages and describes useful tools for creating impressive graphics easily. You'll learn what types of images to use on the WWW and how to optimize them for quality and speed on your Web pages.

In Chapter 8, "Image Map Education," you'll learn how you can build your own clickable image maps. Previously available only with special interaction from the Web server, you'll see how you can build them into any Web page using Netscape 2.0 and some simple HTML tags. Server side image maps will also be discussed in significant detail.

Part III: Multimedia

One of the most innovative Netscape features—Server Push and Client Pull animation—is covered in Chapter 9, "Working with Netscape Animation." With nothing more than a set of graphics that depict an event, visitors to your Web site can see animated sequences of images dynamically load and change within their Netscape window. You'll learn how you can create your own sequence of images, as well as add them to your Web page painlessly.

Continue on to Chapter 10, "Incorporating Netscape Plug-Ins." Adding a new level of interaction to the Web, plug-ins let independent companies release their own products that display information directly from the Netscape Navigator window. Audio, video, and more types of interaction are easily built and added to Netscape enhanced Web pages.

Part IV: Working with CGI Scripts, Forms, and Java

This part focuses on more in-depth issues that can be incorporated into Web pages. Often requiring more of a programming background, CGI scripts, Java, and JavaScript are all discussed in this section, starting with Chapter 11, "Understanding and Using CGI Scripts." Here, you'll be introduced to the Common Gateway Interface (CGI) which lets you build scripts that interact between your Web pages and people who visit them.

Building on your CGI knowledge, Chapter 12, "Figuring Out Where Forms Fit In," is an in-depth discussion on forms. Forms enable visitors to type information into specific fields that you create to get direct feedback. You'll learn the types of forms available, how to build them with HTML, and how to properly use the data that is submitted when your visitors fill out the forms on your site.

Perhaps the hottest innovation on the Web, Java brings a new level of dynamic and graphical display to Netscape. By building simple Java programs, called applets, you have enormous flexibility at your fingertips when enhancing your Web page. Chapter 13, "Making Some of Your Own Java," introduces you to JavaScript, the Netscape preferred strain of Java, and explains several sample applets that you can use on your pages.

Appendixes

Besides the standard chapters just described, there are a few appendixes that are included for your benefit and prove to be useful when creating and enhancing your Web pages.

Appendix A: References Used in This Book

Throughout the entire book, I refer to many different actual pages, products, and tools which you may find useful. This appendix lists all the URLs that are in the book, compiled and organized so you can refer to them easily. You'll also find this same list on the CD-ROM, so you can link to these sites directly from Netscape.

Appendix B: How To Register Your Own Domain Name

Internet domain names—such as **compuserve.com** or **mcp.com**— are quickly being snapped up by individuals and companies across the world. This appendix shows you how to register your own domain name quickly, easily, and in an affordable fashion. I'll step you through the actual process and list the benefits and pitfalls to the registration process.

Appendix C: What's on the CD-ROM?

This appendix provides a comprehensive listing of the files, tools, and utilities that are included on the enclosed CD-ROM. I've spent a great deal of time putting together many of the samples and examples used in this book so you can see them work on your own computer. Explore the CD to see these files in action.

Additionally, there are many sample graphics, sound files, and video clips that you can use on your Web page as well. In fact, the CD-ROM is completely full—that's hundreds of megs of stuff for you to use with your Web page.

What's on the CD-ROM?

Included in the back of this book is a compact disc (CD-ROM) chock full of important and useful files for enhancing Web pages. On this CD-ROM, you'll find dozens of useful programs, sample scripts and applets, and images and icons of all shapes and sizes.

I've tried to include virtually all of the software discussed and referenced in this book as well as much more. Popular HTML editors, external WWW helper applications, and Netscape plug-ins are also included.

Specifically, on the CD-ROM, you'll find the following:

- Dozens of useful images and graphics for your personal use
- Many useful HTML editors and tools for creating and enhancing Web pages
- Hotlists, references, and templates discussed in this book
- Multimedia clips and demonstrations that work with Netscape and/or the Netscape plug-ins
- Netscape plug-in and helper applications
- Many sample CGI and JavaScript snippets—some discussed in the book, many there for your personal pleasure

Tools and Programs Used in This Book

Throughout the book, I focus on using existing tools to help you create and enhance Web pages. Many useful programs exist to help you through the process, and it doesn't make sense not to use them.

Many of these tools are shareware or freeware and are included on the enclosed CD-ROM; some are not. This section describes some of the tools and applications that I talk about in some detail.

Netscape Navigator 2.0

Netscape is the most popular WWW browser being used. Using it is an important requirement for viewing and using many of the enhancements talked about in this book. If you aren't using Netscape 2.0 (or better), point your current browser to **http://www.netscape.com** and follow the instructions for downloading the most current version for your computer.

HotDog

Easily one of the best HTML editors out on the market, HotDog is a shareware product produced by Sausage Software (from Australia). You'll find HotDog on the accompanying CD-ROM or you can visit Sausage's home page at **http://www.sausage.com**. Chapter 2 discusses HotDog in more depth.

Java

Although a programming language, Java is an important enhancement that is becoming more popular daily. Changes that Java is making in the WWW are already being noticed. Chapter 13 spends time talking about Java, but in the meantime, point your browser to **http://java.sun.com** for more information and many sample applications of how Java is used in Web pages.

Additional Tools

Besides those mentioned previously, many other tools and applications are used throughout the book. Image generators, animation developers, client-side mapping programs, and Netscape plug-ins are only some popular examples.

Many of them are on the CD-ROM, and I've included the relevant URL so you can always keep track of the latest version for your own use.

Conventions Used in This Book

As you're reading through the book, I use several different conventions that highlight specific types of information that you'll want to keep an eye out for:

- All HTML codes and tags will appear in FULL MONOSPACE CAPS. That's so you can tell the difference between text that appears on-screen, and text that tells Netscape what to do. Netscape doesn't care whether your HTML tags are in full caps.

■ In addition, all URLs are displayed in **boldface**. You can type them directly into your Netscape window and go directly to the site referred to.

Besides these standard textual conventions, I also use several different icons throughout this book.

Netscape 2.0 Only

This icon means that the specific HTML tags or innovative feature and enhancement are geared towards Netscape 2.0 (or better) only. Other WWW browsers, including previous versions of Netscape, won't be able to use the features indicated with this icon.

On the CD-ROM

You'll find the files, tools, references, or examples referenced with this icon on the CD-ROM enclosed in the back of this book. Check out Appendix C for more information on exactly where the file referenced is located on the CD-ROM.

> ### Tip
>
> Text formatted in this manner offers extra information that is related to the issue being discussed. You'll find personal anecdotes and experiences, specific design techniques, and general information extras in these boxes.

> ### Caution
>
> Actions and commands that could make permanent changes or potentially cause problems in the future are displayed in this manner. Also included are possible security concerns. Make sure you read this text carefully as it could have important information that directly affects enhancing your Web page.

> ### Note
>
> Notes present interesting or useful information that isn't necessarily essential to the discussion. A note provides additional information that may help you avoid problems, or offers advice that relates to the topic.

Keeping the Book's Content Current

Keeping information current and relevant can be difficult when dealing with something that evolves as quickly as the World Wide Web. New enhancements and features are constantly being updated, changed, and released.

Realizing this, I've devoted a significant amount of time to building and maintaining a comprehensive Web site that keeps you, the reader of this book, informed and current. On this Web site, I'll post corrections to the book, keep a list of new and important references that are useful to readers, and add new information that is cutting edge and not talked about in the book.

You'll also be able to leave your comments about the book and how you liked it. I'll keep this site current and you may want to visit it often. I think you'll find it an excellent additional value that you get when purchasing this book. My job as the author doesn't stop when this book gets published; it's continuously evolving.

Stop by the book's home page at **http://www.shafran.com/enhance**. Or, if you'd like to send me some e-mail directly, I'd love to hear from you. Your input and comments are critical to making sure that this book covers all the right information in an easy to use manner. Send mail to me at **andy@shafran.com**.

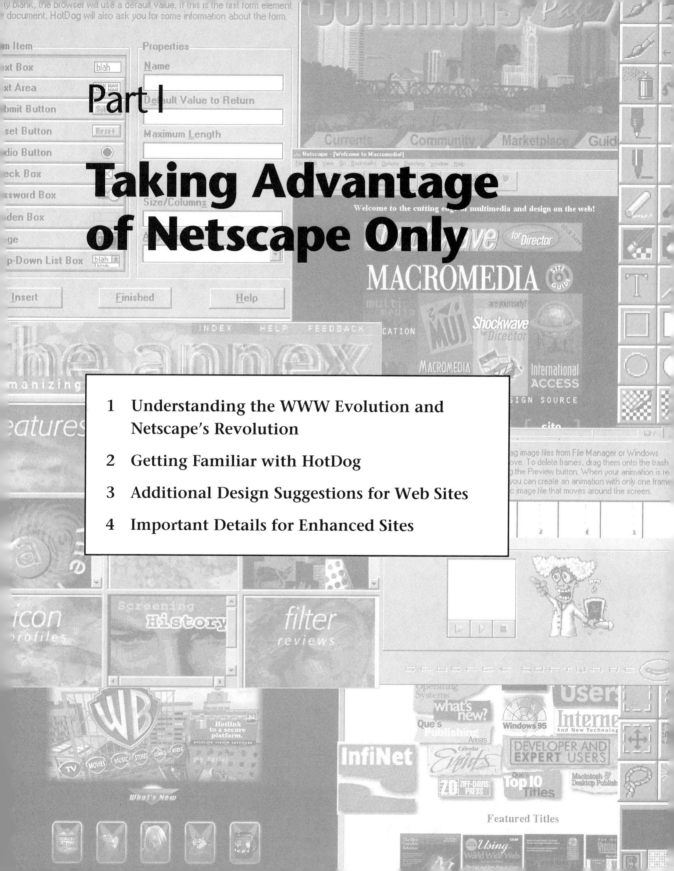

Part I

Taking Advantage of Netscape Only

Chapter 1

Understanding the WWW Evolution and Netscape's Revolution

Have you noticed that when you watch television, all of the advertisers now include their World Wide Web (WWW) address in the commercials? Everyone from Toyota (**http://www.toyota.com**) to Magnavox (**http://www.magnavox.com**) is jumping on the Web page bandwagon. Most of them use some of the exact same features that you have in your Web pages—cool graphics, lots of information, and Netscape enhancements. You also might have noticed people putting their URL on résumés and business cards. It seems as if everyone is going **http://**-crazy.

As you may have gathered, there's a reason for the increased popularity in the Web. Like you, millions of people are becoming more familiar with the Internet and online services every year, and the number of WWW users is growing at an astronomical clip.

In this chapter, I talk about some of these fascinating and important issues. You'll learn why the Web is so popular, where future technology is going, and how one company—Netscape—is riding the WWW's wave of popularity. Specifically, in this chapter, you'll learn about the following:

- The exponential and unprecedented growth of the WWW
- Netscape's unique position in the Web world
- New features you'll use in Netscape Navigator 2.0
- How Netscape stacks up to the other popular WWW browsers
- Common HTML tags you should already be familiar with to get the most out of this book

Why is the Web so Popular?

Only a few months ago, there were about 7 million users that had access to and who used the WWW occasionally. Nowadays, there's an estimated 18 million people—that's a gigantic increase (for more information on these statistics, check out **http://www.cc.gatech.edu/gvu/user_surveys/survey-10-1995/**). In months, the amount of people on the WWW more than doubled, with no end to this skyrocketing in sight. Following almost the same proportions is the number of actual Web pages available to visit. As you're likely aware of, today you have over twice as many different sites to visit, companies to look up, and things to do on the Web than only a few months ago. After three years of unprecedented growth, the World Wide Web is still expanding and reinventing itself.

What is it about the Web that makes everybody want to use it? Businesses like it, individuals like it, even the government has its act together and maintains several great WWW sites. The answer is really quite simple: we've become enraptured with the unique and interactive combination of text, images, audio, and video that's available at our fingertips. You've already become addicted, that's why you bought this book—to enhance your existing Web page into something spectacular.

It's Easy To Use

Using the World Wide Web from your home or business has never been easier. All three major online services—CompuServe, America Online, and Prodigy—include WWW browsers when you sign up; it's part of their membership. Thousands of businesses and universities have added Internet access to their employees' and students' benefits, wanting to take advantage of the enormous research and collaborative opportunities out there.

In addition, hundreds of Internet access providers varying in size offer full Internet and WWW access, all the software you need (including Netscape), and assistance through the installation and setup process for a reasonable monthly fee. Internet access has become so ubiquitous that Congress has even started to evaluate whether it should be regulated as a public service—like the telephone and gas companies.

Where a few years ago, only hard-core computer users logged on to the Internet, millions of people have added "checking their e-mail" and "surfing the Web" to their list of daily activities because the advances in technology have made it easy and plausible for virtually everyone to be "online."

Interaction to a New Level

Unlike television, using the WWW is a truly interactive experience. Users control what Internet sites they visit, how long they look at information, and where they go next. Visiting a different Web page is only a single click away.

In addition, Web pages often interact with the visitors, making it fun and exciting for people to "experience" different pages. For example, the Warner Brothers Web page, (**http://www.warnerbros.com**), shown in figure 1.1, lets you explore current movies, television shows, comic books, musical artists, and more. You can listen to songs, watch sample video clips, and even send e-mail to movie stars and their fan clubs all from your comfortable Netscape window.

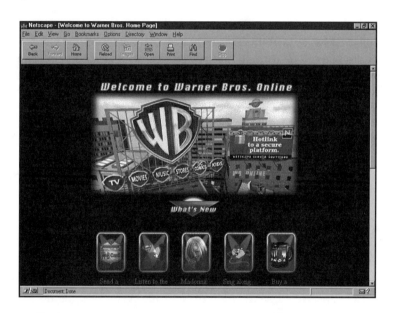

Fig. 1.1
Stopping by Warner Brothers Online is quite an interactive experience.

No longer do you have to sit down on the couch and choose from a few television stations. With the WWW, you can visit *any* site *any* time and see what it has to offer.

Creating Web Pages is Easy

Probably the most significant reason that the Web is so popular is the relative ease in which anyone can create his or her own page. Regardless of age, gender, or occupation, virtually anyone can create their own unique spot on the Web. You probably already know how easy creating Web pages really is—that's why you bought this book. You'll learn how to make your page among the best on the Internet, easily and quickly.

With the right tools, HTML tags are a breeze to learn, and you can add your own pictures, sound, and video clips, just like the deep-pocketed large companies. With minimal time, your Web page can compete with some of the best out there. This type of accessibility is important to the Web—and unique.

Netscape's Continued Dominance

Blazing the trail on the Web is Netscape Communications. With an estimated 80 percent of the WWW population using its acclaimed software, Netscape is the high-tech powerhouse that is shaping where the Internet and WWW is moving toward.

An extremely young company, Netscape issued stock to the general public in the summer of 1995. Within a few months, its stock valued had quadrupled from its original price—this is before the company had even reported any profits! Netscape intends to be the innovative force creating the new WWW technologies and making it easier for people to view, develop, and visit Web pages from across the world.

By giving its software away for free to individuals, educational facilities, and nonprofit organizations, Netscape quickly built up millions of active users. Later on in this chapter, I'll introduce several other popular browsers and point out some differences between them and Netscape.

What are Enhanced Netscape Web Pages?

According to the title of this book, you're going to learn how to create enhanced Netscape Web pages. Enhanced Netscape Web pages are those that take advantage of several unique features that were innovated and work primarily with Netscape Navigator 2.0 or better. Using technologies such as JavaScript, frames, plug-ins, and more, enhanced Netscape Web pages are optimized to be experienced with Netscape 2.0 or better.

This doesn't mean that other WWW browsers, such as Microsoft's Internet Explorer or Mosaic 95, can't be used to see your Web site; it simply means that the best level of interaction with your Web page requires Netscape.

This section focuses on the new features in Netscape 2.0 and highlights some of the best. I'll cover all of them in more detail later in the book, but I want to take you through a quick tour of some of the new innovations Netscape allows.

TML 3.0, the revolving interna-
 the latest release of the Hyper-
 by a worldwide consortium of
d independent Web developers
s can be written onto a Web page

h help you display information
ions, and more. I'll talk more
ur Web page in Chapter 5, "The

u to split up your Netscape win-
 can control how your Netscape
 each of them—giving you signifi-
ce to your Web site (see fig. 1.2).

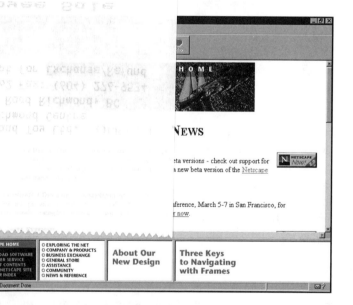

Fig. 1.2
Netscape rede-
signed its home
page with frames
to make navigating
through it easier.

Client-Side Image Maps

The WWW offers people a graphical way to make their way across the
Internet. Often using images and multiple colors, people spice up Web pages
to make them more attractive and usable. Image maps are one way in which
you can add functionality to your pictures. Image maps let you tell Netscape

to bring people to different pages on the WWW depending on where you click in an image. For example, figure 1.3 shows the Que home page (**http://www.mcp.com/que**). Depending on where you click, a different Web page appears. Clicking New Users brings you to a page describing Que's entry-level books, while clicking Internet and New Technologies brings you to an area where you can read about and order this book online.

Fig. 1.3
Image maps make images more useful.

Until Netscape 2.0, image maps could be a difficult thing to create. You had to fiddle with your Web page, create separate files with confusing codes and instructions, and then customize your WWW server to support image maps—an overall pain in the neck. Nowadays, image maps are much easier because Netscape now supports client side image maps. I'll go over the specifics later (in Chapter 8, "Image Map Education"), but the end result is that making your images interactive is much simpler and makes more common sense.

Plug-Ins

Another innovative feature new to Netscape 2.0 is the support of integrated plug-ins. Through Netscape, you can access many different types of interactive information using many different programs. By integrating with Netscape 2.0, these plug-ins work directly from your Netscape window and give you flexibility such as audio, video, and multimedia presentations. Figure 1.4 shows Shockwave, a plug-in from Macromedia (**http://www.macromedia.com**) running directly from Netscape.

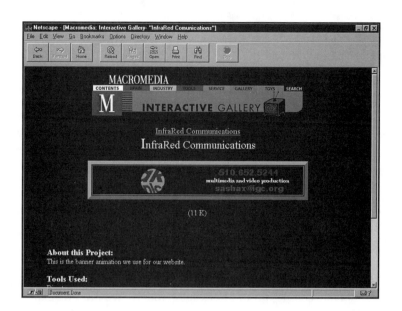

Fig. 1.4
With plug-ins, Netscape opened up new realms of multimedia to companies all across the world.

JavaScript

Out of all the new Netscape 2.0 enhancements, Java and JavaScript are creating the most noise. Java is a new programming language pioneered by Sun Microsystems that allows anyone to create interactive programs that display just like HTML does in your Netscape window (see fig. 1.5). JavaScript is a simplified version of Java that you'll learn how to use and create applets with in Chapter 13, "Making Some of Your Own Java."

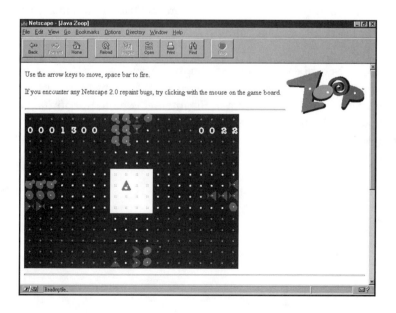

Fig. 1.5
You can play a sample of Zoop! (**http://www.zoop.com**) directly from Netscape.

Where the Other Browsers Are

Although Netscape is by far the most popular browser on the WWW, it certainly isn't the only one. This book spends a lot of time focusing on how you can build enhanced Web pages that use many of Netscape's new features; but, there are some other browsers that you may want to take a look at.

It's important to be familiar with other popular browsers when you are trying to create a Web page that looks good for everyone, not just Netscape users. It's always a good idea to test out your Web page with another browser just to make sure it looks presentable.

This section profiles some of the other popular WWW browsers out there, tells you where you can find them, and describes when you might want to consider using one of them instead of Netscape.

Internet Explorer

On the CD

The most notable competition to Netscape is Microsoft's Internet Explorer. Internet Explorer is another state-of-the-art browser that supports many of the new features introduced by Netscape. Tables, client side image maps, and, soon, Java and plug-ins, all work with Microsoft's Web browser.

Figure 1.6 shows the Microsoft Web page where you can download Internet Explorer (**http://www.microsoft.com/windows/ie/ie.htm**). Internet Explorer is a full-featured Web browser that supports many of the same innovations you'll find in Netscape—and some unique ones as well. Microsoft has introduced several new HTML tags that are only supported by Internet Explorer. These new tags offer advanced picture and background image support as well as innovative ways to incorporate sound and multimedia into Web pages.

Most likely, Netscape will incorporate most of Microsoft's extensions, much as Microsoft supports several tags that were introduced by Netscape. See Chapter 5 for a brief introduction to the Internet Explorer specific tags and how you can add them to your Web page as bonuses to Internet Explorer visitors. I've included a version of Internet Explorer on the CD-ROM in the back of this book.

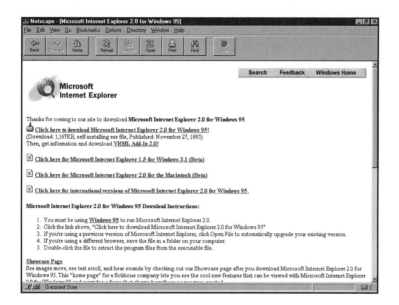

Fig. 1.6
Microsoft's
Internet Explorer
is the best
alternative if you
decide not to use
Netscape all the
time.

Mosaic

The original predecessor to Netscape, Mosaic was developed by students working at the National Center for Supercomputing Applications, the same group of people that went on to write Netscape.

Nowadays, Mosaic has been licensed to many popular companies. Mosaic 95 is the latest and greatest version and compares very nicely to Netscape. Mosaic 95 even supports the new image format PNG which is slowly replacing older GIFs (for more on PNG, see Chapter 7, "Advanced Graphics Issues").

Visit the Spry Home page at **http://www.spry.com** to get a firsthand look at Mosaic 95 and all the features that it includes.

HotJava

During the development of Java, the interactive object oriented programming language supported by Netscape, Sun Microsystems created its own personal WWW browser that was optimized to execute Java programs, called applets.

Although it isn't nearly as robust a WWW browser as Netscape or some of the others mentioned previously, HotJava does let you automatically run and display interactive Java applications. HotJava is destined to be used mainly by people who are Java developers or who spend a lot of time visiting Java specific Web pages. Figure 1.7 shows the Java home page.

Fig. 1.7
The Sun
Microsystems Web
page has a lot of
Java-related
information.

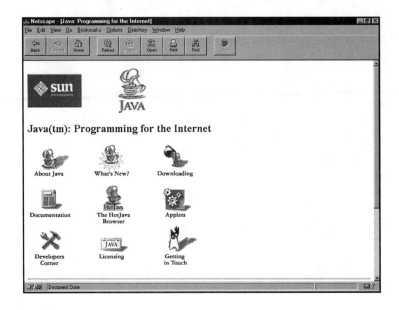

Currently still in testing stages only, HotJava can be downloaded from
http://java.sun.com. As of this writing, HotJava only supports an older
version of the Java language. By the time you read this, there will likely be a
new version of Java designed to support the 1.0 specifications of this new
programming language.

Levels of HTML

HTML is a special set of textual tags that tell programs such as Netscape how
to display information on a computer screen.

Not quite a programming language, HTML has a very specific format that
must be followed in order to properly mark up text accordingly. This format
is set and is a community standard so that everyone in the world recognizes
how HTML tags should be used and formatted. This community standard is
known as the Document Type Definition, or DTD.

The first DTD of HTML was release 1.0 which introduced HTML to the
Internet. Not long afterward, HTML version 2.0 was created. HTML 2.0 was
more robust and well thought-out to better handle some of the issues that
were affecting the WWW. HTML 2.0 introduced many new types of tags and
supported all of the original 1.0 tags, as well

Recently, discussion has been ongoing for the next release of HTML, version 3.0. While not yet finalized, HTML 3.0 is a significant enhancement over the current level of HTML and includes new features that were proposed by Netscape, and individual users from across the world.

> **Note**
>
> As of this writing, debate over HTML 3.0 is still occurring, and it's anybody's guess when all the issues will get hammered out. You can take a look at the complete proceedings of HTML language development and even participate. Go to the Web Consortium's home page at **http://www.w3.org** for more information.

In this book, I cover many new Netscape enhancements that aren't included in HTML 3.0. This means that for you to get the most out of these extensions, you've got to be using Netscape to view your pages. Eventually, many of these new Netscape enhancements will make it into HTML 3.0 or perhaps the next standard level of HTML; but, because they are so new, many people haven't even begun testing them thoroughly yet, let alone used them to enhance their Web pages.

A Quick Review of HTML

As a service to most of the readers who aren't HTML programmers and experts, I've included this section to serve as a hands-on reminder to how to work with many popular and common HTML tags. All of these tags are discussed in much more detail in Que's *Creating Your Own Netscape Web Pages*. This section reviews many popular HTML tags that you should know how to use and are familiar with.

I'll highlight the tags that I feel are important to remember, and show you an example or two of how Netscape displays them. You can use any HTML editor to create these tags—my personal favorite is HotDog, which I talk about in significant detail in the next chapter.

By no means is it a comprehensive list of every HTML tag and their specific quirks and uses. Instead, it is meant to serve as a quick reminder to how many popular tags are used.

The Basic *<BODY>* and *<HEAD>* Tags

When writing and creating a Web page, all your HTML codes and tags should be surrounded by the <HTML> and </HTML> tags. This tells Netscape and other browsers that it can expect to find other HTML tags in this file.

Netscape Only

Similarly, you should also make a practice of using the <HEAD> and <BODY> tags as well to surround the corresponding areas of your Web page. Use <HEAD> and </HEAD> to indicate the Web page's title and important header information. Within the <HEAD> tags, you'll want to specify which text appears in the Netscape title bar at the top of the screen using the <TITLE> tags.

The <BODY> and </BODY> tags should surround the rest of the HTML within your document. Before you type anything else, your Web page should look like this:

```
<HTML>
    <HEAD>
    <TITLE> Welcome to my Home Page </TITLE>
    </HEAD>
    <BODY>
    </BODY>
<HTML>
```

Tip

It's important to use the <HEAD> and <BODY> tags because information that is marked with those specific tags is sometimes added to comprehensive indexes across the Web automatically.

Header

To display headlines on your Web page, you need to use the *heading* tags. There are six different pairs of heading tags ranging from 1–6 (with 1 being the largest). They indicate what size marked text should appear on-screen. For example, I use the <H1> tag at the top of every Web page to present a large headline:

```
<H1> Here's my large heading </H1>
```

Figure 1.8 shows the sample<H1> tag listed above, and a good comparison in size appearance for the other five sizes of headings.

Fig. 1.8
Compare the six different sizes of headings available to you.

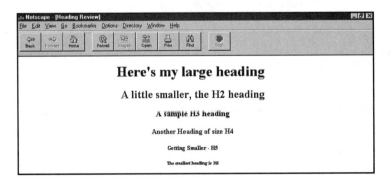

Text Attributes

To indicate how text should be displayed, there are a handful of tags that you use to surround specific blocks of text. Text can appear in **bold**, *italic*, or blinking. The following table lists common tags that affect how text shows up in Netscape:

`<B>` or `</B>`	Makes text appear in **bold**
`<STRONG>` or `</STRONG>`	Similar to bold above
`<I>` or `</I>`	Marks text to appear in *italics*
`<EM>` or `</EM>`	Works the same as `<I>` above—short for adding *emphasis* to text
`<BLINK>` or `</BLINK>`	Text intermittently blinks on and off (should be used in moderation)
`<CENTER>` or `</CENTER>`	Centers a line or multiple lines of text automatically in the Netscape window

Lists

Used to structure and organize information on your Web page, lists come in several different flavors:

- **Ordered**—An ordered list automatically numbers each list element incrementally. Using the `<OL>` and `</OL>` tags, you can surround your list items and create a stepped sequence of information.

- **Unordered**—Similar to ordered lists, unordered lists remove the numbering scheme and replace them with small bullets. Use `<UL>` and `</UL>` when numbering your information isn't important, but keeping the list format and organization features is.

- **Definition**—As you'd expect, a definition list lets you emulate the way a dictionary presents words of information. By using the `<DL>` and `</DL>` tags, Netscape displays two lines of information for each item in a list.

Within each list, you specify each element separately using the `<LI>` tag (except for a definition list, which uses `<DT>` and `<DD>` to define each title and definition of your list elements). Take a look at the following simple unordered list:

```
<UL>
     <LH> Some of my favorite classes
     <LI> Art History
     <LI> French Culture and Civilization
     <LI> White Water Rafting (not with the Clintons)
     <LI> World Wide Web Programming
</UL>
```

Figure 1.9 shows how this simple list looks from Netscape, and also displays an ordered and a definition list as well.

Fig. 1.9

Lists are one of the most important basic features to be familiar with.

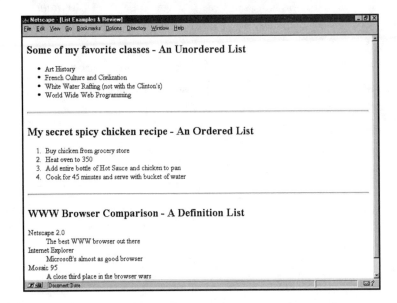

Tip

Netscape has several cool enhancements when you use lists on your Web page. Make sure you learn about those innovative HTML tags by reading *Creating Your Own Netscape Web Pages*.

Tables

Another way of organizing information on a Web page is by creating a table. Tables look similar to spreadsheets because they have multiple rows and columns, and you've got to specify what information goes in each and every cell.

Tables require several tags to work properly. First, you've got to surround the entire table with the <TABLE> and </TABLE> tags. Then you've got to build the table row by row—one cell at a time. Take the following simple example:

```
<TABLE BORDER=4>
    <TR>
       <IH> President Name </TH>
       <TH> Election year </TH>
       <TH> Party </TH>
    </TR>
```

```
    <TR>
        <TD> John F Kennedy </TD>
        <TD> 1960</TD>
        <TD> Democrat </TD>
    </TR>
    <TR>
        <TD> Jimmy Carter </TD>
        <TD> 1976 </TD>
        <TD> Democrat </TD>
    </TR>
    <TR>
        <TD> George Bush </TD>
        <TD> 1988 </TD>
        <TD> Republican </TD>
    </TR>
</TABLE>
```

This table has four rows and three columns. Each row is specified with the <TR> and </TR> tags. Within each row, I've indicated each cell with either the <TH> and </TH> (table header) tags or the <TD> and </TD> (table data) tags. Figure 1.10 shows how this table looks in Netscape.

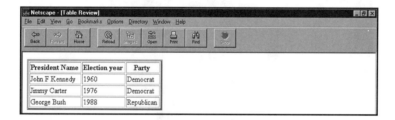

Fig. 1.10
My political table is simple, to the point, and organized better than if I used a list.

Horizontal Rules and Paragraph Attributes

Other popular tags you'll undoubtedly use on your Web page separate paragraphs of text from one another. Because HTML is a formatting language, you've got to tell Netscape where to add blank line carriages and mark the beginning and ending of paragraphs of text. Use the following tags:

- <HR>—Adds a simple horizontal line that extends all the way across the screen. It's useful for logically separating different groups of information on a single Web page.

- <P>—Used to separate all paragraphs of information. It tells Netscape that your paragraph is finished and to display a blank line before the next paragraph of text is displayed. Without this tag, Netscape doesn't know how to format your text.

-
—This line break tag separates lines of text. It works the same as <P> except that it doesn't add an additional blank line on the screen.

Adding Images

One of the most common tags you'll use is <IMG>. This tag lets you indicate what image or graphic should appear. You can embed JPEG and GIF images directly into your Web pages, like the following:

```
<IMG SRC="BETH.JPG">
```

This tag tells Netscape to add an image which is named BETH.JPG to the screen. It assumes that the file BETH.JPG resides in the same subdirectory as the HTML file that is referring to it. Figure 1.11 shows how Netscape displays my image on-screen using this tag.

Fig. 1.11
A picture of my sister Beth is displayed when I used the tag listed above.

Working with URLs

Perhaps the most important tag about which you want to jog your memory deals with linking your Web page to others across the WWW. Unlike most of the others, this tag has several different parts which I'll outline below.

To add a link to another Web page, first you've got to start with <A HREF="">. From there, type in the complete Uniform Resource Locator (URL) of the page you want to link to. For example, the URL of my home page is **http://www.shafran.com**:

```
<A HREF="http://www.shafran.com">
```

Then, you type in the text that should be linked to the URL listed above. Finally, close the tag with </A> for a complete result:

```
<A HREF="http://www.shafran.com"> Link to Andy Shafran's Web Page
</A>
```

You have significant flexibility when linking your Web page. Local files can be linked without typing in the complete URL—just the path and filename. Of course, a local file must be in the same file subdirectory as the calling link to work properly:

```
<A HREF="moreinfo.html"> More information </A>
```

Or, you can even link to other popular sources of information on the Internet such as e-mail, Gopher, UseNet newsgroups, or files using FTP (file transfer protocol).

My Web Page as a Review

Add up all of these different components, and you get a complete Web page. HTML has many different tags and unique components that are used to display information. You'll have to create your own page using some of the tags listed previously and experiment with how you want to use images, display text, and organize information on your Web page.

To get an idea of how all the different components come together to make a complete page, take a look at figures 1.12 and 1.13. Figure 1.12 shows the home page for *Creating Your Own Netscape Web Pages* when viewed with Netscape—which is accessible from my home page listed previously. Now select View, Document Source from the menu bar. Netscape displays the HTML source code of my Web page in figure 1.13.

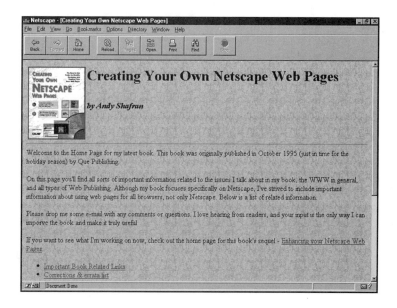

Fig. 1.12
My personal home page.

Fig. 1.13
The HTML source
code of the same
page.

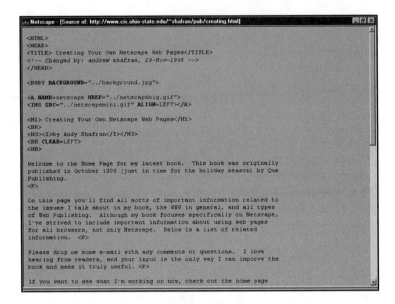

Tip

You can view the HTML source code for every page on the WWW you visit. Use this method to learn how Web pages do neat things. By examining the source code of different pages, you'll learn advanced techniques that you can use on your page in no time.

Chapter 2
Getting Familiar with HotDog

Creating and enhancing Web pages can be difficult for most people because of the sheer volume of HTML tags there are to know and remember. There are literally hundreds of different tags available that you can add to your Web page, and keeping track of them in your head just doesn't work.

That's why most people use some sort of HTML editor or assistant when creating Web pages. HTML editors are optimized programs whose goal is to make it easy for you to quickly and easily create a Web page. Many different HTML editors exist. Some integrate with existing word processors such as Microsoft Word or Lotus Word Pro, while others are separate stand-alone programs.

In this chapter, you learn about using one of the best HTML editors out there—HotDog. HotDog is a robust and comprehensive HTML editor that fits the needs for virtually all WWW developers from beginning to advanced. It's my personal HTML editor of choice, and you'll soon learn why.

I'll show you how to quickly get HotDog up and running and use it to create HTML files using most of the common tags you're already familiar with. Then, you'll learn about some of HotDog's advanced features—which make it ideal for individuals who are creating enhanced Web sites.

Specifically, in this chapter, you'll learn how to do the following:

- Install HotDog from the accompanying CD-ROM
- Get familiar with the basic, but important, buttons and commands
- Use HotDog's graphical interface to add tables, hypertext links, and form elements to your Web pages
- Customize HotDog to fit your specific needs
- Manage and publish entire sets of HTML files with built-in file project management features

Installing HotDog Standard

On the CD

HotDog Standard version 1.3.1 can be found on the included CD-ROM. Insert the CD into your drive and do one of the following:

■ For Windows 3.1, select the file menu title and the Run menu item.

■ For Windows 95, click the Start button and choose Run.

Type **D:** and hit return. You can replace the *D* with another drive for your CD-ROM if *D* isn't correct. HotDog will start the automatic installation process and set itself up. HotDog allows you to use its software for up to 30 days before the shareware version expires.

The nature of books about software and the WWW is such that they are almost immediately out of date in some capacity. In this book, I talk about HotDog Standard version 1.3.1. Since publication, a new edition may have been released and would be available for downloading. Visit Sausage Software's home page at **http://www.sausage.com** to make sure you are using the most recent version of HotDog Standard (see fig. 2.1).

Fig. 2.1
You've got to visit the Sausage home page just to see the animated car moving across the screen!

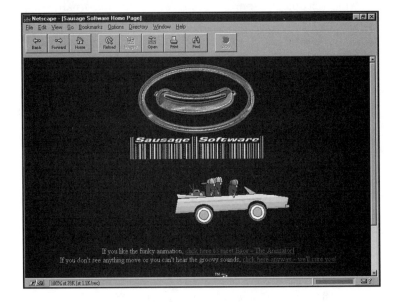

Note

On the CD-ROM, you'll only find a version of HotDog which works under Windows 3.1 and Windows 95. Soon, HotDog will have a custom-built version for 32-bit Windows platforms, Macintosh, and UNIX systems.

Besides HotDog Standard, you have another option available to you along the same lines—HotDog Professional (HotDog Pro). HotDog Pro combines all of the enhancements of HotDog Standard together with many impressive new features that advanced Web developers will want to look at. Unfortunately, HotDog Pro isn't on the CD-ROM in the back of this book—but you can download it for a free 30-day evaluation at Sausage Software's home page. For more in-depth information about several HotDog Pro features, see Chapter 4, "Important Details for Enhanced Sites."

Extending Your Registration Period

HotDog is a shareware software package—this means you are allowed to try it out for a while before you decide whether or not to make an investment and purchase it. This try-before-you-buy plan is extremely useful for people who want to make sure they get their money's worth out of a piece of software.

Once you install HotDog on your computer, you have 30 days in which you can decide whether or not you want to register and purchase HotDog. At the end of a month, HotDog will simply stop working if you haven't registered it. All you need to do is uninstall it from your computer.

If, after 30 days, you still haven't made up your mind, or your registration number hasn't arrived yet, send e-mail to **evaluation@sausage.com**. Sausage will send you instructions to use HotDog for another 30 days, free of charge.

> **Note**
>
> In order to calculate whether or not your 30 days have expired, HotDog adds a small hidden file onto your computer. This file will always be there regardless of whether or not you uninstall HotDog. This prevents you from uninstalling it on day 29, and then reinstalling the software. This practice of leaving a file or two behind on your computer is standard. Virtually every software package you place on your computer adds special files to your Windows or system directory—and rarely do they ever clean up after themselves.

Registering HotDog

Once you've decided to register HotDog, break out your wallet. At the time of this writing, HotDog Standard costs $29.95, while HotDog Pro costs $99.95. If you aren't sure you need all of the features of HotDog Pro, my recommendation is to simply register HotDog Standard, because any time in the future, you can simply pay a $70 upgrade fee to register the Professional edition. If you're serious about creating and enhancing Web pages, HotDog Standard is likely to be enough editor for you; but, as you'll learn later on, HotDog Pro has several attractive features built in.

The easiest way to register HotDog is online via Netscape. Point your browser to **https://www2.rucc.net.au/sausage/gocc.htm**, which is a Netscape secure server (see fig. 2.2).

Fig. 2.2
Notice the whole key in the bottom left hand corner? That means your credit card transaction is encrypted and safe.

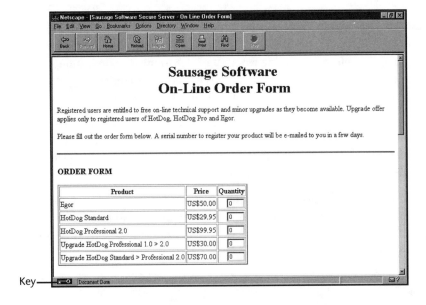

Key

Caution

This transaction is only secure if you are using Netscape version 1.1 or better. If you are using an initial version of Netscape, or Mosaic, upgrade immediately, then come back and try to register. Otherwise, you'll be sending your credit card information unprotected across the Internet. Usually, secure Web pages use **https** instead of **http** when defining the WWW URL.

Note

If you prefer to register the old-fashioned way, or want to use a check or money order, search the HotDog Help Index for registration information. You'll find the address and price of registering HotDog there.

What Can You Do with HotDog?

Now that you know how to install and register HotDog, let's take a few moments learning how to use some of the most useful and important features—adding basic HTML tags.

If you read *Creating Your Own Netscape Web Pages*, you'll recall that I spent most of the entire book showing how you can build most HTML tags with HotDog, instead of typing them yourself. Figure 2.3 shows the main HotDog Standard screen that appears when you first start the program.

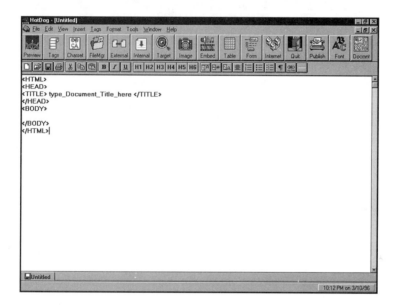

Fig. 2.3
HotDog starts you off with a bare-bones HTML document.

Notice the two rows of icons that line the top of the screen. The larger set at the top brings up secondary windows which let you add more HTML codes to your Web page, while the smaller set translates directly into HTML tags.

For example, type the following into your Web page:

- Baseball forever
- In past generations, baseball was more than a sport, it was a religion. Baseball and apple pie, that's what people subsisted on. Babe Ruth, Ty Cobb, and Pete Rose will always live in our hearts forever.

Now, highlight the words *Babe Ruth* and click the Boldface icon (the heavy *B*). HotDog adds a set of tags around those words automatically. Now highlight *Ty Cobb* and click the Italics button. Highlight the first line of your text and click the icon marked H1, which sets the surrounded text as a large heading. Your simple HTML code now looks like this:

```
<H1>Baseball forever</H1>

In past generations, baseball was more than a sport, it was a
religion. Baseball and apple pie, that's what people subsisted on.
<STRONG>Babe Ruth</STRONG>, <EM>Ty Cobb</EM>, and Pete Rose will
always live in our hearts forever.
```

Figure 2.4 shows this Web page in Netscape.

Fig. 2.4
Here's my own tribute to America's favorite pastime.

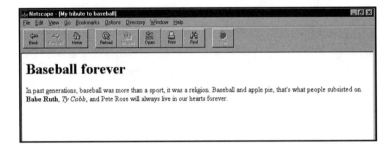

You'll find yourself using many of the icons shown at the top of the screen to create and modify Web pages.

Note

On your computer, you may not see all the icons that I'm displaying here—that's because my screen resolution is running at SVGA, or 800×600 pixels. If your monitor is only running at VGA (640×480), the last icon you'll see at the top of the screen is Quit.

Set Document-Wide Defaults

You can change your document-wide default settings by clicking the Docmnt icon (or choosing Format, Document from the menu bar) to bring up the Format Document dialog box shown in figure 2.5.

You can type in your HTML document's title and base URL, and choose from among several other options (unfortunately, the Banner option doesn't work in Netscape 2.0—yet).

In addition, you can set the base colors of your document's background and text by clicking the tab marked Graphics/Colors. You can select the type of text you want to colorize and click the Color button in the bottom right corner. HotDog brings up the Color dialog box with a selection of 48 default colors you can choose from (see fig. 2.6). Change the colors for your Web page to make it seem more exciting and fun to look at. Be careful not to use a bad color combination (such as lime green and orange).

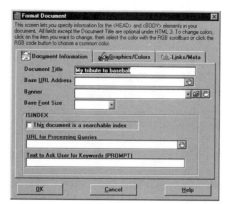

Fig. 2.5
Set your document-wide settings here.

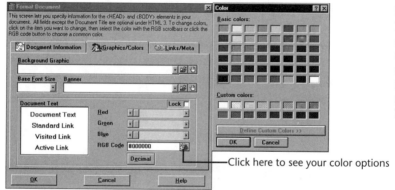

—Click here to see your color options

Fig. 2.6
I love controlling all my default text and background colors from the Format Document and Color dialog boxes.

For more information on using text color effectively in your document, see Chapter 7, "Advanced Graphics Issues."

Add Basic HTML Tags

Besides the many different icons that line the top of the screen, you can choose any HTML tag available and add it directly to your Web page. Click the Tags icon to bring up the Tags dialog box. From there, you can scroll through the window until you find the tag you want add to your Web page.

Then, using your mouse, double-click the tag from your Tags dialog box. HotDog adds that tag automatically. Take a look at figure 2.7 to see the Tags dialog box working in conjunction with my HTML document.

Fig. 2.7
Choose tags from
this default dialog
box so you don't
have to memorize
them all.

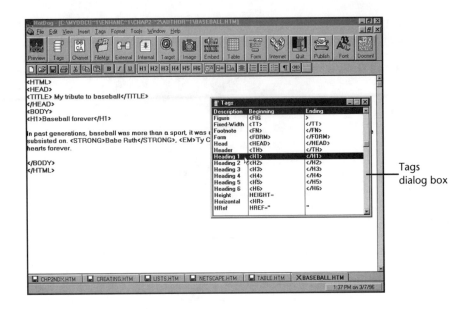

Tags
dialog box

Text Formatting and Lists

Other useful icons that you'll use often include the list-building ones, which
are on the second row of icons at the top of the HotDog screen towards the
right hand side.

Each of the icons in Table 2.1 adds the necessary code to add a list to your
Web page.

Table 2.1 List Formatting Icons	
Icon	**Description**
	Creates the necessary ordered list HTML tags and readies you to type in the first item
	Same as above, only it adds the HTML tags for an unordered list instead
	Creates the two-tiered HTML tags for a definition list—including the term and definition tags

Figure 2.8 shows the results of clicking these three small icons to add lists to
your Web page. Similarly, figure 2.9 shows how the lists appear in Netscape.

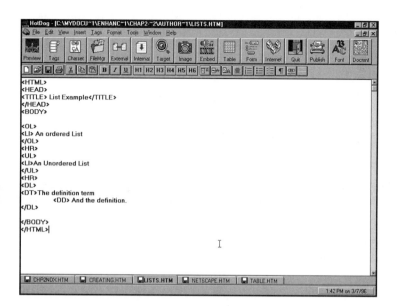

Fig. 2.8
This HTML code shows three extremely simple types of lists.

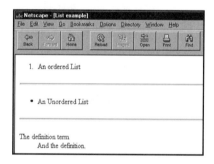

Fig. 2.9
Here are the same lists, only Netscape-ized.

Manage Your Hypertext Links

Another popular way to use HotDog is to create your hyperlinks to other documents across the WWW. Click the External icon to bring up the Build External Hypertext Link dialog box (see fig. 2.10). Of course, you need to know the complete Internet path, filename, and domain name of the document you are referencing. Without that information, you can't create a correct hyperlink across the Web.

You can also use HotDog to build and manage internal references, or anchors, within the same HTML document. Click the Internal icon to work with internal document references.

Fig. 2.10
Now my Web page is linked to some baseball information.

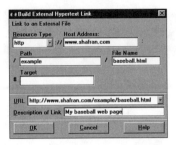

> **Tip**
>
> To avoid retyping URLs, you can copy and paste them from Netscape into HotDog. Pressing Ctrl+C copies text from Netscape, and Ctrl+V pastes it into the Build External Hypertext Link dialog box.

Link to Other Internet Resources

Besides creating links to other HTML pages, you can also create hyperlinks to all sorts of Internet services including newsgroups, Gopher, and even e-mail. Click the Internet icon to bring up the Create HyperText Link dialog box (see fig. 2.11).

Fig. 2.11
Don't forget that Web pages can link to all sorts of Internet resources.

Select the Internet service of your choice, and HotDog lets you type in the unique URL and then adds the entire link to your Web page.

Build Tables Graphically

My personal favorite feature of HotDog is the ability to graphically build tables. Instead of trying to negotiate through all the <TH>, <TR>, and <TD> tags, click the Tables icon instead to bring up the Create Table dialog box (see fig. 2.12).

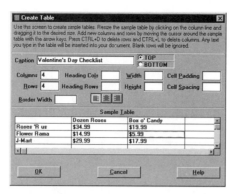

Fig. 2.12
Making tables has
never been easier.

From this dialog box, you can actually enter the information you want to appear on a cell-by-cell basis. Once you click the OK button, HotDog builds all
the HTML tags for you. Figure 2.13 shows the simple table I built when
viewed in Netscape.

Valentine's Day Checklist		
	Dozen Roses	Box o' Candy
Roses 'R us	$34.99	$19.99
Flower Rama	$14.99	$5.99
J-Mart	$29.99	$17.99

Fig. 2.13
Better buy my
sweetie's gifts at
Flower Rama!

Once you use the HotDog table builder, you'll wonder why you ever built
tables from scratch—it's that easy.

Build Forms Easily

Creating and adding interactive forms is a two-step process. You've got to create a complete HTML file, and then build a separate program telling your
Web page what to do with data once it's been entered. HotDog helps you
through the form building process by letting you add all the HTML tags
graphically.

Click the Form icon to bring up the Design Form Elements dialog box (see
fig. 2.14). From here, you can choose the type of form elements you want to
add and place them on your Web page directly. HotDog supports all of the
different types of form elements so you don't have to memorize the unique
keywords for each one of them.

Fig. 2.14

Choose from all ten different form elements for your Web page.

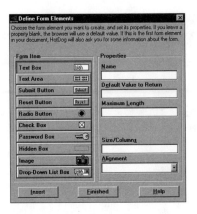

Tip

For more information on building forms yourself, check out Chapter 12, "Figuring Out Where Forms Fit In."

Publishing Your Web Pages

One innovative concept that Sausage Software has developed into HotDog is the concept of publishing your HTML files. Publishing occurs once you're finished making changes to your document. You click the Publish icon, and HotDog scans through your file and makes several changes that you specify. Then it saves your file and it's ready to be added to your Web page.

HotDog can automatically read through your file and update important pieces of information for you. For example, many people like to include the date a Web page was last modified in their file. Normally, they have to retype the date each time they make changes—and hope they don't forget. By using HotDog's publishing features, you can have the last modified date automatically updated every time your document is saved.

To use publishing features in HotDog, your first step is to customize your personal publishing options. Choose Tools, Options from the HotDog menu bar to bring up all of your personal options in the Options dialog box. Click the Publishing tab (see fig. 2.15).

There are several options you can customize. The two you want to pay attention to are Extension for Published Documents, and the grid at the bottom of the dialog box. When HotDog publishes a document, it processes through the whole file and then saves it with the extension you specify here. Set your file extension for published document. I set mine to .HTM because that's the WWW default extension for HTML files.

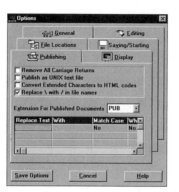

Fig. 2.15
Here are your publishing options.

Then, in the grid at the bottom of the screen, you can tell HotDog which words and phrases you want it to replace. Figure 2.16 shows a good general use for this feature. I tell HotDog that I want to replace all instances of the text [home] with a complete link to my home page. For me to add a link to my home page, all I have to do is type in [home] within my HTML file.

Fig. 2.16
Notice how [home] is defined.

Another way you can add published information is by adding a predefined field to your Web page. To add a last modified date field, choose Insert, Special, Date/Time from the menu bar (see fig. 2.17). HotDog brings up the Date/Time dialog box as shown in figure 2.18.

Netscape Only

Fig. 2.17
You can insert several different types of fields from here.

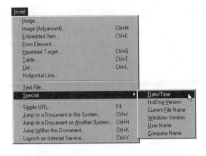

Fig. 2.18
So many ways to display the date.

Make sure the Update when Publishing checkbox at the bottom of the dialog box is selected, and click OK. HotDog adds a line of text that looks like the following to your Web page:

```
{{PUBLISH AUTO[[DATE("Long Date")]]}}
```

Once you've finished adding all the publishing information to your Web page, click the Publish icon. HotDog reads through your file and saves it according to the options you set earlier, interpreting your special fields along the way. The date field you specified now lists today's date.

Managing Projects

Another powerful HotDog feature enables you to manage multiple HTML files and manipulate them as a single project. By now, your Web page is likely to have been split into several different files—creating a Web site. Within each file, you probably have references to many different graphics and images.

As you've most likely experienced, keeping track of multiple files and images can be hairy, especially if you edit and create your Web pages on your personal computer, and then upload them to a WWW server. HotDog has many advanced and special built-in features that enable you to quickly manage an entire Web site, images, HTML files, and all. These advanced tools are discussed in more depth in Chapter 4, "Important Details for Enhanced Sites."

Using HotDog Help and Reference

One important characteristic of HotDog that is often overlooked is the extremely useful and informative Help system. HotDog has a comprehensive Help Index that goes into extreme detail on every feature built in.

Beyond that, HotDog also has examples for all of the HTML tags it supports, and shows you how to add them to your Web page. New and experienced users alike can benefit from looking through HotDog's multiple examples. HTML 2.0, HTML 3.0, Netscape extensions, and Microsoft extension tags are all covered in excellent detail. Figure 2.19 shows the HotDog reference manual for the new Netscape extensions.

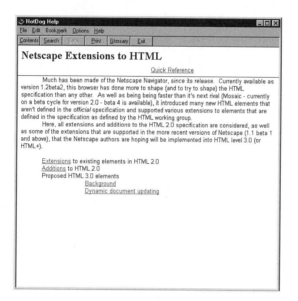

Fig. 2.19
HotDog's HTML and WWW reference is among the best out there.

You can browse through HotDog's help system by choosing Help, Search from the HotDog menu bar.

Preview Your HTML File with Netscape

HotDog is simply an HTML editor, not a WWW browser. So the text and information you type in your HotDog window always looks like regular text. Often, when creating Web pages, you want to test out your HTML and see what it would look like from a WWW browser. HotDog lets you preview your HTML code with the click of the Preview button.

Before the Preview button works properly, you've got to tell HotDog where it can find Netscape on your computer. Choose Tools, Options to bring up a list of your customizable options in the Options dialog box. Click the File Locations tab to set Netscape as your Preview browser (see fig. 2.20).

Fig. 2.20
This window lets you set all of your default HotDog directories.

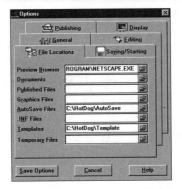

In the box marked Preview Browser, type in the full path name to Netscape. Alternatively, you can click the file icon and find your Netscape program by wandering through your hard drive. For me, my full Netscape path and filename was the following:

```
C:\NETSCAPE\PROGRAM\NETSCAPE.EXE
```

Your own path is likely to be different, but your filename (NETSCAPE.EXE) should remain the same. You can also customize HotDog to preview documents with Mosaic or Internet Explorer if you choose.

Note

If you don't want to specify any default WWW browser, you can also have HotDog prompt you every time you click the Preview button. This is useful for testing files in multiple browsers. To set this option, select Tools, Options from the menu bar and click the tab marked General. Then, select the checkbox marked Choose Browser before each Preview. Then save your options.

Chapter 3
Additional Design Suggestions for Web Sites

As you've gathered by now, creating a Web site is usually pretty easy—but creating a *good* Web site can be extremely challenging and time-consuming. That's what this chapter is all about—making your existing Web page look good.

This chapter helps you realize how to use many design strategies and concepts in your Web page. You'll learn how to create useful and attractive Web sites regardless of the Netscape enhancements you choose to work with. I'll compare Web page developing with desktop publishing and show you how to incorporate true multimedia aspects into your Web page while building a high-quality site.

More importantly, I'll introduce you to several important design concepts and methodologies. You'll be able to evaluate your Web page for yourself and see how well you follow many standard "common sense" design concepts. I'll show you several advanced and impressive tips that professional developers use on their Web pages.

Specifically, in this chapter, you'll learn how to do the following:

- Borrow desktop publishing strategies when making WWW pages
- Use popular common sense strategies when evaluating and designing your Web page
- Keep your Web page from being overwhelmed by new Netscape features and enhancements
- Interact with Web visitors in a logical and entertaining fashion

Sharpening Your Design Skills

Because the WWW is a graphical way to display information and interact with visitors, nearly every page is unique and uses a different style. Some Web pages resemble a relaxed and elegant atmosphere while others look more like an eclectic collection of text, images, and other innovative Netscape enhancements.

Regardless of the overall style for your Web page, there are several important universal details that should always be followed when it comes to creating and building Web pages.

The WWW vs. Desktop Publishing

Desktop publishing is the process of using your computer to customize the layout and presentation of information once it's printed. Posters and fliers are desktop published to integrate pictures and text in a colorful and graphical manner. This book was desktop published to display consistent columns of information and effectively add the sample screenshots, drawings, notes, and tips. In the computer world, desktop publishing has become an art with thousands of people performing these activities daily.

The whole concept behind desktop publishing is that by using your computer and mouse, you control exactly how information should appear on a piece of paper—so when the sheet is printed, there aren't any surprises. WYSIWYG (what you see is what you get) is technology that directly translates on-screen information into a printed page. Programs such as Adobe PageMaker and Microsoft Word are often the tools of choice for desktop publishers. Figure 3.1 shows a sample flier created in PageMaker that would be extremely difficult to reproduce on the WWW. With PageMaker, you get precise placement techniques, can twist and turn bits and pieces of text, and can manually control the different fonts and sizes of text that appear on the page.

Fig. 3.1
Don't even try to
create this type of
flier on the WWW.

The WWW is much different. The whole concept behind the WWW is that
everything is strictly text based. Within a text file, you use certain HTML tags
to mark how you would like information to appear on-screen. It is up to programs such as Netscape and Mosaic to decide how HTML tags are interpreted.
Web developers have significantly less control over appearance of information in this new electronic format.

For example, let's say you wanted to make text appear bold. A desktop publisher would simply highlight the desired text and change its font to become
bold. They would instantly know whether that was the desired effect for their
publication. Web developers have their hands tied. All they can do is add the
<B> and </B> or <STRONG> and </STRONG> tags around their desired text, and
hope that WWW browsers display information the way they want. Some
browsers might do a fine job bolding text, while others could achieve an
undesirable effect when interpreting the <B> and <STRONG> tags—it's out of
your control.

As you can tell, there are fundamental differences between how desktop publishers and Web developers create pages of information for display. One uses
a physical formatting to see a page being built, and the other method uses
logical formatting, relying on another program to display HTML tags properly.

Nowadays, the differences between desktop publishing and Web developing are shrinking. New Netscape and Microsoft HTML tags geared for physical formatting (such as tables and frames) make it easier to specifically plan the appearance of a Web page. There are many different desktop publishing conventions that can be easily and effectively used on the WWW without much trouble.

Logically Placing Images

One common design characteristic comes into play whenever you use images and pictures on Web pages. It's important to place the image on a Web page in such a manner so that it draws a visitor's line of attention towards the center of the screen, not to the edge. Let me show you an example to explain what I'm talking about.

Figure 3.2 shows a sample Web page describing a European vacation. Notice the picture at the top of the screen (it's me standing in front of Napoleon's tomb). See the cannon behind me pointing to the right? It's important that this image was placed on the Web page properly. Logically, when someone sees this Web page, they'll notice the picture at the top. Because the cannon points to the right, most people's eyes automatically look in the direction the picture is pointing. In this case, they are immediately drawn towards the title of the Web page on the right hand side of the picture. Simply put, when someone looks at an image, they will logically look in the direction a picture is pointing towards.

Fig. 3.2
Design your Web pages with the image in mind.

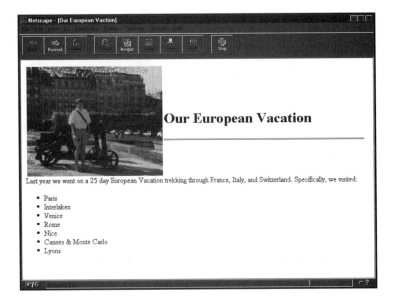

Figure 3.3 shows the same Web page, only this time the image is on the right. It just doesn't have the same effect. When you look at this page, the visitor's line of vision moves towards the right, off the screen.

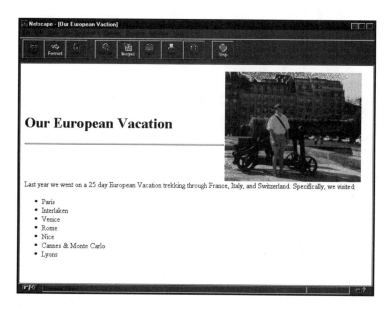

Fig. 3.3
This way doesn't follow the visitor's logical line of vision.

I call this method image visioning. Whenever you use an image on your Web page that has something that points or has a person facing a particular direction, make sure it points towards the rest of the text on the Web page. This creates a more cohesive Web page that uses the text and images to tie itself together.

Quick-n-Dirty Headlines

Learning a lesson from the newspaper industry, it's important to create concise, yet informative, headlines for your Web pages. Even though Netscape will format your headlines automatically and wrap them to the next line on the screen, in general, you want your headlines and titles to be as short as possible.

I like to think of a headline as an introduction to what I'm going to read on the rest of the page. If the introduction appeals to me enough, then I'm willing to spend an extra moment or two to read the related information. Think of the way you read a newspaper. Most likely, you scan through the stories and pick out the headlines that interest you. Then you start reading the article. If a headline is boring, too long, or confusing, you might not even look at the story.

Creating headlines for Web pages uses the same philosophy. Use headlines to draw visitors into your Web page. Make them want to scan through your entire page instead of clicking the Back button or selecting a hypertext link to another page.

What makes a headline good? That's a subjective question. Figures 3.4 and 3.5 show you one extreme example between a Web page with a good headline and a not-so-good headline.

Fig. 3.4
This headline is long-winded, unclear, and wordy.

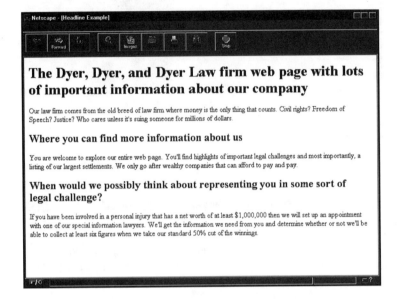

Fig. 3.5
This is a much better headline for the same Web page.

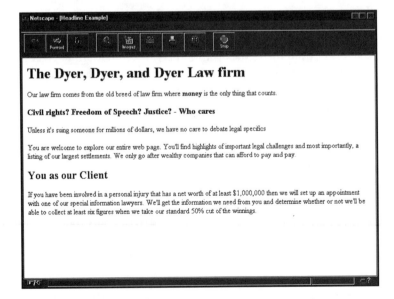

> **Note**
>
> Another way to gauge headline effectiveness is how well it stands out. Headlines can be effective tools for splitting up different sections of a Web page. With HTML, you have seven different headline sizes (<H1> through <H7>). Don't be afraid to place a large headline at the top of your page and smaller ones sprinkled throughout the rest.
>
> This has a twofold effect—it lets visitors immediately go to the subsection that interests them, and it spreads out your Web page making it easier to read.

Netscape Only

Using Lines and Boxes Effectively

Another common feature that desktop publishers tend to use is simple lines and boxes to separate and organize text on a page. Effective use of lines and boxes is more difficult when it comes to Web pages, but it can be achieved.

To add a simple line to your Web page, you can use the <HR> tag. Remember that there are several Netscape specific enhancements to how this horizontal line appears on your Web page. I use the <HR> tag to logically split up sections of my Web page.

Some people look at HTML tables as the ability to create square shaped boxes on their Web pages. By adding the BORDER keyword to your <TABLE> tag, you can force Netscape to always display the black border around each square in your table.

Figure 3.6 shows my home page using both horizontal lines and boxes (a simple table) effectively. The horizontal line separates the heading of the page from the rest of the information. It's not important that I show the table's border in figure 3.6, but it adds a succinct graphical representation of modularizing my Web page. In case you were wondering, the HTML for this particular horizontal line is the following:

```
<HR WIDTH=80% ALIGN=CENTER NOSHADE>
```

Using Empty Space Effectively

One of the most common mistakes Web developers make when designing Web pages is trying to cram too much information and too many images in a small space. They often have the mentality that a single Web page is all they have to work with and they'll fit every piece of information imaginable on it.

Desktop publishers have long valued the concept of empty space—an area on a page that is left blank to create aesthetically-designed projects. Experienced Web developers can also borrow this rule and incorporate blank space when designing their Web page.

Fig. 3.6
Lines and boxes
are important
design elements.

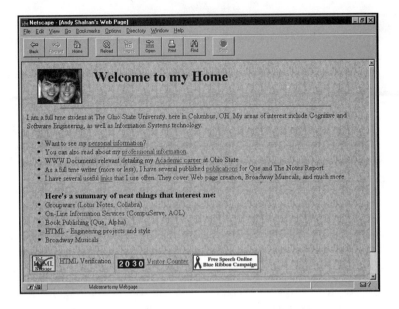

One example of a Web site which uses blank space well is Yahoo! (**http://www.yahoo.com**) as shown in figure 3.7. At Yahoo!, the Web developers have created a very simple, yet informative and easy-to-use, Web site. Notice how there is plenty of blank space on either side of Yahoo!'s list of information? That's by design, to keep the page uncluttered.

Fig. 3.7
Empty space can
be an effective tool
when used
properly.

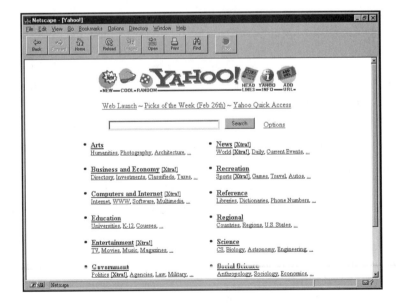

Caution

Although empty space can make a cluttered Web page appear more spacious and less intimidating, be careful when using this concept on your Web pages. You must strike a happy medium between a Web page that uses empty space to enhance its appearance and one that uses empty space to make it look sparse and uninteresting.

Mixing Multimedia

One new aspect that desktop publishers haven't had to deal with is incorporating true multimedia in a single experience. In your Web pages, you can have text, images, sound clips, and video clips all being displayed (and heard) at the same time.

Working with multimedia is a new and difficult task to master. When you add a video clip to your Web page, you want to make sure it doesn't interfere with any audio plug-ins or background sounds playing. Here's a simple recipe that you should always follow when building a multimedia enabled Web page:

1. Plan what the final "experience" should be like. Decide whether sound, images, and video clips really go with one another. Take into effect colors and styles of all images sound and video clips. Remember that you can change the color and appearance of any text as well.

2. Add all the text to your Web page. Format and colorize it properly. Make sure that text is readable when using background colors and images.

3. Add images next. Decide where images should be placed, what size they are, and make sure they are a reasonable file size to download so visitors don't wait forever to see your Web page. Take advantage of the image compression, interlacing, and alternatives suggested in Chapter 7, "Advanced Graphics Issues."

4. Now add sound. Sound is easier to work with than video and animation because it's one-dimensional. Video clips often have their own soundtracks. If you use a background sound, make sure it's not too loud. Ensure that the sound clip you pick fits with the style of your Web page—i.e., don't add the *Overture of 1812* to a Web page dedicated to Metallica. If you're using a plug-in, make sure there is a link to that plug-in's Web page so it can be downloaded immediately. See Chapter 10, "Incorporating Netscape Plug-Ins," for more information on this new technology.

5. Mix in video and animation. Often, you won't have audio clips on the same page with video clips and animations because they can interfere with one another. Check the performance of your video/animation clip to make sure it downloads quickly.

One last thing you can do is read the following section. I talk about some other issues that you should be aware of when using all of these new forms of multimedia in Web pages.

Be Aware of Creeping Featurism

Creeping featurism is one of the largest dangers that face Web developers and WWW pages. Creeping featurism is when you slowly add new and innovative features to your Web pages—one at a time (they creep into your Web pages), until eventually your Web page is full of gimmicks and features that don't look or work well together. The overall effect is that, while your Web page becomes full of "neat" features, it no longer is fun to visit, easy-to-use, or informative for visitors.

Because the Web is so exciting and has literally endless possibilities for Web pages, Web developers often fall into the trap of needing to include *every* cool innovation on their Web pages. Figure 3.8 shows a sample Web page that demonstrates a large reservoir of HTML knowledge but little effort put into good design. This example just demonstrates that you shouldn't use a new Netscape enhancement because it's there.

You'll see the creeping featurism phenomenon pop up all over the Web—particularly in sites that use video and audio clips integrated into Web pages. Many times, people are impressed with how easy it is to add multimedia to Web pages, and all their carefully laid plans for a good Web page are ignored when they get the opportunity to add a "neat" new feature.

Caution

I'm not saying you should not take advantage of any or all of these new Netscape enhancements; it's just important that you keep an aesthetic perspective when building them into your Web pages. Use them, but use them carefully.

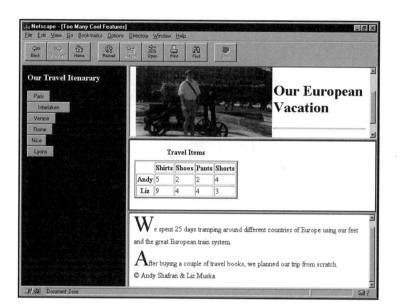

Fig. 3.8
I get a headache just looking at this page and there's no audio or video clips!

Be aware that creeping featurism isn't necessarily a bad idea, as long as you take into effect the new changes. For example, splitting your home page up with several different frames can be good—and bad. If you redesign your site to be frame dependent, you could end up with a nice effect—a well-organized and easily-navigated Web page. Unfortunately, frames also can make your page look worse—if your frames aren't large enough or if there are too many frames on the screen. You just have to control which new features creep into your Web pages and how you end up using them.

One excellent example of a WWW site that had many new features creep in is the Walt Disney Web page (**http://www.disney.com**). Originally, this site was designed to offer visitors a peek into the world of Disney. Several months ago, Disney redesigned its entire site to take advantage of new multimedia enhancements made possible with Netscape 2.0. The overall result is spectacular. Figure 3.9 shows the current Disney home page—but who knows, by the time you read this, they may have redesigned yet again.

Fig. 3.9
You'll find just about every type of WWW feature imaginable here in the Magic Kingdom—and used well.

Note

On a personal level, I get asked all the time why my own home page doesn't have spectacular animations, use lots of plug-ins, and have many integrated CGI scripts and JavaScript applets. The reason is that it is very, very difficult to build all of those features into a single Web page or Web site.

The goal of my page is to let people know who I am and provide them ample resources when they stop by after reading a book—not to impress people with my knowledge of using every Netscape enhancement. So I choose to limit what features are placed in my Web page for simplicity reasons.

On top of that, creating a good Web site that has multimedia, scripts, plug-ins, tables, frames, and more all working together in a good manner takes a lot of time and effort—more than most people (including myself) are willing to put into a Web page. For me, I simply chose a few WWW features that I liked personally and used only those.

Common Sense Design Strategies

In this section, I've put together a list of what I call "common sense design strategies"—a set of good standards that all Web pages, regardless of their purpose and style, should follow. These strategies are a list of what I think is important when you are evaluating your Web page and making it available on the WWW.

Many of the items in this section will seem like common sense—some you may not have thought of—while others will seem like second nature to you. Read through each of them for important and easy ways you can evaluate your Web page to see if you've followed common sense design.

Create a Consistent Look

Every day when you wake up and get dressed, you've got to put together an outfit. Whether you're simply wearing jeans and a t-shirt, or slacks and a dress shirt, you always make sure your outfit has some semblance of coordination. For presentation purposes, it's important you have matching shoes, socks, pants, a shirt, and even a belt.

Building Web pages often requires that same type of coordination. You want to make sure that every separate page on your Web site maintains a consistent style of appearance and usability so that they match, or fit well together.

The two easiest ways to create a consistent set of Web pages are the following:

- By sticking with the same colors and header styles on all your Web pages. For example, if you are going to use a background color or image on one Web page, it makes sense to use that same color for all of them. Giving each page in your Web site a different background color isn't usually an ideal style (unless you're a rainbow-loving leprechaun).

- By creating the same type of header for all of your Web pages.

Take a look at the set of figures in figure 3.10—they're Web pages about *Creating Your Own Netscape Web Pages*. Notice how they have a consistent look and feel about them. Each has the same background pattern, a similar header and footer, and I use the cover of the book in the same spot.

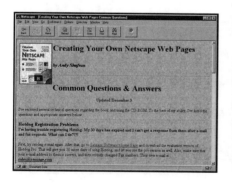
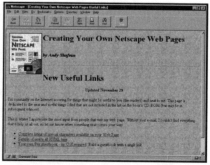

Fig. 3.10
It's easy to tell these Web pages are both related.

Besides color and header style, another way to ensure consistency across Web pages is by creating the same type of header and footer for each page. In the previous figures, each Web page has the same general style of header (an image, headline, and by-line). At the bottom of each page, there's also a similar footer—with my name, e-mail address, and a link to the previous page.

Don't Hide Links and Features

Another common sense strategy to follow is making sure that your advanced and cool features aren't hidden, or difficult to find for visitors to your Web page. What's the point of building cool plug-in examples, interactive image maps, and advanced JavaScript applets if no one even knows they exist?

Image maps are particularly bad about hiding links to other Web pages because often they aren't delineated well enough to know what all the links actually are (see Chapter 8, "Image Map Education," for more information). The Warner Brothers home page—**http://www.warnerbros.com**—is a good example of this (see fig. 3.11). It's pretty easy to figure out where you'll visit if you click the shield labeled DC Comics; but did you know that if you click the globe at the top of the building in the top right corner of the image that you also link to DC Comics (presumably the Superman theme is the reason)? How would you know that? Image maps are only useful if you know what Web page you are going to visit *before* you click on an area in the picture.

Fig. 3.11
Although a great Web site, this image map makes it difficult to find all the possible links available.

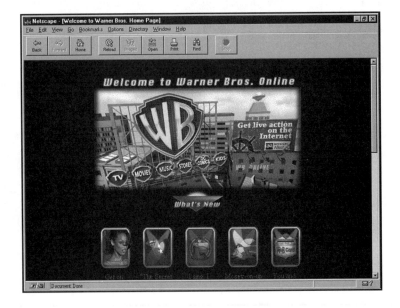

To get around this problem, many Web sites list each possible link beneath the clickable image map, to make sure you don't miss out on one particular section of the image map that you may not think is clickable. Warner Brothers follows this philosophy—to a point. At the bottom of its home page is a listing of all the main sites accessible from the image map (see fig. 3.12). You can almost match up the items listed with the various sections of the image map.

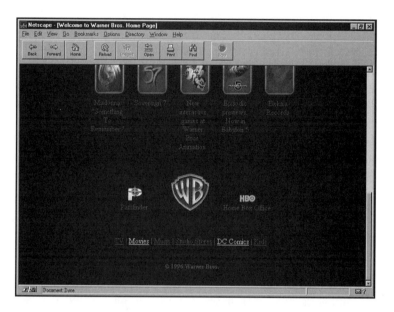

Fig. 3.12
Warner Brothers tries to list all the links available from the image map.

Even more important than using image maps, make sure all of your textual links are easy to spot. Usually you want to link an entire word or phrase instead of a single character or number. Some people don't like hypertext links appearing all over their Web pages, so they will link a single character, or the period of a sentence instead of an appropriate word. This is a bad idea and defeats the purpose of linking various Web pages together.

Get Feedback from Visitors

Adding simple HTML forms to your Web pages enables you to get direct feedback from visitors who stop by (you learn more about this in Chapter 12, "Figuring Out Where Forms Fit In"). This feedback is valuable because you allow visitors to answer questions and share their own opinions about your Web page.

If you're truly interested in hearing what other people think of your Web site, make sure you include a feedback form or at least your e-mail address so people can contact you. I try to add my e-mail address to every page on my site so that people can send me a suggestion or correction regardless of which page they happen to be visiting.

Note

Don't worry if most people don't take the time to send a response telling you whether or not they liked your Web page design. Typically, most people won't bother sending mail unless they have suggestions for improving (or complaints about) your Web page. In this case, I like to think of no news as good news.

Be a Visitor, not a WWW Developer

Once you've finished your initial page, it's time to take off your WWW developer hat and put on a WWW user hat. It's important to take the time to go through and check each and every page on your Web site. The reasons for this are twofold:

- You can catch all simple errors such as misspellings, bad links, typos, and other easy mistakes to find.
- You want to evaluate your entire Web site experience.

Imagine that someone stopped by your home page and tested everything out. They tried out your video clips, listened to a sound plug-in, even looked at pictures of your family that you made available. Only after exploring your site can you get a true feel for how a visitor might enjoy it. Some things you want to look for include the following:

- Are links to other spots on the WWW useful and fitting?
- Is the performance of visiting various pages in your site reasonable to the average visitor?
- Do your colors and images match one another?
- Could you improve your page by using some desktop publishing strategies?

Proper Interaction with Visitors

One new field of design and evaluation on the WWW that has recently become much more widespread is the integration of Java and JavaScript in Web pages. When building simple applets, oftentimes you bring up dialog boxes of information asking visitors particular questions. Depending on their answers, your applet performs a certain set of tasks.

Once you start building and creating these interactions with users, it's important that you make it easy for visitors to understand questions and know how to answer correctly. As a good example, let's take a closer look at one of my JavaScript applets I use in Chapter 13, "Making Some of Your Own Java." In this example, I introduce the Confirm dialog box inside of a JavaScript applet. I show you how to ask visitors a question (see fig. 3.13).

Fig. 3.13
This is a poorly worded question.

By reading this question, visitors have two choices. They can click the OK button or click the Cancel button. If they choose OK, the JavaScript applet continues and asks them the same question again (just to make sure). If Cancel is chosen, Netscape brings them back to the previous page that referred them.

The problem with my JavaScript applet is that the possible answers don't make sense. When I ask them "Did Anyone Follow You Here?," they should be able to choose from Yes and No instead of OK and Cancel. I'm assuming that visitors to my Web page understand that by clicking the OK button, they are indicating that nobody has followed them and mean to answer "yes."

To get around this, I could have reworded the question (see fig. 3.14).

Fig. 3.14
Now visitors know exactly which button they should click to continue.

Explore Other Sites—Borrow Design Concepts
Although I try to point out many important design concepts, you will invariably find Web pages that you do—and don't—like on the WWW. One of the best parts about the WWW is that you can completely view the source code for all pages available with the View, Document Source command from Netscape.

Whenever you are surfing the Web and exploring new sites, you should always make it a priority to keep your eyes open for new and innovative design and layout ideas for your Web pages. Feel free to borrow concepts from other sites on the WWW. The only way to learn and improve your Web site is through experience.

Where To Find Other Design Information

This chapter has only touched upon some easy-to-implement design features that all experienced Web developers should be aware of. There are many other resources out there which are solely dedicated to instructing readers how to create and design information into a usable format. The following are two of my favorites that should go into anyone's library if they're serious about learning more design concepts. Although neither one of them is geared specifically toward WWW design, it's easy to appreciate common design concepts and apply them to your own Web pages:

- *The Design of Everyday Things* **by Donald Norman**—This book is literally the bible of all things when it comes to design. It shows you, through many practical examples, the differences between good and bad design concepts. This book also shows you how you can put yourself in the user's perspective and evaluate your products (Web pages) quickly.

- *User Interface Task Centered Design* **by Lewis and Rieman**—This book is available electronically on the Internet. You can download it from **ftp://ftp.cs.colorado.edu/pub/cs/distribs/clewis/HCI-Design-Book/**. It is a shareware book that offers a practical and logical explanation of how to design interfaces, and is particularly useful when it comes to working with interactive information such as the WWW. It's worth the time to download and read. ❖

Chapter 4
Important Details for Enhanced Sites

Once you've finished the rest of this book, you're likely to have created a fantastic and impressive looking example of a WWW page. By adding many new Netscape enhancements and following the important design suggestions peppered through the book (and the previous chapter), you're one of the most experienced and advanced Web developers out there. Your pages will compare to some of the best professional Web pages.

This chapter discusses some important concepts that experienced Web developers will find handy. By this point, you've probably created many different Web pages and have had the experience of linking them together and keeping track of all your different HTML files and images. I'll show you several ways you can keep track and manage multiple Web pages.

While you may create and manage a fantastic WWW site, it's always a challenge to attract new people to stop by for a visit. Although you're already familiar with traditional publicity methods, I'll introduce you to the concept of advertising on the Web and show you where to go if this is how you want to attract visitors for your Web site.

As an experienced Web developer, it is also important that you make yourself aware of several important legal issues that could effect your Web pages. This chapter talks about copyright and pornography issues that all Web users should be familiar with.

Specifically, in this chapter, you'll learn how to do the following:

- Create a flowchart and directory structure to show how your Web site links together
- Use advanced HotDog Pro features that let you manipulate sets of Web pages easily

- Verify the links and images for each Web page at your site
- Learn where to go to create advertisements for your Web page

Managing Multiple Web Pages

Originally, you might have started with a single Web page describing just a little bit of information about yourself—maybe even including an image or two. Eventually, your Web page started growing as you added more and more information, until finally you started splitting it into several different Web pages—now you've got a Web site.

Each page has its snippet of text and information, and each one has links to different images and other HTML files. If you're like most people, you'll quickly have yourself immersed in a mess of HTML and GIF files all pointing back and forth to one another.

In *Creating Your Own Netscape Web Pages*, I talked about several different strategies for splitting your Web page into a Web site. You learned a number of possible ways to structure your Web site so that visitors can easily navigate their way through your collection of pages. Unfortunately, one of the major side effects of creating multi-paged Web sites is the confusion that can be caused.

Take my Web page as an example. I have seven different HTML pages all focused on different interests. On each page, there are links to other HTML pages in my site, embedded images and pictures, and sometimes even audio and video clips linked directly into a page. After a quick count, I realized that—including my HTML pages and multimedia files—I have over 25 separate files to keep track of. That's a lot! Imagine if I was creating a Web page for a business. I could easily have hundreds of separate files that all need to work with one another to avoid any problems.

Managing this collection of files doesn't have to be hard, but it takes patience and organization in order to keep all of your links working properly. This section describes a few popular methods for managing your entire Web site and keeping track of all your files. Then you'll learn how to use HotDog Pro—the advanced version of the HotDog HTML editor—to manage your Web site for you.

The Flowchart Method

You probably already use this method—even if you aren't aware of it. The flowchart method is when you create a large map—either in your head or actually on paper—and draw all of the HTML pages and files in your Web site.

This method is particularly useful when you have a medium-sized Web site (7–10 pages and under 20 images), because you can chart out your whole Web site on a single page. Figure 4.1 is a sample flowchart for my Web site.

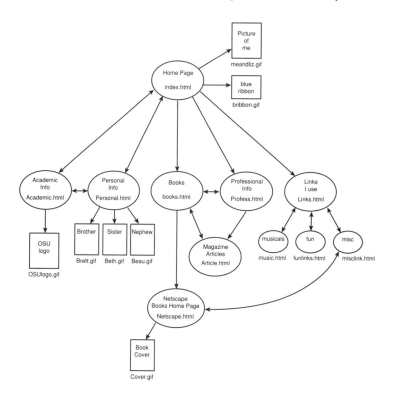

Fig. 4.1
Creating a flowchart of how your pages link together is vital to managing your Web site.

Notice how in my flowchart I use circles to represent HTML pages and squares to represent images. Each circle and square on the flowchart is connected with a line. The arrow at the end of the line indicates that a link to that file is built into a particular HTML page. Most of my links between pages work both ways—meaning that I can go back and forth between these Web pages. But some of them only work one way. For example, there is a link from the Professional Info page to Magazine Articles, but not one back to Professional Info—that's just how I set up my Web site. I've included the filenames on my flowchart so that I know which particular file is associated with a particular image or topic.

Try creating a flowchart for your Web site—it isn't difficult or time-consuming. Now, you have a map of how your pages are organized and how they link to one another. But the real benefit to flowcharting your Web site is achieved when you start to make changes to your pages.

Take my flowchart as an example. What if I changed the OSU logo that is saved as an image? I want to replace OSULOGO.GIF with NEWLOGO.GIF. By looking at my flowchart, I instantly know that I've got to update two pages—Academic Info and Personal Info—to reflect the new image's filename. Without the flowchart, I might have only made one change and forgot about the other. As you can tell, the flowchart comes in handy when you start making updates and modifications to your Web site. Can you imagine if I renamed my Books page without having some sort of flowchart? There'd be no way I'd remember to update each and every link that points to that HTML file.

Common Directory Structure

Besides creating a flowchart, another common way to keep track of your Web site is to organize all of your HTML files (and images) into file subdirectories. By creating subdirectories, you can keep all related images and files together and easily identifiable (see fig. 4.2).

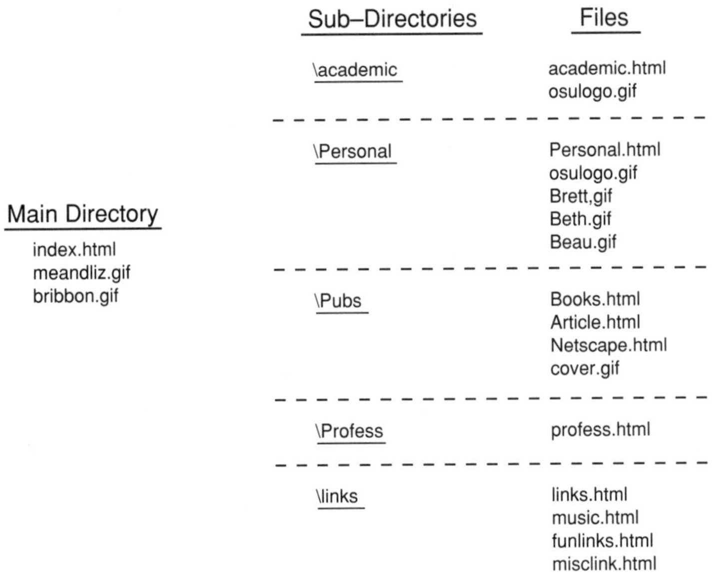

Fig. 4.2
Even if you aren't a neat freak, you can see how important organizing your files is.

Sub–Directories	Files
\academic	academic.html
	osulogo.gif
\Personal	Personal.html
	osulogo.gif
	Brett,gif
	Beth.gif
	Beau.gif
\Pubs	Books.html
	Article.html
	Netscape.html
	cover.gif
\Profess	profess.html
\links	links.html
	music.html
	funlinks.html
	misclink.html

Main Directory
index.html
meandliz.gif
bribbon.gif

This method is similar to flowcharting because now I have a report that I can refer to whenever I want to create links to other pages, or update information. For example, if I wanted to create a link from MUSIC.HTML located in my \LINKS subdirectory to \Pubs\books.html, I could instantly look at my simple directory listing and add the following link:

```
<A HREF="../Pubs/books.html">Link to my Books Page</A>
```

Using HotDog Pro To Manage Your Web Site

Regardless of how organized you are, managing a Web site can cause numerous gray hairs. Compensating for this difficulty, HotDog Pro 2 has several built-in features that make it easy to keep track and work with multiple page Web sites. HotDog Pro is the advanced (and more costly) version of the HotDog HTML editor. HotDog Pro has all of the features that HotDog Standard has, with several other important characteristics. You can download a shareware version of HotDog Pro from Sausage's Web Page (**http:// www.sausage.com**). Unfortunately, HotDog Pro costs $99.95—quite a few nickels and dimes. But if you are trying to manage a Web site, or want to use some of HotDog Pro's other features, it is a price well worth paying. Feel free to try out HotDog Pro and see whether or not it fits your advanced needs.

By organizing sets of Web pages into "projects," HotDog Pro lets you open and close multiple HTML files at the same time, generate a list of all of the embedded hypertext links and images within each file in the project, and upload your entire set of HTML files to the Internet in a single step.

All you have to do is tell HotDog which files should be saved as a single project. You can specify HTML files, forms, and even CGI scripts saved as text files, and manage them as a single project. Once you've created a project, HotDog Pro will go through and verify that it can find every HTML file and image that is referenced in your Web site. Then, it will compile a master list of all the HTML files and images. In this fashion, HotDog Pro keeps track of building and verifying a flowchart for you.

Web developers may want to use this innovative new feature to manage their multi-page Web sites. Not only can you open and close sets of HTML files within HotDog with a single command, but you track all links and images for easy reference.

Create a Project

When working with HotDog Pro, the first step is to create a project. A project allows you to open, close, publish, and upload an entire set of files at one time—instead of working with them individually.

When creating a project, you need to tell HotDog Pro which files you'd like to group together. The easiest way to accomplish this is to open each and every HTML file so that they are all open simultaneously (see fig. 4.3).

Fig. 4.3

First you open all of the files that will be in the project.

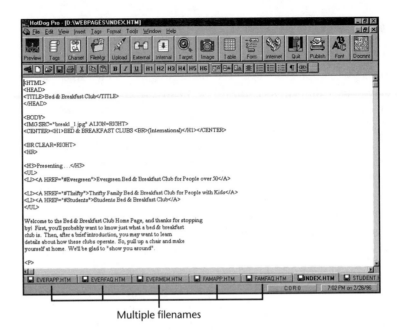

Multiple filenames

Then choose File, Project Manager to bring up the Project Manager dialog box (see fig. 4.4). In this dialog box, you need to type in pertinent information for this set of HTML files. First, name your project; then indicate where on your hard drive your files are stored.

Fig. 4.4

Name your project so you can refer to it at a later date.

The second part of this dialog box deals with automatically uploading it to the WWW. These boxes are useful if you make changes to your Web pages on your personal machine and then upload them to the WWW via FTP (File Transfer Protocol). This allows you to upload the entire project—all of the files and images—with one command instead of FTPing them individually.

Type in your WWW server and the subdirectory these files are stored in (if any). Then, to automate the FTP process, include your user ID and password in the boxes provided. If you're not sure how to FTP your HTML files to the Internet, check with your Web or Internet provider for more detailed instructions on the WWW server or your user name.

Now, click the Files tab at the top of this dialog box to specify the files you want to mark for this project. Click the Add Opened Docs button and HotDog adds all of the currently open HTML files to this project. Figure 4.5 shows the files in my Bed & Breakfast Club Project.

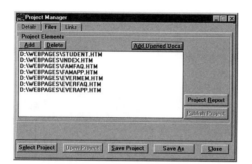

Fig. 4.5
Specify the files you want to include in this HotDog project.

Netscape Only

Note

You can also add files to a project without opening them in HotDog. Click the Add button and HotDog lets you select unopened files from your computer to include in this project.

Tip

To remove a listed file from your project, click the file with your mouse and click the Delete button. The file isn't actually deleted; it is just removed from your project listing.

Once you've added all the files to your project, click the Save Project button to bring up the Project Name dialog box (see fig. 4.6). Type in a filename and click OK. HotDog saves your project listing in a separate file that you can refer to in the future.

Fig. 4.6
Simply give your
project listing a
filename.

Opening and Closing Existing Projects

Now that your project is saved, you can refer to your entire set of HTML files
by simply opening and closing your single .PRJ file. HotDog always lists the
project(s) you have open in the toolbar at the bottom of the screen, as shown
in figure 4.7.

Fig. 4.7
HotDog shows the
filename of your
open project.

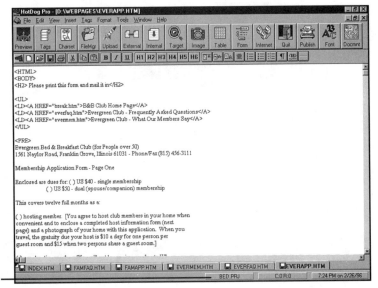

Project name

By clicking the project name that I pointed out in figure 4.7, HotDog brings
up the Project Manager dialog box that you are already familiar with.

To close your entire project, choose File, Close Project from the HotDog
menu bar. All of the HTML files associated with that project are closed.

Caution

Make sure you save all of your files before closing an entire project so you don't lose
any data. HotDog reminds you to save every file that has had changes made to it,
but it's better to be safe than sorry.

Similarly, to open an existing project, choose File, Open Project from the menu bar. HotDog brings up the Open Project dialog box which lists project titles and filenames (see fig. 4.8).

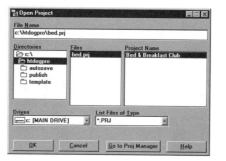

Fig. 4.8
HotDog lists all of your available projects here.

Reporting Your Projects

After you familiarize yourself with making and working with HotDog projects, let's start using some other project-related features. One of the most useful is the ability to create a project report, which is a file-by-file listing of all hypertext links and embedded images (and audio and sound files, if any) itemized for each entry in your project. In the Project Manager dialog box, click the Files tab and then select the button labeled Project Report. HotDog creates a separate file immediately, and gives you the option to look at it. Figure 4.9 shows a part of the project report for this particular set of HTML files. As you can tell, this report comes in handy when building flowcharts and keeping track of all the links and images for my Web site.

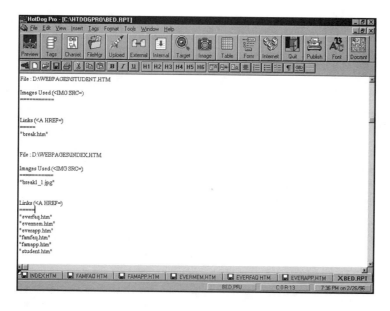

Fig. 4.9
Print your project report so you always have a copy of the infrastructure of your Web site handy.

Uploading Your Project

Another useful feature of HotDog is the capability of uploading your entire set of HTML files—including image files—with one command. HotDog Pro comes with a built-in File Transfer Protocol (FTP) Program named HotFTP that will connect with your WWW server and send your requested files to the Web site. By clicking the Upload icon from the HotDog Pro menu bar, the Uploading Web Pages dialog box appears (see fig. 4.10).

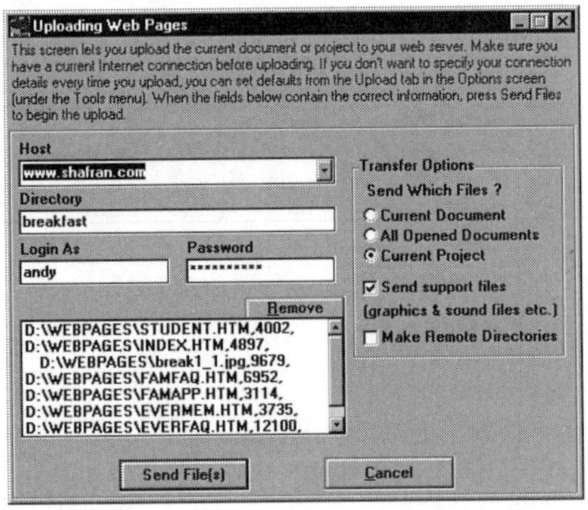

Fig. 4.10

Send your entire set of files to your Web site with one command.

> **Tip**
>
> You can specify whether HotDog uploads a single file or an entire project by clicking the appropriate Transfer Option in the Uploading Web Pages dialog box.

Notice how HotDog lists all of the HTML files in my project, and the embedded GIF and JPG files, as well. Every file related to this particular project gets sent when I choose to upload my pages to the WWW. Make sure that your Host, Directory, Login, and Password information are correct, and click the Send File(s) button.

> **Note**
>
> In order to get the HotFTP program to work properly, you will have to already be connected to the Internet with a SLIP/PPP account. A SLIP/PPP (Serial Line Input Protocol/Point-to-Point Protocol) is how WWW browsers exchange information with the Internet. Basically, you've got to be logged on before you can upload any files.
>
> Additionally, before you can upload files for the first time through HotDog, you may need to run HotFTP on its own, separate from HotDog Pro. This initial time sets several important FTP options that pertain to your Web site—your host, login name, and password.

Create HTML Templates

HotDog Pro also allows you to create several HTML files and mark them as default templates. That means when you create a new file, you can choose one of your templates to be modeled after. This process is exceedingly useful if you are creating several similar HTML pages. For example, on my home page, I have several different pages that are all similar in style. On each page, I have a default picture, headline, and footer that I always want to appear. So, after making the first file, I made it a HotDog template. Then when I create the rest of my files, they have the same HTML tags.

To create a template, first you've got to make your own HTML file in HotDog. Figure 4.11 shows all of the HTML codes that I want to appear on each Web page created from my template.

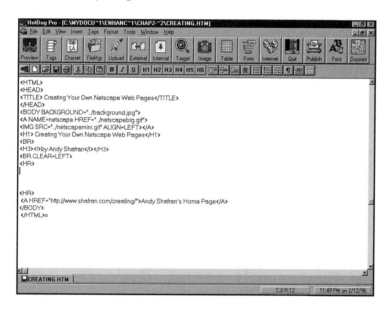

Fig. 4.11
Here's the standard template I'm using.

Then, choose Tools, Make Template from Document from the HotDog menu bar to bring up the Create Template dialog box (see fig. 4.12).

Fig. 4.12
Give your template a unique name.

Type in your new template name and click OK. HotDog informs you that a new template has been created. Now, to create a new document based on your template, choose File, New from the menu bar. HotDog displays a list of templates you have to choose from in the New Document dialog box (see fig. 4.13).

Fig. 4.13
Select the template
you want to use.

Highlight a template from this list and click the OK button. HotDog brings up a new document that is based exactly on the template. This saves you a vast amount of time and effort when you are creating many similar Web pages.

> **Note**
>
> This is the actual template I used when I created a set of Web pages for the book *Creating Your Own Netscape Web Pages*. Each page has a picture of the cover and a simple headline at the top, and a referencing URL and my e-mail address at the bottom. Visit **http://www.shafran.com/creating** to see how I created a whole set from this template.

Legal Issues with Web Pages

The whole concept behind society is that human beings can live together with certain rules, or laws acceptable by the majority governing the way life is led. This powerful concept is the basis of nearly every society and has been documented for thousands of years. In today's day and age, laws are particularly pertinent—especially for people who use and create information found on the Internet and World Wide Web.

> **Caution**
>
> Although I have attempted to describe some important and intense legal issues that are affecting the Internet and WWW developers, I am not a lawyer, nor am I the definitive source for all things legal in cyberspace. In addition, the points of view

from this chapter are based on current United States laws. International readers should be careful to examine their own legal specifics. One of the reasons legal issues have become such a hot topic is precisely because there are no international pornographic and copyright standard laws that hold true in each and every country of the world.

Enjoy this section of the book and feel free to look for more advanced resources on legal issues in cyberspace, and what is and is not permitted. If you are ever in doubt, contact your local lawyer or Bar Association to get the up-to-date information on cyberspace laws.

Many laws governing copyright and pornography issues have been in place and are well known throughout the United States and across the world. However, with the dawning of electronic communications, many of these laws are, as of yet, untested when dealing with information found on computers and worldwide networks such as the Internet. In general, you'll find that laws dealing with electronic information are vague, at best, and confusing and possibly unconstitutional, at worst. The government is still trying to develop an effective and logical strategy for protecting rights for Internet users and applying existing laws without being too overprotective.

Note

Although some laws aren't clearly defined when it comes to the online world, most are just as effective. One prime example is protecting the President of the United States. It is against the law to threaten the Commander-in-Chief. Whether you attack the president's residence or send threatening e-mail, both methods are illegal and subject to punishment in a court of law.

What Does Copyright Mean?

Many people understand how copyright laws apply when it comes to books and magazines. For example, as a reader of this book, you couldn't take the text from an entire chapter, type it into your computer, and then publish it in your own book—because I already have. Copyright laws protect the intellectual and physical rights of individuals who produce information.

However, when it comes to electronic information, the copyright laws are not as clearly defined. Typically, information and images produced by someone else are copyrighted by them and you must have their permission to use that information on your Web page. Unfortunately, enforcing copyright laws on the WWW is difficult. Anyone who stops by a Web page can save their own copy of all text, scripts, applets, and images without the original owner even knowing.

This makes it almost too easy for people to "borrow" text and images from Web pages and put them on their own sites. In Chapter 6, "Framing Your Work," I build a simple frame example linking to various cartoon sites on the WWW. As a visitor, you can easily save your own copy of these daily cartoons using features built right into Netscape—but the very act of saving these images to your computer breaks the copyright laws that protect the original artist.

As a general rule of thumb, it is against the law for you to borrow text, images, and scripts from other Web pages unless the author has explicitly announced that his or her information is free of use. You'll find that many individual sites on the Internet follow the philosophy that "information wants to be free" and encourage users to borrow their examples at their convenience. On the other hand, many large companies tend to be very protective of their icons, logos, and trademarks and vigorously pursue individuals who illegally infringe on their copyright.

> **Note**
>
> Although many Web pages and businesses commonly add a copyright notice to their Web sites, it's really unnecessary. In the United States today, all information that is produced either electronically or printed is automatically copyrighted to the original creator. So whether or not you notice a © or not, get permission from the original author before using text or images from other Web pages.

Are Links OK?

Besides borrowing images from other Web sites, another new issue that the Web makes possible is the ability to easily link individual Web pages to images stored at different Web sites. For example, add the following link to your Web page (see fig. 4.14):

```
<IMG ONC="http://www.ohafran.com/~andy/lizandmo.jpg">
```

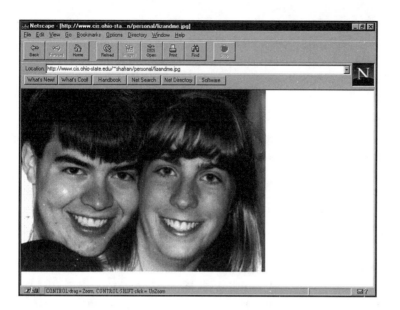

Netscape Only

Fig. 4.14
Here's an enlarged
version of the
image you'll find
on my Web page.

In your Web page, you've just inserted the exact same image that you'll see when you stop by my personal page. You aren't actually "borrowing" my image for your Web page, you are accessing the version that is saved at my Web site. But then again, you are using the image on your Web page in a way that I didn't originally intend. Does this break copyright laws? The answer is maybe. The judicial system can't give a solid answer to that question. No one is stealing my image, but yet I don't have control over how it is referenced.

This is a prime example of how there is no legal precedent for sharing and distributing information on the Internet. While I might not care if you added pictures of me to your Web page, Walt Disney Pictures might if you linked to a picture of Pocahontas from its Web site.

Before you go and start linking to images and information on other Web sites, stop. Although the legal ramifications of this aren't clearly defined, the social effects are. Using someone else's image without his or her permission should be avoided. In addition, it puts additional stress on his or her WWW server. If everyone who reads this book added the above link, it would bring my WWW server to its knees because of the constant requests for the image.

Pornography

The most explosive legal issue on the Internet certainly centers around the issue of pornography. These legal debates revolve around defining pornography, how existing pornography laws should be interpreted online, and how to protect minors from information that is not appropriate for their eyes.

The current pornography debate came to a head on February 8, 1996, when President Bill Clinton signed into law the 1996 Communications Decency Act (CDA). This act strives to pinpoint what pornography is, and describes legal liability for individuals and businesses that allow pornographic information to be available to minors.

Basically, the problem is that most people enjoy their rights of free speech and see those rights naturally transferred to the Internet and WWW. Unfortunately, information and images that are available legally to adults are just as easily available to minors, or those under 18. With the 1996 CDA, the government has attempted to place liability on information providers who allow access—known or unknown—of pornographic material to minors.

Immediately after the CDA was signed into law, several legal challenges by many online companies and civil rights organizations filed suit against the bill, attempting to overturn the bill in court. As of this writing, the CDA has been temporarily restrained until these lawsuits are resolved. It will likely be several months, if not years, before this situation is resolved.

Pornographic material usually deals with text, video clips, and images that deal with adult issues in a manner not appropriate for minors. Be aware that including that type of information on your Web pages could be construed as against the law should the 1996 Communications Decency Act be upheld.

Note

As part of a massive campaign against Internet censorship and liability, the Electronic Freedom Foundation (EFF) started a "blue ribbon" campaign. They encourage WWW users and developers across the world to add an image of a blue ribbon to their Web page indicating that they support free speech. Stop by the EFF's Web page at **http://www.eff.org** for more information on the blue ribbon campaign.

World Wide Issues

The most confusing part of these legal issues focuses on the "world" part of the World Wide Web. That's because laws that control what type of information is available in the United States don't necessarily hold for other countries across the globe. Take pornography, for example. Information and images that are illegal in the United States are legal in some other countries.

This disparity in laws often causes confusion in how laws are interpreted and applied, and creates all sorts of new questions. Is it illegal to access pornographic information from another country? (Maybe.) Is it illegal to save that information on your personal computer? (Probably so.) How do international copyright laws work when it comes to adding information to the Web? (They don't.)

These types of issues are only the tip of the iceberg when it comes to understanding how laws affect our interactions in the global world.

WWW Advertisements

Getting people to stop by and visit your Web page can be the most difficult and challenging part of creating a cool Web site. Even though there are literally millions of people surfing the Web daily, they won't stop by your Web page unless they know it exists—and it attracts their interest.

There are many different comprehensive indexes of WWW pages that exist. Most of these indexes accept virtually any new submission to publicize and advertise your Web page. Once listed in these online indexes, your Web site is listed whenever someone does a search for a related topic. For example, when someone stops by Yahoo and searches for "creating Web pages," they'll find a list of pertinent Web pages under that topic—with mine listed as one of them.

Adding your WWW pages to these large indexes isn't often the best way to publicize them because your Web site is just one of the masses listed—but it's usually a free service.

To attract more people to their Web sites, some Web developers have turned towards advertising on popular Web sites. These advertisements usually consist of simple images that, when clicked, bring visitors immediately to a specific Web page. Figure 4.15 shows an advertisement as it appears on the Netscape home page.

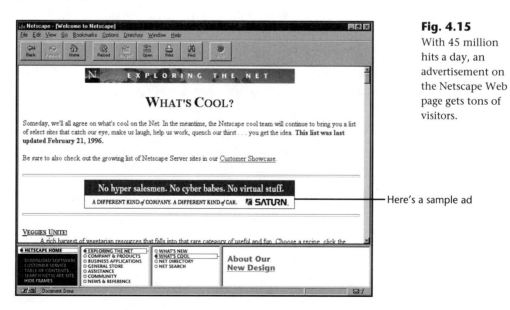

Here's a sample ad

Fig. 4.15
With 45 million hits a day, an advertisement on the Netscape Web page gets tons of visitors.

Unfortunately, advertising on popular Web sites can be expensive. At Yahoo's Web site, a week long advertisement starts at $1,000. Netscape advertisements are significantly more expensive—most businesses can't even afford them. Figure 4.16 shows WebLaunch, Yahoo's costly, but effective, advertising service (**http://www.yahoo.com/weblaunch.html**).

Fig. 4.16
WebLaunch is my favorite advertising locale on the Web—it's well designed and easy to use.

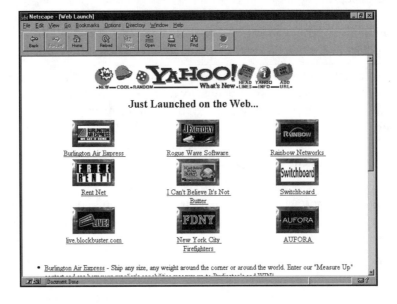

Many popular Web sites allow advertising, usually ranging from $50 to $1,000, for any period of time ranging from a week to a few months. Any spot on the WWW that sponsors advertising should be able to give you detailed information about the number of visitors that stop by (thus seeing your advertisements)—if not, you don't want to advertise there.

Advertising your Web pages is usually left to businesses who are willing to make a financial investment to get people to stop by their pages. This usually means that they are selling a product or service.

If you don't fit in this category, your best bet is to stick with the free catalogs and indexes of Web sites and attract visitors that way.

Note

One extremely affordable way to advertise your Web site is by trading links with another site. For example, if you create a Web page for selling light bulbs, you might want to send e-mail to another company that sells light fixtures. On your page, you can include a link to that related Web page, and their page will link to yours. This creates good advertising for both of your sites. You might want to consider trading these types of advertisements depending on your Web situation.

Netscape Only

Part II

Livening Up Your Web Page

Chapter 5
The New Generation of HTML Tags

In the early '80s, buying a VCR wasn't such an easy choice. They were expensive, unreliable, and you had to choose between Beta and VHS videotape formats. Both sides of the VCR debate preached that their format was superior and would become the industry standard. In the end, the VHS format won, leaving many old Beta VCRs gathering dust in garage sales, basements, and junk piles.

On the WWW, a similar type of war is currently raging. This war is slightly different though, because instead of trying to get you to purchase one type of equipment over another, companies such as Netscape, Microsoft, and Spry are all vying to *give away* their software for free. The company that can give away the most copies of its software becomes the winner. It will then support more users on the WWW and have more marketing information at its disposal.

Who's the real winner? You, the consumer in the middle of these WWW browser wars. Practically every few months, new HTML tags are introduced to the Web community, usually by Netscape or Microsoft.

Thus far, Netscape has been at the forefront, creating innovative new tags that make your Web pages look spectacular—but only when viewed with its software. This chapter shows you how to add and incorporate many of these new tags into your enhanced Web page.

Recently though, Microsoft has introduced a plethora of multimedia, special effects driven HTML tags that really add some zip to your Web page—you'll love them, guaranteed. While over 80 percent of WWW users use Netscape to explore the Web, it's important to stay up with new technology, because Microsoft's Internet Explorer is quickly gaining popularity. After talking about new Netscape tags, I quickly introduce some of the impressive new Microsoft tags—that only work with Microsoft's Internet Explorer.

Specifically, in this chapter, you'll learn how to do the following:

- Control the relative font size of text compared to other snippets on your Web page
- Add subscript and superscript text
- Change the color of text on screen
- Incorporate special characters—such as the copyright symbol—into your Web page
- Build Microsoft-only features in your Web page for dazzling multimedia special effects

New Netscape Formatting Tags

Leading the pack with new and innovative tags, Netscape 2.0 supports many new text formatting tags that give you more control over how text is displayed on the screen.

Realizing that Web developers wanted more control over font size and color, Netscape added several new tags that let you control these attributes. This section will show you how to control the color and relative size of text on-screen, change the colors of "hot" or linked text, and add text that appears subscript or superscript.

Making Your Text Slightly Larger or Smaller

Sometimes when you add text to your Web page, you want to slightly emphasize certain portions of text to make it stand out to the reader. HTML offers you several alternatives. You can bold text (<B> and </B>), italicize it (<I> and </I>), or use any number of other tags at your disposal.

Now, Netscape offers two new tags that help you make text look slightly different on-screen—the <BIG> and <SMALL> tags. Neither one of these two tags drastically changes the way words are displayed, but instead makes slight, but noticeable, changes to the thickness and size of text marked with these attributes.

Surrounding text with the <BIG> and </BIG> tags makes it appear slightly larger and bolder on-screen. As you'd expect, the <SMALL> and </SMALL> tags have the exact opposite effect. Text surrounded with this set of tags is slightly smaller in font size.

Here's the best way to think of the <SMALL> and <BIG> tags. Assume without any special tags, your regular text appears at 100 percent size. Using the <SMALL> tag reduces the text size by about ten percent on-screen while, conversely, the <BIG> tag increases the text size by about ten percent.

The following is an example of the <BIG> and <SMALL> tags in action:

```
<BIG> Here's some BIG text</BIG> <BR>
Here's some REGULAR text <BR>
<SMALL>Here's some SMALL text</SMALL>
```

When used within large blocks of text, these tags can be significantly more subtle than using any of the other text attribute tags (see fig. 5.1).

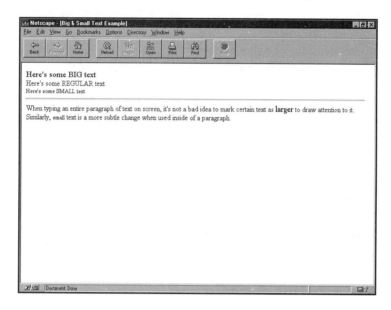

Fig. 5.1
These two new tags allow for increased flexibility when displaying text with Netscape.

Controlling Font Size Dynamically

The most flexible new Netscape tag is <FONT>. Using the <FONT> tag, you can set specific text size and color for a specific piece of text. You'll love the new flexibility that <FONT> gives you when creating your Web pages. You can change text color on-the-fly, mark certain phrases as important by increasing the size on-screen, and much more. This section introduces you to the three different ways you can customize text appearance using the <FONT> and </FONT> tags.

Tip

The font attributes you have control over now are just the tip of the iceberg. Soon, you'll be able to specify different fonts for your text, build in default icons that can appear alongside your text, and create animation that makes your text move around on the screen. Keep an eye on the Netscape home page (**http://www.netscape.com**) for more information on these innovative new ways to use the <FONT> tag and new forthcoming HTML tags.

Setting Actual Font Size

Remember how you could control the size of headings on-screen? Using six different sets of tags ranging from <H1> to <H6>, you could specify exactly how a heading should appear on-screen. The only drawback was you only used the <H1> tags for headlines. You didn't have that kind of flexibility with regular text on the screen.

Now, with the <FONT> tag, you have the same flexibility with regular text. Text can appear in seven different sizes on-screen ranging from 1 (the smallest) to 7 (the largest). Normally, without using the <FONT> tag, text appears in size 3. That means Netscape gives you four new settings to make text larger (4–7) and two to make text smaller (1–2). All you have to do is surround the text whose font size you want to change, and add the SIZE= keyword like the following example:

```
<FONT SIZE=5> Here's text displayed in Size 5 </FONT>
```

The previous <FONT> tag sets the surrounded text to be of size 5, two steps larger than text normally appears on-screen. Figure 5.2 shows you how all seven font sizes compare against one another.

Fig. 5.2
This figure compares the multiple text sizes.

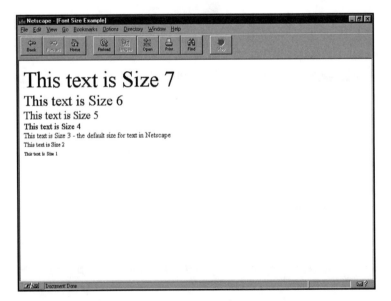

Tip

Just like using headings, make sure you change font sizes step-by-step. Jumping from size 1 to size 6 on subsequent lines makes a Web page look odd and out of place. Differentially sizing text should be used carefully and scrutinized closely.

Setting Relative Font Sizes

The <FONT> tag also has slightly more flexibility when setting the actual size of your text on-screen. Instead of setting your text size to be a specific number, you can give it a relative size, such as +3 or –1. Netscape takes your relative size tag and adds to (or subtracts it from) the default font size being used (size 3). Take a look at the following examples:

```
<FONT SIZE=+3> A Relative Font Size Example </FONT>
<FONT SIZE=-2> Another Font Size Example </FONT>
```

Since the normal font size of text is size number 3, the first line above makes the surrounded text display on-screen in size 6 (3 + 3 = 6), while the second line displays text in size 1 (3 – 2 = 1). Figure 5.3 shows how Netscape interprets the previous two lines of HTML.

Fig. 5.3
Relative font sizes let you tell Netscape to increase or decrease the size of fonts on a step-by-step basis.

You also can embed <FONT SIZE> tags within one another—but they don't work as you might assume. Let's say you wanted to make three words appear subsequently larger, like this:

Big Bigger Biggest

Your first reaction might be to embed three <FONT> tags inside of each other, like the following:

```
<FONT SIZE=+1> Big <FONT SIZE=+1> Bigger <FONT SIZE=+1> Biggest
</FONT> </FONT> </FONT>
```

That way the first word, *Big*, would be enlarged by one size; then *Bigger* is enlarged another size; and *Biggest* is enlarged for a cumulative total of three sizes—but that's not how Netscape works. <FONT> tags are not cumulative in nature. Each of the <FONT SIZE=1> tags sets the surrounded text to be one size larger than regular—the result being that all three words are the same size.

To make cumulative changes in font size, you would have to create your HTML like this:

```
<FONT SIZE=+1> Big <FONT SIZE=+2> Bigger <FONT SIZE=+3> Biggest
</FONT> </FONT> </FONT>
```

Figure 5.4 shows how Netscape displays these two examples.

Fig. 5.4
Remember that
<FONT> tags are
not cumulative
in nature.

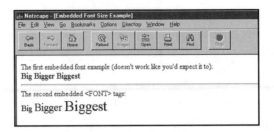

Tip

If you change the relative size of text to be larger than +4 or smaller than –2,
Netscape just assumes you want to display the information in the largest (or smallest)
size available.

Changing the Displayed Font Color

One of my favorite new ways to customize text is being able to change the
color of any piece of information being displayed. Now, you can set a word or
sentence in a paragraph, an item in a list, or a snippet of text to automatically
appear in any of millions of different colors. Netscape lets you choose from
16 different default colors, or you can create your own particular color creation by mixing and matching different shades of red, green, and blue.

Font Colors

Changing the color of displayed text is one of the easiest things you can do
to enhance your Web page. Using the new COLOR= keyword in the <FONT> tag,
you can specify several different colors for your text to appear in, like the following:

```
<FONT COLOR=RED>Some Red Text</FONT>
```

You have 16 different default colors at your fingertips that are named and
recognized within Netscape. You can use them as often as you like on your
Web page—just be careful not to make your text unreadable.

The 16 colors you can identify directly by name are as follows:

Black	Maroon	Green	Olive
Navy	Purple	Teal	Gray
Silver	Red	Lime	Yellow
Blue	Fuchsia	Aqua	White

Besides using the 16 named colors, Netscape enables you to specify colors by mixing different shades of red, green, and blue. This gives you literally millions of different colors to choose from. See the section "Color by Hexadecimal" later in this chapter for more information.

Tip

Use the <FONT> tag to change text color for a small piece of your Web page. If you want to modify the text color for the entire page, see the following section.

Other Ways To Change Color

Changing text color on-screen is an advanced feature that you'll want to take advantage of. Primarily, the <FONT> and </FONT> tags are used to change the color of a small piece of text on your Web page.

In this section, you'll learn how to change the default text color for the entire page by adding new keywords to your <BODY> tag. Each of these keywords uses the exact same color formula as described previously—where you name the color you want to use from the named colors.

You'll want to customize these options when you start using background images and colors on your Web page. By default, the Netscape text color is black, and the background is gray or white. But if you set your background color to become black using the <BODY BGCOLOR=> tag, or use a dark background image, then you won't be able to read any text on the screen. In this case, you need to change the color of text to something light—like white. Figure 5.5 shows one of my own sample Web pages that has a black background and white text.

Text Color

To change the default color of text on your screen, add the TEXT= keyword to your <BODY> tag, like the following:

```
<BODY TEXT=Lime>
```

The above tag sets all text on my Web page to lime green (how ugly).

Note

Colors specified using the <FONT> tag as described above override your default color setting from the <BODY> tag.

Fig. 5.5
With my background set to a dark color, I've got to change the text color for my Web page.

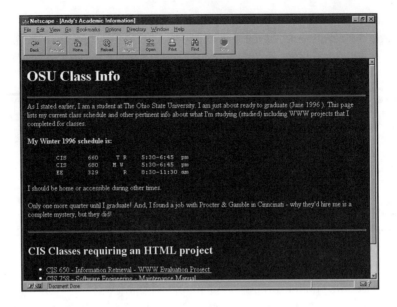

Link Color

You can also change the color of "hot" text that links your Web page to another spot on the World Wide Web. Use the LINK= keyword just as you used the TEXT= tag previously. The following is an example:

```
<BODY TEXT=LIME LINK=AQUA>
```

All linked text on my page now appears in aqua to match my lime green specified for regular text.

Visited Link Color

You may have noticed that sometimes linked text appears in a slightly different color, indicating that you've already traveled that particular thread of the WWW.

You can change the color of visited link text on your Web page with the VLINK= keyword, like the following:

```
<BODY TEXT=LIME LINK=AQUA VLINK=SILVER>
```

The color of links on this Web page tones down silver when you've visited it already.

Active Link Color

The final color customization you can make is what color text appears as it is being clicked upon. This text is signified as active link text and uses the ALINK= keyword. When someone visits your Web page, the color of linked text is set with LINK=. But when it is clicked on, for a brief moment it changes to the color you specify with ALINK=:

```
<BODY TEXT=LIME LINK=AQUA VLINK=SILVER ALINK=YELLOW>
```

To go along with the other atrocious colors I've selected for this example, active linked text is now set to bright yellow.

Note

These color settings can be overridden manually in Netscape by choosing Options, General Preferences, and setting them individually on the Colors tab. By setting these traits in Netscape, visitors ignore the background and color settings on your Web pages.

Color by Hexadecimal

Many times, you might want to use other colors not specified in the default named 16 provided. Just like a painter, you want to mix and match different hues and shades to come up with your own color concoction.

Another way to set your COLOR= keyword inside of the <FONT> tag is by using the six-character hexadecimal equivalent. Specific colors are indicated by a six-character hexadecimal combination which tells Netscape how it should mix red, blue, and green together to get your specified color. Hexadecimal numbers range from 0–9 and A–F. If this sounds confusing to you, don't worry. I'll step you through the color process and show you how to figure out the six-character combination for many popular colors.

Here's how it works. All colors are a mix of red, green, and blue. Each of these three primary colors controls two of the six hexadecimal characters. By mixing and matching different shades of these colors, you have literally thousands of different possibilities to choose from. For example, let's say you wanted to use a pure shade of red on your Web page. For this, you'd use <FONT> in the following manner:

```
<FONT COLOR=FF0000>Some Red Text</FONT>
```

Notice the six-character color tag. Each primary color—red, green, and blue—is assigned to two characters correspondingly. So the above tag, interpreted, says to mix 100 percent full vibrant red with zero percent of green, and zero percent of blue. Similarly, true green and blue are defined below:

```
<FONT COLOR=00FF00>Some Green Text</FONT>
<FONT COLOR=0000FF>Some Blue Text</FONT>
```

Unfortunately, this book doesn't appear in color, otherwise I could demonstrate how these colors work visually (I have several color examples linked to my home page, though). For a more complete listing of colors and examples, visit **http://www.infi.net/wwwimages/colorindex.html** (see fig. 5.6).

Fig. 5.6

Here's a good cross section of the 16 million color options available to you.

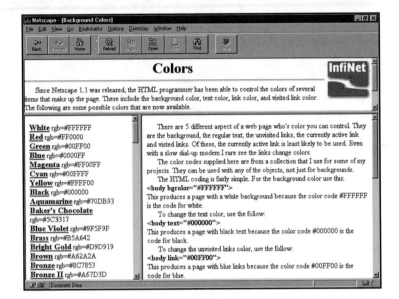

Below, I've listed a short table of some of my favorite colors and the corresponding six-character codes. Feel free to experiment with your own creative mixes of colors (each character can be a number 0 through 9 or a letter A through F).

Color	Six-Digit Code
Black	000000
White	FFFFFF
Yellow	FFFF00
Gray	C0C0C0
Maroon	8E236B
Hunter Green	215E21
Pink	BC8F8F
Navy Blue	23238E
Violet	4F2F4F

Subscript and Superscript

Two other new tags have been introduced with Netscape 2.0—subscript and superscript. These two tags give you increased flexibility for displaying information in Netscape.

You'll find yourself using these two tags sparingly, but they come in handy when you need to display information like chemical formulas (H_2O) or street addresses (1400 W 13th).

Use the _{and} tags to mark text that should appear in subscript in Netscape, and the ^{and} tags for superscript information. The following are examples:

```
The chemical formula for water is H<SUB>2</SUB>O—Two parts
Hydrogen and one part Oxygen.
Stop by the holiday party this weekend. My address is 1400 W
13<SUP>th</SUP>.
```

Figure 5.7 shows how Netscape displays subscript and superscript marked text.

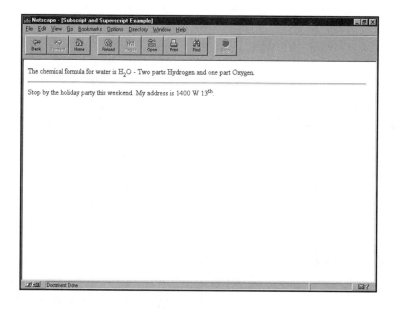

Fig. 5.7
Useful for specific pieces of information, the superscript and subscript tags aren't used very often.

II

Livening Your Web Page

Adding Special Characters

Sometimes, you may have trouble making certain characters display within Netscape. Characters such as &, ", <, >, =, and more are integral to the definition of other tags. Other tags are not in the normal alphabet—such as ", ", —, or b. Still other characters are present in foreign languages, but not English—for example, to correctly insert *français* in your Web page, you need to use a character called the *cedilla* instead of the *c*.

To include these individual special characters on your Web pages, you need to refer to them individually, each with a special HTML tag. Netscape and the HTML standards agree on a default set of HTML tags that represent characters when found inside an HTML file.

The following table lists several popular characters that you may want to include on your Web page, and the appropriate HTML you must use—each beginning with & for them to appear.

Character	HTML tag
<	&lt
>	&gt
&	&amp
"	&quot
"	&copy
'	&reg
—	&emdash

Tip

For a more complete listing of all the special characters you can include on your Web page, visit the following site:

http://ncdesign.kyushu

Microsoft's New Tags

As I alluded to in the opening paragraphs of this chapter, there are several other new and innovative tags that can be used on your Web pages. These new tags, released by Microsoft, only work with Internet Explorer, the Microsoft WWW browser.

Even though this book is entitled *Enhancing Your Netscape Web Pages*, I've decided to add a section that shows you how you can add some of these new tags to your Web pages. My reasoning is listed as follows:

- I fully expect Netscape to announce support for some, if not all, of Microsoft's new tags. Netscape leads the pack in HTML support and wants to remain the best all-around browser.

- These new tags are really cool. Microsoft added several new innovations that add multimedia special effects and better control over several aspects of your Web pages.

- Many people use more than one WWW browser. Although the lion's share of individuals use Netscape, Microsoft's Internet Explorer is becoming a viable alternative. Since both of these leading browsers are available for downloading for free (see Chapter 1 for information about downloading them), you might want to consider using them both intermittently, to take advantage of the best features in each of them.

- Even if you use Netscape only, some visitors to your home page might not. They can enjoy the special features you've built in just for them (this is what I do on my home page).

This section will quickly introduce my favorite of the Microsoft HTML extensions and show you how to add them to your Web page. You'll have more control over sound, color, and video objects on your Web page.

New Background Features

Microsoft has introduced several new keywords that work along with the <BODY> tag to determine some characteristics of your Web page. Using the new Microsoft extensions, you can add a watermarked image, instead of a background, and a default audio clip that plays whenever someone stops by your Web page for a visit.

Watermarks

You're probably already familiar with using background images on your Web page. Background images are small pictures that are tiled to cover the entire screen behind your text. This creates the illusion of wallpaper on your Web page.

To add a background image to your Web page, you used the following tag:

```
<BODY BACKGROUND="myback.gif">
```

Your WWW browser looks for `myback.gif` and covers the entire background of the screen with that image. New to Internet Explorer is the Watermark feature. By using the BGPROPERTIES keyword along with BACKGROUND, you can specify an image that should load in the background of your Web page that appears fixed, liked a watermark.

II

Livening Your Web Page

This watermark image doesn't move as you scroll up and down through the page. You can add a watermark to your Web page by adding BGPROPERTIES=FIXED to your <BODY> tag, like this:

```
<BODY BGPROPERTIES="mywater.gif" BGPROPERTIES=FIXED>
```

Background Sounds

The other new background feature is the <BGSOUND> tag. Using this tag, you can identify a default audio file that is downloaded and played automatically when a visitor stops by your Web page.

You can add a welcome clip, a sound effect, or any type of audio experience you'd like to incorporate as part of your Web page. Use the <BGSOUND> tag, like this:

```
<BGSOUND SRC="myaudio.wav">
```

When Internet Explorer stops by this Web page, it first loads all the text and images. Once finished, it starts downloading myaudio.wav, a Windows sound clip, and plays it automatically on the visitor's machine.

You can also control how many times your sound is played on the visitor's machine. Using the LOOP= keyword, you can tell Internet Explorer to replay the downloaded sound clip over and over and over. By default, Internet Explorer only plays a sound clip once unless specified, such as the following:

```
<BGSOUND SRC="myaudio.wav" LOOP=10>
```

Visitors to this Web site won't forget this sound clip—this tag tells it to play ten times.

Tip

If you want a sound clip to repeat endlessly, set LOOP=INFINITE instead of giving a particular number.

Caution

Use this keyword sparingly. Visitors may not want to hear long or inappropriate sounds—in fact, they may not want to hear anything at all. If you want to use this tag, a short and useful sound bite is best suited.

Scrolling Text Marquee Style

My favorite Microsoft HTML extension is the <MARQUEE> tag. Using this tag, you can specify words and phrases to scroll across your Web page. All you

have to do is surround the text you want to serve as your marquee with the
<MARQUEE> and </MARQUEE> tags:

```
<MARQUEE> Here's some scrolling text.</MARQUEE>
```

Figure 5.8 shows the marquee in three stages across the screen.

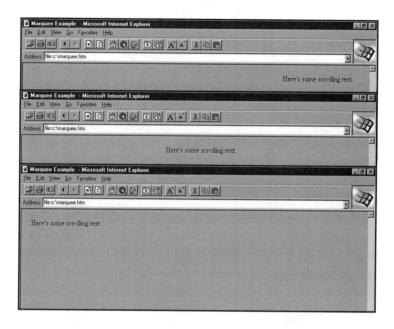

Fig. 5.8
Here's the marquee
in action.

By default, marquee text scrolls from the right hand side of the screen to the
left and keeps repeating indefinitely.

Of course, there are several ways in which you can customize the behavior of
marquee text. By using the BEHAVIOR keyword, you can tell Internet Explorer
to SLIDE the text across the screen and stop moving once it hits the left hand
margin, or even ALTERNATE—that is, bounce back and forth from each margin, like the following:

```
<MARQUEE BEHAVIOR=SLIDE> Here's some sliding text.</MARQUEE>
<MARQUEE BEHAVIOR=ALTERNATE> This text bounces back and forth off
each margin.</MARQUEE>
```

Video Clips

The most significant multimedia Microsoft extension enables you to directly
embed video clips into your Web page. Using the <IMG> tag, you can tell
Internet Explorer to display a video (in Microsoft AVI format) instead of a
standard image.

II

Livening Your Web Page

To add a video image to your Web page, use the DYNSRC (short for Dynamic Source) keyword in the <IMG> tag:

```
<IMG SRC="andy.gif" DYNSRC="andy.avi">
```

Internet Explorer first downloads andy.gif to be displayed on your Web page. Once all of the images and text have been downloaded, it starts downloading the animation file named andy.avi and starts playing it automatically in the same location where the original image was loaded. Pretty amazing, huh?

Figure 5.9 shows Internet Explorer displaying a simple AVI file I created with Web3D (see Chapter 7, "Advanced Graphics Issues," for more information). Don't worry about Netscape users. They'll only see the image pointed at by the SRC keyword and will ignore DYNSRC.

Fig. 5.9
Here's my animation in action.

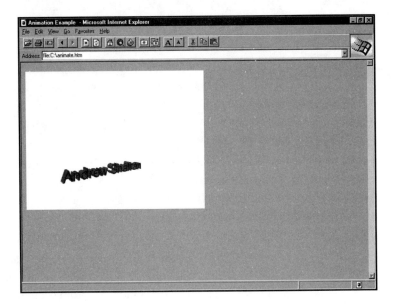

Two other keywords that may come in handy are CONTROLS and LOOP. The CONTROLS keyword adds video playback controls to the bottom of the animation as shown in the following tag (see fig. 5.10):

```
<IMG SRC="andy.gif" DYNSRC="andy.avi" CONTROLS>
```

Additionally, you can also set how many times you want the animation to repeat itself using LOOP just like the background sound tag. By default, your animation will play itself one time.

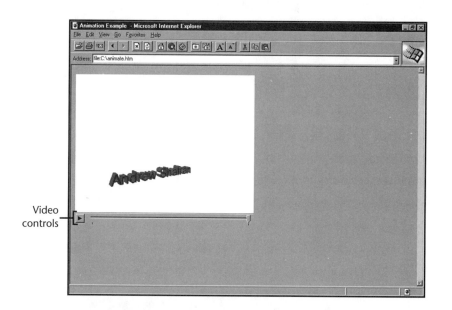

Video controls

Fig. 5.10
These standard video control buttons appear when you use the CONTROLS keyword.

Tip

Check out the CD-ROM for a fantastic collection of video clips in AVI format that you can directly add to your Web pages today!

On the CD

Chapter 6
Framing Your Work

If you're like most people, you can do more than one thing at a time. Some people can type while talking on the phone, and almost everyone can listen to the radio while driving. In the computer world, operating systems now multitask, letting you run two (or more) programs at once. The latest televisions have picture-in-picture support, letting you watch two shows simultaneously.

Not wanting to be left behind, Netscape now allows to you display multiple HTML files on-screen at the same time. Using frames, you can create different areas within the Netscape window that display separate HTML files. You can link to many different sites across the world at once!

This chapter introduces you to frames and shows how you can use them in your Web pages. You'll learn the proper HTML for frames, useful techniques for adding them, and when you should—and shouldn't—use frames for your Web pages.

Specifically, this chapter shows you how to:

- Understand what frames are and how they work
- Decide when using frames makes sense
- Create a simple frame layout for your Web page
- Use advanced techniques for designing with frames
- Evaluate practical alternatives to frames on your Web page

What are Frames?

Netscape frames give you significantly more control over how your Web page appears to visitors. By using special HTML tags, you can create multiple independent frames within your Netscape screen, with each frame pointing to a different HTML file and linking to different sites on the Web.

This allows you to control the presentation of your page and make it easier for users to navigate through your site. Here's an example of how frames can be used. For my home page, I have several different pages linked together. On every page I have the same general header and footer. Because each page is in a separate HTML file, I have to retype the common information for each of them. Figure 6.1 shows my home page before I used frames.

Fig. 6.1
The header and footer are the same on every page at my site.

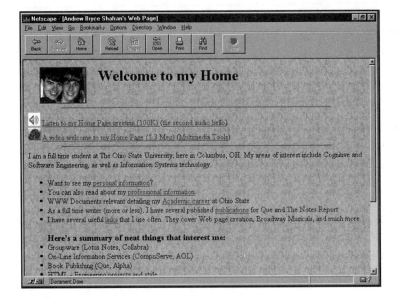

However, by using frames on my Web page, I can freeze the header and footer information into separate frames—because they never change—and let people browse through my Web page as usual. Figure 6.2 shows the same home page, now divided into three frames.

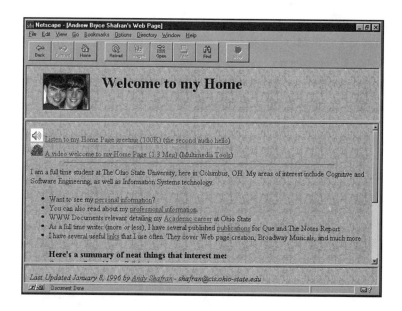

Fig. 6.2
Here's my home page broken into three frames.

Each of the three frames points to a different HTML document, so you're actually seeing three separate files at once! To navigate through my site, you still can click the hypertext links (underlined text) and see the corresponding Web pages, but the header and footer frames never change. That's because I want a title, as well as footer information (my e-mail address), on every page of my Web site.

Tip

Coincidentally, this makes it much easier to maintain and update the site. Let's say my e-mail address changes. With frames, I only have to update my e-mail address on one page, **footer.html**. Before I began using frames, I had to change the e-mail addresses on every page—what an inconvenience!

Freezing standard text is just one use of frames. In this section, I'll discuss several other ways you might want to use frames on your Web page. You'll learn that frames can be used for informational purposes, navigational reasons, or to keep material organized.

Remember that frames are only supported by Netscape 2.0 or later. Other browsers ignore your frame-related HTML tags, so you should take special steps so that other browsers don't see a blank screen. I'll point out how you can design a framed site that's friendly to users with other browsers in a few moments.

Useful Navigational Tools

Probably the most useful way to implement frames is as a navigational tool. You can create a frozen set of icons that appears at the bottom or side of the Netscape screen that lets users work their way through your Web site.

A great example of this is at the Netscape Navigator 2.0 home site (**http:// home.netscape.com/comprod/products/navigator/version_2.0/ index.html**) shown in figure 6.3.

Fig. 6.3

Netscape uses frames to make a standardized navigation bar.

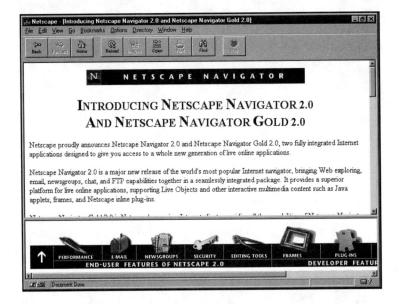

Notice how the screen is split into two sections. At the bottom of the screen, there are several different icons that you can click; these never change, no matter where you are within the Netscape site. When you click an icon at the bottom, the top frame changes to bring up the information you've requested.

Thanks to this unique navigation system, visitors can enjoy the Netscape site without having to work their way back and forth through a string of Web pages to jump from section to section. The navigation frame is always right there!

Organizing a Lot of Information

Another good use for frames is to sort and organize a lot of information. Figure 6.4 shows Bill Gerrard's home page (**http://ourworld.compuserve. com:80/homepages/DigitalDaze/**). Bill is a regular person like you and I, but he had a lot of information to put on his Web page. He decided to use Netscape frames to keep track of all that information and tie it all together.

Fig. 6.4
Visit Bill's site to take a look at how individuals can use frames on their personal Web pages.

Tip

If you like how Bill's page is organized, choose View, Document Source from the Netscape menu bar to see exactly how his HTML code is structured.

On the left side of the screen, Bill has created a simple table of contents for the information available on his Web page. When you click an item from the TOC, that information appears in the window on the right. The TOC is always there (like the navigation bar at the Netscape home page) but is structured in a different format. Just like my home page does, Bill's home page has a standard header and footer that never change.

Playing Tic-Tac-Toe: A Unique Frame Experience

The impressive thing about frames is that they are extremely flexible and allow you to structure Web pages in just about any way you choose.

For example, one innovative way to use Netscape frames would be to create a tic-tac-toe board. Using nine separate frames, figure 6.5 shows how you can play a quick game of tic-tac-toe from Netscape.

Fig. 6.5
Tough game.
Where should I
move next?

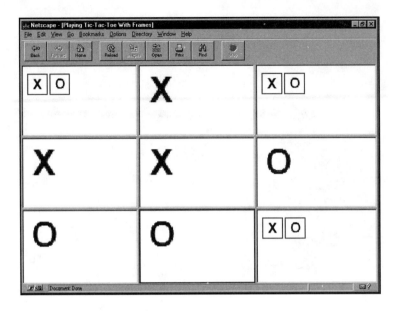

This example of frame use is interesting because each frame points to the exact same HTML file. All that's in the file are two small images, an "X" and an "O." When you click one or the other, Netscape redraws that frame with a large "X" or "O." There are not separate HTML files for each frame. Since all nine frames work the same way, there only needs to be a single HTML file, of which as many as nine separate instances may be open at once.

Frames are not Perfect for Every Situation

As with all new technology, you need to be careful where you choose to use Netscape frames. As you can see, there are a lot of different places where frames let you build custom interfaces to your Web site and make it more exciting and interesting, but don't add frames to your Web page just because you can. For an example of what I mean, take a look at the fictitious Web page shown in figure 6.6.

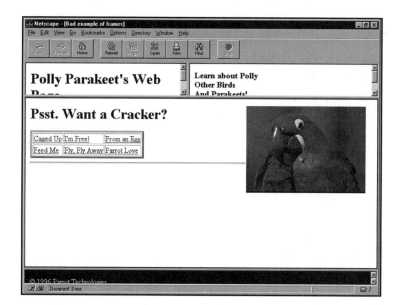

There are a lot of neat Netscape enhancements used here, including a colorful image and tables. Now, notice the two frames at the top of the page. This is seemingly to logically divide the two types of headlines for Polly's Web page. Unfortunately, it doesn't succeed. The headlines are not sized correctly to fit in the frames. Actually, these two frames serve no purpose. This same information could just as easily be incorporated without using frames, and be simpler to read. Also notice the copyright symbol in the bottom frame—again a bad use of frames. This simple frame is too small to display all of the information on screen, and generally isn't useful to visitors.

I'm not saying that using frames is a bad idea for this particular parakeet, but an important lesson should be learned. Don't use frames just because they are available, and test and evaluate a Web page interface to make sure it is usable and presentable. With a redesigned organization of the frames, this site could be great!

> **Note**
>
> Using frames on your home page tends to significantly increase the required time to download and see the entire page.
>
> Netscape itself learned this painful lesson early in 1996. It redesigned its site to take advantage of new frame capabilities. Unfortunately, instead of streamlining the interface to its site, its use of frames was difficult to use and required visitors to wait several minutes before the entire home page was downloaded. So, it removed frames off its Web pages in order to rethink and reengineer how to use them effectively. Using frames on a large site—especially one as big as Netscape—can be a daunting task.

Frame Navigation Differs from Standard Web Navigation

As you start encountering more frames, you might notice that there are some important differences in how you can navigate through them with Netscape.

On a Web page without frames, you can easily use the Back button to return to the previous page you visited. On a framed Web site, however, Back works a little differently. To move backward in a specific frame, you need to use the right mouse button.

Put your mouse in the frame within which you want to backtrack, then right-click and hold the button. Netscape brings up a list of options you can choose from (see fig. 6.7). Choose Back in Frame and the most recent previous text that appeared in that frame is displayed again.

Similarly, you can choose Forward in Frame from the same pop-up menu when applicable.

> **Note**
>
> Actually, the Back button at the top of the Netscape screen works as you'd expect it to, as long as you understand how frames work. When you visit a Netscape site with frames, the first HTML file that Netscape loads tells it how to split up the page, and where frames should appear. That file then points to other, separate HTML files to appear within those frames. From Netscape's point of view, you have loaded only the initial file, splitting up the page into different frames. It treats each smaller window differently, so clicking Back brings Netscape to the HTML file that was loaded before the first frame. Unfortunately, that's usually not what you meant to do—to move back within a single frame, you need to get in the habit of right-clicking.

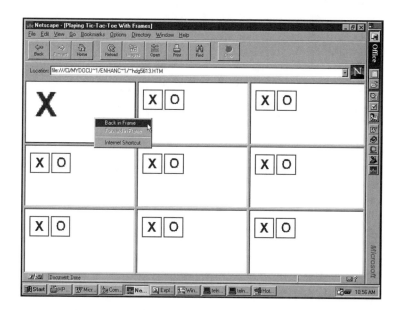

Fig. 6.7
Select your
mapped image in
this dialog box.

Building Simple Frames

Now that you're familiar with how frames can be used, let's start learning how to create them. There are just a couple of simple tags to learn; the tricky part is using them properly so that the frames appear the way you want them to.

This section takes you through creating a simple Web page that is divided into two frames. You'll learn what the HTML tags are, how to use them, and what files you need to create.

The First Step

When you want to add frames to your Web page, the first step is to think about how you want the frames organized, and how they should be displayed. Once you have a model in your mind, creating the actual HTML is relatively simple.

For this example, I'm going to create a new section on my Web page that lists all my favorite cartoons that are available on the Web. It doesn't have to be spiffy, but I want to create two frames—one to serve as a navigational table of contents, and the other to see the cartoon Web pages. In figure 6.8, I've drawn a quick sketch of how I want the frames to work.

Fig. 6.8

Before you start messing with HTML, plan, plan, plan.

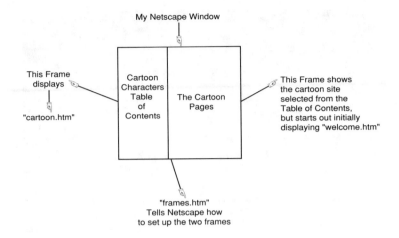

Basically, I want a table of contents on the left side. Visitors can click any entry, and the corresponding Web page appears in the window on the right. That way, you can always see the TOC, and can jump back and forth between cartoons.

To build this example, I need to create three separate HTML files. The first (cartoon.htm) is for the TOC, the second (welcome.htm) is for the frame on the right that appears when no cartoon pages are selected, and the third (frames.htm) tells Netscape how to organize the frames on-screen.

First You Add the <*FRAMESET*> Tag

The first file you must create tells Netscape how to divide the screen logically using some new tags. The first pair consists of the <FRAMESET> and </FRAMESET> tags. In your Web page, this pair of tags replaces the <BODY> and </BODY> tags.

When you use <FRAMESET>, you need to use additional keywords to signify whether you are splitting the Netscape window into different rows or columns. For example, to split your Netscape window into two columns of equal width, use COLS= as follows (see fig. 6.9).

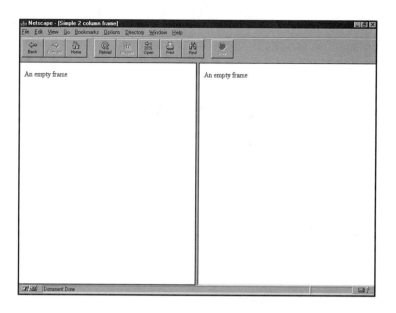

Fig. 6.9
These two
columns of frames
are of equal width.

```
<FRAMESET COLS="50%,50%">
</FRAMESET>
```

Likewise, to create two distinct rows on your Web page, use ROWS= as follows
(see fig. 6.10):

```
<FRAMESET ROWS="60%,40%">
</FRAMESET>
```

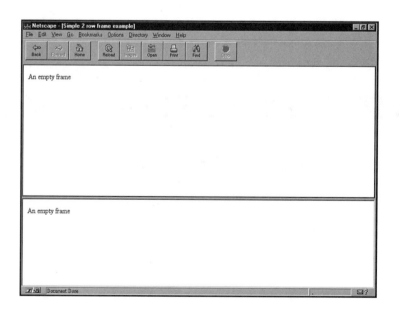

Fig. 6.10
These two rows of
frames are of
different height.

II

Livening Your Web Page

You are telling Netscape that you want to split the screen into two rows that take up 60 and 40 percent of the screen, respectively. You can tell Netscape to create as many rows and columns as you want, as long as the total percentages adds up to 100 percent.

Tip

In case your percentages don't quite add up to 100 percent, Netscape recalculates the proportions for you. For example, you might accidentally use the following:

```
<FRAMESET COLS="33%,33%,33%,33%">
</FRAMESET>
```

Netscape assumes that you want to have four columns of 25 percent each. Although Netscape tries its best to figure out what you mean, you should spend extra time to make sure that your numbers add up, to avoid surprises on the finished page.

Using Pixels Instead of Percentages

Instead of using percentages, you have other options when creating the dimensions of frames. You can indicate specific pixel counts. On standard VGA screens, the monitor displays 640 pixels horizontally and 480 pixels vertically. Super VGA dimensions are 800×600, and extremely high-resolution monitors can display 1024×768 or higher. If you use actual pixel counts on your Web pages, it's best to assume that everyone is using a standard VGA monitor at 640×480.

Thus, to create four even rows of frames on-screen using pixel coordinates, you could use the following pair of tags (see fig. 6.11):

```
<FRAMESET ROWS="120,120,120,120">
</FRAMESET>
```

Tip

Notice how my total pixel amounts adds up to 480—this implies I am using a VGA screen (640×480). Netscape automatically interpolates the meaning of this for SuperVGA and more intense resolutions.

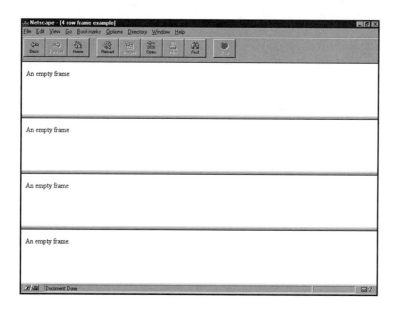

Fig. 6.11
Four frames of
exactly the same
pixel height.

Use the Asterisk

When telling Netscape to divide your screen, you can also use the asterisk (*)
as a wild card when specifying the height or width. Consider the following
example:

```
<FRAMESET ROWS="100,*,100">
</FRAMESET>
```

These tags create three rows of frames. The top and bottom rows are exactly
100 pixels tall, and the middle frame is the leftover amount. This method is
extremely useful when building frames, because you can disregard whether
the visitor's screen resolution is 640×480 or 1024×768. The top and bottom
frames are always the same size, and the browser makes sure that the variable
number adds up correctly. Figure 6.12 shows this example on a screen that
has a resolution of 800×600.

Fig. 6.12
The asterisk can create a "remainder" frame size so you don't have to worry about the exact numbers in pixels or percentages.

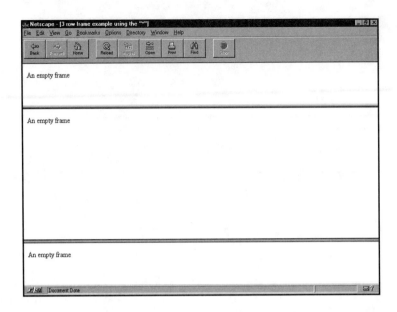

Note

The asterisk also can be used to create frames of relative sizes. Consider the following example:

```
<FRAMESET ROWS="*,2*,*">
</FRAMESET>
```

Here, you are requesting three frames. The first gets 25 percent of the screen, the second gets 50 percent, and the third gets 25 percent.

How does Netscape figure this? It creates a simple algebraic equation using * as a variable, and using 100 percent for the total screen height (for rows) or total screen width (for columns). In this example, the equation is:

```
* + 2* + * = 100%
```

When this equation is solved, * = 25%, Netscape replaces * with 25 percent to figure out the frame sizes, and ends up allocating frames of 25 percent, 50 percent, and 25 percent.

Using an asterisk this way lets you develop frames that work for every visitor regardless of screen resolution.

Caution

Be careful not to divide your screen into too many frames, lest they become unusable. Consider this pair of tags:

```
<FRAMESET COLS="10%,10%,10%,10%,10%,10%,10%,10%,10%,10%">
</FRAMESET>
```

The above tag does add up to 100 percent, but displaying ten separate frames on a single Web page is overkill. As a general rule, more than five rows or columns on a single page tends to be too much—and even less frames than that can be overwhelming, depending on what's in them.

Include the *<FRAME>* Tag

Once you've decided how to split up your screen into multiple frames, the next step is to tell Netscape which HTML file to display in each frame, and set several options for how the file should appear on-screen. The syntax of the <FRAME> tag is similar to incorporating an image on your Web page, and this tag must appear within the <FRAMESET> and </FRAMESET> tags.

The number of <FRAME> tags must correspond to the number of frames indicated by the <FRAMESET> tag. Consider this example:

```
<FRAMESET COLS="30%,70%">
<FRAME SRC="cartoon.htm" NAME="Navigation Window">
<FRAME SRC="welcome.htm" NAME="Cartoon Window">
</FRAMESET>
```

Here, you tell Netscape to divide the screen into two frames (columns). The left hand frame displays the HTML file named cartoon.htm and the right-hand frame displays welcome.htm. Figure 6.13 shows these frames in Netscape.

Notice the NAME= keyword within the <FRAME> tag. This keyword names each frame for Netscape's benefit, and lets you access the frames separately. I'll talk more about NAME= in a moment. With my new frame setup, the TOC always stays on the left, while the frame on the right changes, depending on which link I select. Figure 6.14 shows my Netscape window after I click Winnie-the-Pooh.

II

Livening Your Web Page

Fig. 6.13
These two frames
are the backbone
for my cartoon
Web page.

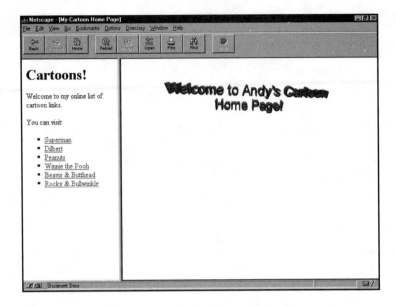

Fig. 6.14
With these two
frames, I can easily
visit every cartoon
site within
moments.

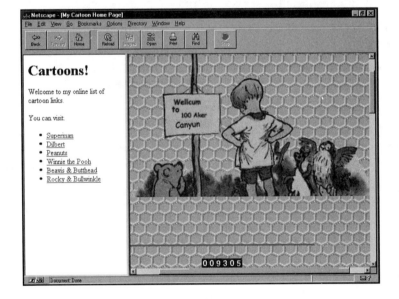

Note

When completing the SRC="" portion of the <FRAME> tag, you can insert any valid URL between the quotation marks. In this example, I simply referenced two local files that are stored in the same subdirectory as the file for the page.

To access a file within the CARTOON subdirectory, for instance, you would use the following tag:

```
<FRAME SRC="CARTOON/cartoon.htm">
```

To access a directory one level above the current directory you would use .. as follows:

```
<FRAME SRC="../cartoon.htm">
```

You can use this concept to access files several directories above the current directory. The following example points to a file three directories above:

```
<FRAME SRC="../../../cartoon.htm">
```

You can even link to other Web pages on the Internet. For example, you would link to my copy of the cartoon file with this tag:

```
<FRAME SRC="http://www.shafran.com/enhancing/cartoon.htm">
```

For more information on valid URLs, refer to Chapter 1, "Understanding the WWW Evolution and Netscape's Revolution."

The *NORESIZE* Keyword

Several other keywords can be added to the <FRAME> tag, including NORESIZE. Without this keyword, visitors to your Web page can shift and move the column and row boundaries if they want to.

To ensure that your frames appear exactly as you've specified, add NORESIZE to the <FRAME> tag:

```
<FRAME SRC="cartoon.htm" NAME="Navigation Window" NORESIZE>
```

In most situations, you don't need to add this keyword. People generally won't resize their frames. Think carefully before adding this tag, because it means that visitors with different screen resolutions will not be able to make your page work better for them by changing how the frames appear.

Control Scrolling

Another keyword you can add is SCROLLING. This keyword indicates whether or not scroll bars should be added to frames in which some text or image is too big to fit, given the frame size specification. You can set SCROLLING to YES, NO, or AUTO. By default, it is set to AUTO, meaning that Netscape adds scroll bars when it deems them necessary.

II

Livening Your Web Page

Usually you won't bother with the scroll bar settings, but sometimes you might want to permanently suppress them by adding SCROLLING=NO to your tag. Figure 6.15 shows you what scroll bars look like within Netscape.

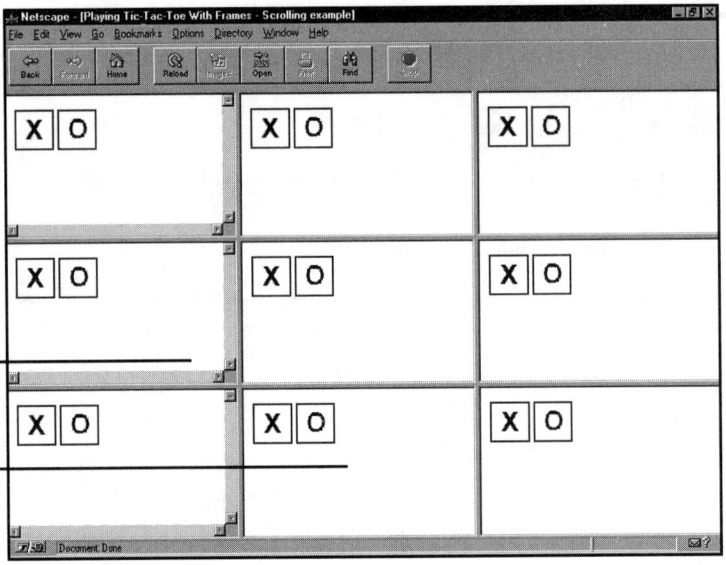

Fig. 6.15
In this case, scroll bars get in the way of playing the game, but usually you want to leave SCROLLING set to AUTO.

Frame with scroll bars ——

Frame without scroll bars ——

Creating Links to Each Frame

Once your frame is built, you're almost finished. The last step is to learn another keyword that Netscape recognizes when creating hypertext links. With the <A HREF= > tag, you can use the TARGET= keyword to tell Netscape which frame you want the linked text to appear in; the default is the current frame that's selected. Remember how you named the frames above? You use those names to explain to Netscape which frame you want to use for loading certain things.

For my cartoon example, I always want the left hand frame to stay on-screen as a TOC. When a visitor clicks a specific cartoon in the left hand frame, therefore, I want the appropriate link to appear in the right hand frame. When building my list of links on the left, each one uses TARGET=. Here's a snippet of HTML from my cartoon.htm file:

```
<UL>
<LI><A HREF="http://www.unitedmedia.com/comics/dilbert"
TARGET="Cartoon Window">Dilbert</A>
<LI><A HREF="http://www.unitedmedia.com/comics/peanuts"
TARGET="Cartoon Window">Peanuts</A>
<LI><A HREF="http://www.midtown.net/~olen/pooh" TARGET="Cartoon
```

```
Window">Winnie the Pooh</A>
<LI><A HREF="http://mindlink.net/charles_ulrich/frostbite.html"
TARGET="Cartoon Window">Rocky & Bullwinkle</A>
</UL>
```

Whenever one of the links is selected from the TOC listing, Netscape goes out and retrieves the linked text, then displays it in the frame named "Cartoon Window," leaving the TOC frame unchanged.

> **Tip**
>
> Make sure that the value you use for the target is exactly the same as the value you typed when naming the window earlier.

Other Target Keywords

When building links and targets, there are a few other options you should know. Netscape recognizes certain values that always work the same with TARGET=, regardless of how you have named your frames:

- TARGET="_blank"—This brings up an entirely new window of Netscape to display the linked information.

- TARGET="_self"—This tells Netscape to display the linked information in the frame where this URL is displayed (useful for my tic-tac-toe example).

- TARGET="_parent"—This tells Netscape to display the linked information in the frame previous to the current document; this is seldom used.

- TARGET="_top"—This tells Netscape to load the linked information into a complete new screen of Netscape, not divided into any frames.

> **Tip**
>
> Remember to add TARGET="_top" to any links that take the user away from your Web site. Without this being specified, the frame characteristics you have set for your screen will remain the same as users go on to browse other parts of the Web.

Advanced Frame Features

Now that you're familiar with adding simple frames to your Web page, you're ready to learn some advanced ways that frames can be used.

This section shows you how to include both rows and columns on your Web page (like the tic-tac-toe board), and how to build recursive frames. I'll also show you how to set up your page so that users without Netscape 2.0 don't see a bunch of gibberish when visiting your frame-enabled site.

Working with Multiple Frames

So far, you know how to add rows or columns to your home page, but sometimes you may want to use both. All you need to do is to embed additional <FRAMESET> tags within the first pair of tags, and make sure that they work together.

Let's say I want to add two new rows to my cartoon screen, one across the top and one across the bottom. The top one is my standard header that I include on every Web page at my site, and the bottom one is the footer that includes my e-mail address and other valuable information.

First, I define the number of rows that I want on-screen; it's three. Next, I want to split the middle row into two columns, so I need to build two levels of <FRAMESET> tags:

```
<FRAMESET ROWS="70,*,50">
    <FRAME SRC="myheader.htm" NAME="Header Window">
    <FRAMESET COLS="30%,70%">
        <FRAME SRC="cartoon.htm" NAME="Navigation Window">
        <FRAME SRC="welcome.htm" NAME="Cartoon Window">
    </FRAMESET>
    <FRAME SRC="myfooter.htm" NAME="Footer Window">
</FRAMESET>
```

Figure 6.16 shows the new cartoon Web page after clicking Superman.

Fig. 6.16
With four frames, my cartoon Web page is just about finished.

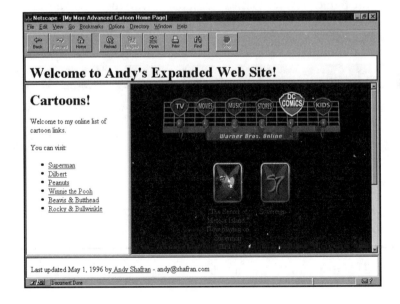

> **Caution**
>
> Every time you embed tags within tags, make sure you have the appropriate closing tags in your HTML file. In this example, for instance, I need to use </FRAMESET> twice or Netscape won't display my frames.

Another Example Using Multiple Frames

I usually give only one example of how to perform an operation, but you'll almost always use multiple frames on a Web page, so we need another example of how they can be used.

For the tic-tac-toe game shown earlier, I divided the screen into equally spaced rows. Then, I created three equally spaced columns within each row. The HTML is still relatively simple, and you can see how each frame is specified:

```
<FRAMESET ROWS="33%,33%,33%">
    <FRAMESET COLS="33%,33%,33%">
        <FRAME SRC="choose.htm">
        <FRAME SRC="choose.htm">
        <FRAME SRC="choose.htm">
    </FRAMESET>
    <FRAMESET COLS="33%,33%,33%">
        <FRAME SRC="choose.htm">
        <FRAME SRC="choose.htm">
        <FRAME SRC="choose.htm">
    </FRAMESET>
    <FRAMESET COLS="33%,33%,33%">
        <FRAME SRC="choose.htm">
        <FRAME SRC="choose.htm">
        <FRAME SRC="choose.htm">
    </FRAMESET>
</FRAMESET>
```

This section of HTML produces the table that you saw earlier in this chapter. The HTML within choose.htm is extremely similar:

```
<BODY>
<A HREF="bigx.gif"> <IMG SRC="littlex.gif"> </A>
<A HREF="bigo.gif"> <IMG SRC="littleo.gif"> </A>
</BODY>
```

All that this file does is display two small images for each frame—a small x and a small o. If the small x is clicked, for example, then the frame links to an image of a larger x.

> **Note**
>
> You might have noticed that I don't use NAME= for my nine individual frames. It's unnecessary. Because they're not named, Netscape automatically replaces the frame that has the file linked to it. So, as the game is played, the big X or 0 replaces the two smaller letters in whichever frame is clicked.

Frames Within Frames

Another innovative way to include frames on your Web pages is by recursively adding frames within frames. You can build frames within frames within frames, and so on. All you have to do is add the appropriate <FRAMESET> and <FRAME> tags.

On the CD

For example, in the tic-tac-toe file, I have each of the nine frames display an X or an 0. Figure 6.17 shows how Netscape appears when I tell each of the nine tic-tac-toe frames to build another set of nine frames inside of itself.

Fig. 6.17
This super tic-tac-toe board has two levels of recursive frames so that 81 separate areas appear on-screen.

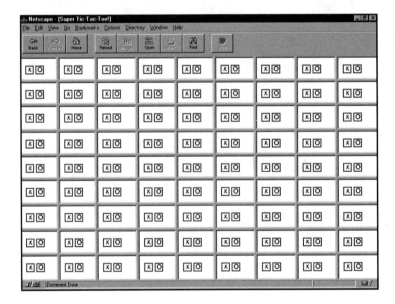

Use recursive frames carefully, because too many different frames on-screen can easily confuse visitors to your Web site.

Designing for Non-Frame-Capable Browsers

Realizing that not all Web browsers are created the same, Netscape has built in an additional tag to make sure your Web pages look good to non-frame-capable users. Using <NOFRAMES> and </NOFRAMES>, you can mark text that will appear only when a visitor stops by your Web site with a browser that doesn't support frames.

When a Netscape 2.0 visitor stops by, he or she automatically ignores the text specified in the <NOFRAMES> tag. When a non-Netscape 2.0 browser stops by, he or she ignores the commands within the <FRAMESET> and <FRAME> tags, and only displays the information specified by <NOFRAMES>. The <NOFRAMES> tag is ignored by these other browsers, but they display the text you want them to.

With the <NOFRAMES> tag pair, you can create regular HTML files, including lists and tables, and even link to images and other sites. Some sites spend time creating two sites—a frame and non-frame site, but this can be difficult and time-consuming.

Alternatively, use the <NOFRAMES> tag to display a short message to non-Netscape 2.0 users urging them to get the newest version of Netscape and then return back to this Web page. The decision is yours—to exclude non-Netscape users, or to work twice as hard for a simple Web page:

```
<NOFRAMES>
<H1> This page is no fun for you. </H1>
<HR>
Because I use frames on my Web page, you won't be able to experi-
ence my page as I've designed it. Try downloading Netscape 2.0 or
better and then coming back here to see my site in its full glory.
<P>
<B>Andy Shafran</B>
</NOFRAMES>
```

Make sure that your <NOFRAMES> tags appear between the <FRAMESET> and </FRAMESET> tags in order to work correctly with Netscape 2.0.

Tip

Because frames are a relatively new technology, many Web sites develop their pages twice—one set for browsers that support frames, and one set for browsers that don't. This ensures that your Web pages are accessible to everyone. That's how I've designed my home page, because I didn't want someone to be unable to enjoy my site just because he or she wasn't using the latest version of Netscape. For me, it was worth the extra work.

II

Livening Your Web Page

Alternatives to Frames

The presentation possibilities with frames are spectacular. With this new Netscape enhancement, you have significantly more control over how your page appears, and can make it easier for people to peruse your whole site.

Frames are not, however, the perfect solution to every situation. Sometimes, you'll want to design Web pages for people who use a non-frame-capable browser, and other times frames just won't fit the purpose you are trying to achieve. This section takes a quick look at some practical alternatives to frames, and shows you how they can be used in your Web pages.

Tables

Tables and frames have a lot in common with each other. They both require a handful of HTML tags, help you to line up the correct number of rows and columns on-screen, and give you a lot of flexibility when displaying information.

Tables let you split the parts of your screen into different cells of information. They work differently than frames because tables don't link to separate HTML files to be displayed in the corresponding cells. All the information for building a table is in a single file.

I could easily build a table for my cartoon home page, but it would have to be designed much differently. Because tables don't actually split the screen, I could never view two different sites at once. Whenever I clicked a cartoon listed in the table, my whole window would be replaced by the new site.

As a general rule, tables are a great idea for displaying information in Netscape. The cell display and formatting capabilities make it ideal for comparing information, or listing it in a usable fashion—but not for creating an interface to your Web pages. Keep in mind also that many browsers that don't support frames won't support tables, either.

Navigation Button Bars

The precursor to frames was the technique of creating a customized navigation bar at the top or bottom of the screen. Several icons were displayed, and when clicked, each icon would take you to a different URL.

These bars were nice because you could use them to link from page to page easily. Such bars still make sense when letting users navigate your Web site, but these days many people are putting them in a frame that stays put at the bottom of the screen (recall the Netscape home page we looked at earlier). That way, no matter what information is displayed in the top window, the navigation bar stays put and is always available for clicking.

If you use a customized button bar, however, don't feel obligated to start including support for frames in your site. Think through how people will visit your Web site, and be sure it makes sense before you build a special frame for the navigation icons.

Well-Organized Web Sites

The best alternative to using frames at your Web site is careful and thorough planning. Using frames introduces a different way to display Web pages that might not fit in with what your site already has available. For example, if the first thing visitors see is a big picture of you or your company's logo, then adding a frame to split up the page may distract the user from what you want them to see.

If you keep close track of how your pages link to each other, and make it easy for people to browse your site, then there may be no need to add frames. Test your Web page and see if there is an appropriate number of hypertext links, if information is displayed in a concise and simple format, and if your progression of links follows a logical order. These factors are usually enough to make a site successful. ❖

II

Livening Your Web Page

Chapter 7
Advanced Graphics Issues

Imagine going to a symphony concert that had no music. There would be no point to watching the conductor wave his baton or observing the musicians fiddle with their instruments. The whole point of a concert is hearing the music. Similarly, graphics and images lie at the heart of the World Wide Web's existence. Without colorful images and interesting graphics, there would be no mass of people using the Web, and no influx of people creating home pages.

On the same note, you wouldn't like to listen to a concert where the musicians were horrible. It's no good if you can hear sounds coming from the symphony, but cannot distinguish between Pachelbel's *Canon in D* and Tchaikovsky's *The Overture of 1812*. Likewise, the key to having satisfying Web pages is using good, high-quality images that are useful, entertaining, and informative.

This chapter teaches you several innovative techniques for using images on your Web pages. Specifically, you'll learn how to:

- Enhance your page's appearance with good graphics
- Incorporate existing images into your pages
- Build and scan interactive images from scratch
- Take advantage of new file techniques when using GIF and JPEG images
- Learn about new image formats on the horizon
- Use an enhanced Netscape tag to optimize performance when using images

Graphics Make or Break a Page

In *Creating Your Own Netscape Web Pages*, I spent considerable time explaining the necessity of using images on Web pages. In this section, I'm going to follow up on what I said there, and discuss some guidelines you should be aware of when building and enhancing your Web page.

Many of these qualities aren't of much concern when you create a simple Web page, but come into play when you are using the newest Netscape features and understand more about how the Web works.

Number of Images

File size is perhaps the most important trait when working with images on Web pages. Most users who will browse your site are using a 14.4 or 28.8 baud modem—fast, but not that fast. You should keep this in mind when adding images to Web pages.

Using a 14.4 baud modem, a 30K image takes about 45 seconds to download. A 28.8 modem works faster, but still takes 20–30 seconds. Add up everything on your Web page and see how many bytes visitors have to download when they stop by. Don't forget to include the size of your background images, icons (such as buttons or arrows), and the size of the HTML text file. Try to keep this total in the 40K–75K range—you'll find my home page pretty close to 40K.

Don't panic if you can't get the sum of all your images to a reasonable number. Later in this chapter, we'll look at several techniques that make a significant difference when you're using GIF and JPEG images, so that total file size isn't as critical.

Fits Inside of Frame

With Netscape 2.0, many people are starting to incorporate frames into their Web pages. Frames are very neat, useful tools (see Chapter 6, "Framing Your Work," for more detailed information), but can affect the images you want to use on your Web site. That's because your Netscape window can now be split into multiple frames of different sizes. Banners and graphics sometimes don't fit when you change the height and width of your Netscape frames.

Figure 7.1 shows a site (**http://www.pcworld.com/annex/**) named The Annex. This is a prime example of how creating images for frames can be difficult. The designers of this site obviously spent a tremendous amount of time putting lots of different images inside of each frame, but didn't think through the whole process. Notice how some of the images fit perfectly in a frame, while others don't? The whole point of using frames here was to provide a graphical way to explore the site, but you can't even read some of the images.

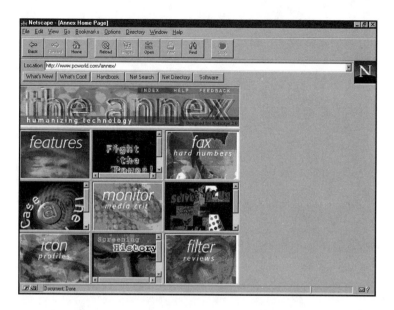

Fig. 7.1
A great site...
almost. The Annex
needs to look at its
frames with a view
to improvement.

Mixing frames and images makes sense in this situation, but you need to make sure they work correctly with one another. The Annex could fix its Web page easily by shrinking the size of the graphics that don't fit in a particular frame, or adding the SCROLLING=NO keyword when defining the frame.

Remember, also, that when you start using frames, you might use different types of graphics than you would use with a non-framed page. For example, you might want to create customized navigation icons for your Web page, similar to what Netscape does at their site (refer to Chapter 6, "Framing Your Work").

Unpredictability of Visitors' Resolutions

An important point I neglected to mention in the first book was designing for users with all types of screen sizes and resolutions. This rule is especially important because you can have visitors to your home page who use Windows, Macintosh, or UNIX versions of Netscape—all with different screen sizes and resolutions.

There are three typical resolutions to be aware of that are commonly found among Windows users. Each displays a certain number of pixels on the monitor. Figure 7.2 shows an example of how resolutions can vary.

II

Livening Your Web Page

Fig. 7.2
This drawing
compares VGA,
SVGA, and
enhanced SVGA.

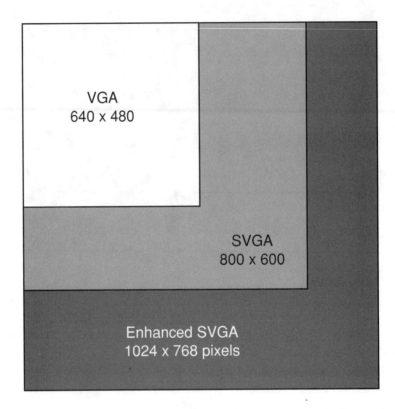

When creating and editing images, you want to cater to the lowest common denominator—in this case, VGA. No image should be larger than about 600 pixels wide and 440 pixels tall. Notice how I subtracted 40 pixels in each dimension from the standard VGA setting. That's to ensure that an image completely fits inside of the Netscape window.

Be aware that visitors to your home page will arrive using all three types of screen resolution. If your images are too big to be seen, Netscape includes scroll bars that let visitors scroll up and down (or left and right) to see the rest of the image, but that is extremely inconvenient for the visitors.

Remember that, as a general rule, the larger an image is displayed on-screen, the larger its file size is. Most users don't want to wait a long time to see some gigantic image on your Web page.

Creativity

It almost goes without saying how important creativity is when designing and creating a Web page. I'm not insinuating that the images on your Web page need to be masterpieces, but creativity does make a difference.

Take a look at figure 7.3. Each icon and image here is hand-designed, and you can tell. Although this Web site is mostly useful only to people who live in Columbus, Ohio, it's a good example of how spending a little extra time working on your images can go a long way. Also notice how they effectively use the image to create an elegant look on this Web page. Instead of adding a huge image, they have a reasonably sized home page picture and let empty space on the sides of the page draw your eyes to the center and focus on the word "Welcome."

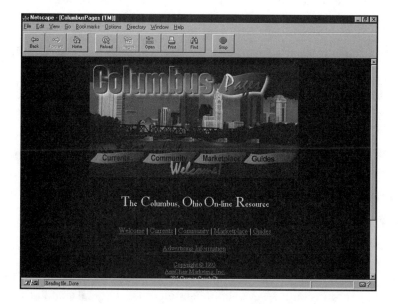

Fig. 7.3
The ColumbusPages (**http://www.columbuspages.com**) site is a homegrown page that shows a lot of creativity.

II

Livening Your Web Page

Fresh Graphics

Another important aspect to keep in mind when creating Web pages is the need to keep your images fresh and constantly changing. If you add and replace images periodically on your Web site, then people will come back and visit more often.

By constantly updating the images on your Web site, you indicate that you are interested in maintaining a current and up-to-date page on the Web. Generating new images or pictures for your page makes it more fun for the visitor who frequents your site, but also more fun for you, because you get to redesign your site on a regular basis.

I try to change the images on my Web page every few months. Since it is my personal Web page, I like to keep pictures of myself, family, and friends, and updating them more often than every few months is a real inconvenience. You have to decide how often to update your Web page to fit your own needs and requirements.

Also keep in mind that you should continually change the text of your Web page as well. Simply changing the images is nice, but by adding new information, people will be excited about stopping by for multiple reasons. Changing images is usually an indication that the Web developer is keeping the whole site current.

> **Tip**
>
> Another way to keeping your images fresh is by keeping a standard set of images, and having Netscape display a different one every time someone visits your Web page. I talk about this type of advanced scripting and HTML development in Chapter 11, "Understanding and Using CGI Scripts."

Getting Cool Images for Your Web Page

The most difficult aspect of creating a Web page for most people is finding the perfect graphics and images to use. Everyone has their own preferences when it comes to images, icons, bullets, graphics, buttons, and pictures. The following sections outline several different methods that make finding and using graphics on your Web page easier.

On the CD-ROM

Included on the CD-ROM accompanying this book are many different icons and images of various shapes and sizes. I've spent a lot of time looking for neat and advanced-looking icons and images to help enhance your Web page. Feel free to use as many of them as you like.

Besides the standard icons and images, you'll also find a sample collection of 3D icons, banners, buttons, and graphics. These sample pictures were provided by Asymetrix, an advanced multimedia software company, to show you some examples of its products that can help you create great images for the Web. I'll talk about Asymetrix again later when I show you how to create great images from scratch.

Appendix C, "What's on the CD-ROM?," contains more details on the images and pictures that are available on the CD-ROM.

Borrowing from Other Web Pages

Another, more common way of finding images for your Web page is by "borrowing" them from someone else's site. Netscape allows you to save any image you see while cruising the Web directly onto your computer; all you have to do is right-click the image and choose Save this image as from the pop-up menu.

Caution

While many people on the Web don't mind if you borrow icons and images from their Web pages, businesses and corporations often have a different point of view. Usually their images are custom-developed, and they—and the court system—view saving a copy of their images as stealing. Be careful when taking images from sites around the Web. Many images and graphics are copyrighted, and the owners can—and sometimes do—take legal action against people who infringe upon their copyrights.

If you ever are unsure whether an image is copyrighted or not, send e-mail to the person in charge of the Web page and ask.

A different way of borrowing images from other Web sites is to link your page to an image on another site. To do this, right-click the image you want to link to, and choose Copy this Image Location from the pop-up menu (see fig. 7.4).

This copies the URL of the image you selected to your computer's internal
Clipboard. From there you can go to your HTML editor and choose Edit,
Paste (or press Ctrl+V). The URL of the image you want to display appears
wherever you perform the paste operation. Make sure you build the <IMG> tag
properly. For example, if you want to include a link to an image of me on
your Web page, you'd first copy the URL to your Clipboard, and then paste it
into the following <IMG> tag:

```
<IMG SRC="http://www.shafran.com/meandliz.gif">
```

Whenever someone visits your Web page, Netscape also retrieves the image
you linked to when displaying your Web page.

Caution

This practice of linking your Web page to images elsewhere on the Internet is in the
hazy gray area of the legal world. By linking to an image, you are giving credit to the
original owner, but may be using the image in a manner not originally intended by
the author/creator. I am not a lawyer, however, and the application of copyright law
to the Internet is not very clearly defined. Be aware that some individuals and companies may request that you do not link to images and pictures on their Web page.

Read the section "Legal Issues for Web Sites" in Chapter 4, "Important Details for
Enhanced Sites," for an in-depth discussion of these issues.

Other Existing Images

Although I have tried to put a reasonable collection of images, tools, and
multimedia clips on the CD-ROM accompanying this book, it is hard to ac-
commodate everyone.

You may want to take a look at the book *Internet Graphics Gallery* by Paul
DeGroot and Dick Oliver. This book lists literally hundreds of different sites
on the Internet and WWW where you can find images of all kinds. You'll be
impressed with the encyclopedic approach this book takes towards finding
creative and unique images on the Internet.

Another possibility is using stock images and clip art for your Web pages. Stock images are those which are sold in bulk quantity—usually on CD-ROM—and can be used in any manner once purchased. You can find stock CD-ROMs (for the Mac and PC) for all types of different images in your local computer store. One of my favorites comes from Expert Software. For $19.99, I purchased a CD-ROM that came with 3,000 full color and professional photographs. They have similar CDs full of clip art as well. Many of the examples and images used in this book come from those CD-ROMs. If you are interested, you can contact Expert Software directly at 1-800-759-2562 (or 305-567-9996 for international callers).

Create Amazing Images from Scratch

Probably the best way you can enhance your Web page is by creating your own innovative, customized, and creative graphics from scratch. Making your own graphics offers several advantages:

- You don't have to worry about copyright violations.
- Your images are a product of your personality.
- You don't have to spend a lot of time looking for images to borrow on the Web.
- You have complete flexibility over how images appear and are displayed on your Web page.

This section talks about several great, easy-to-use ways to create your own unique images for your Web page.

3D Images with Asymetrix's Web 3D

Realizing that there are millions of people who want to create their own customized images, Asymetrix, a multimedia company based in Seattle, recently released a product named Web 3D. Web 3D is a simple, powerful software package that creates excellent 2D and 3D graphics.

Unfortunately, Web 3D is not a shareware software package, and could not be included on the CD-ROM accompanying this book. Instead, on the CD, I've included some sample icons, banners, and images that were created with Web 3D, though, so you can get a taste of the types of images you can make for yourself.

On the CD

Even better, Asymetrix sponsors an online demo area where you can interact with the Web 3D software through Netscape, and build a small handful of graphics for your Web page—to build custom graphics for yourself. Combining the online demo with the sample images on the CD-ROM, you should get a nice feel for how Web 3D can enhance your Web pages.

Using the Online Demo

I'm going to step you through using the demo version of Asymetrix Web 3D. The first step is browsing **http://web3d.asymetrix.com** as shown in figure 7.5.

Fig. 7.5
The Web 3D home page is where the complimentary demo starts.

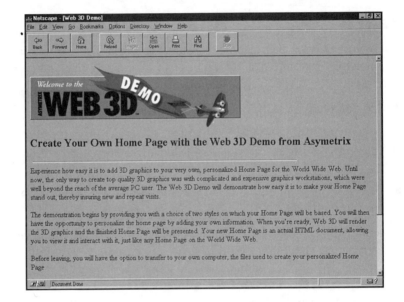

At the bottom of that Web page, Asymetrix lists three distinct styles in which you can create your sample images (in the actual product, there are many more styles for you to choose from). I like style B the best, so I'll choose that. You can select whichever of the three you prefer. Figure 7.6 shows the new screen that appears when you select a style.

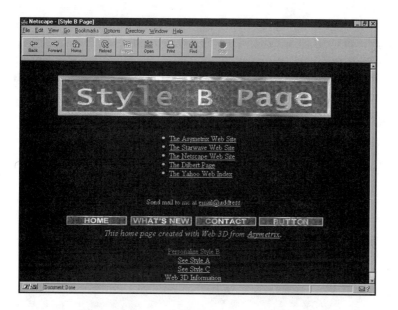

Fig. 7.6
Here's a more thorough example of the types of images Web 3D is about to create for you.

At the bottom of this screen choose Personalize Style B (or A or C, if that's what you chose). A form appears, letting you fill out exactly what you want your customized banner and buttons to look like (see fig. 7.7)

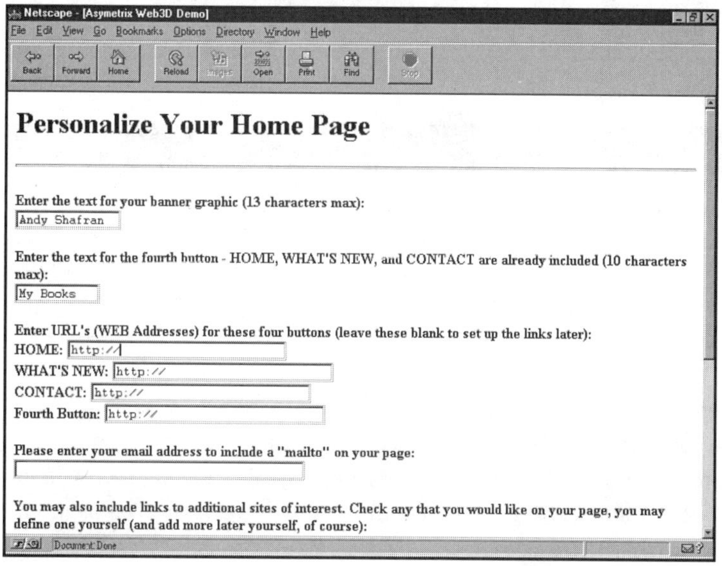

Fig. 7.7
Filling out this form lets you customize your images.

II

Livening Your Web Page

When you've completely filled out this form, click the Create a Home Page button. Asymetrix goes out and builds your own 3D images on-the-fly and then inserts them into your Web page. Figure 7.8 shows the final product. From here, Asymetrix lets you download the images, or you can right-click and use Netscape's pop-up menu to save the images one at a time to your local drive.

Fig. 7.8

Here's the final product—pretty cool images, huh?

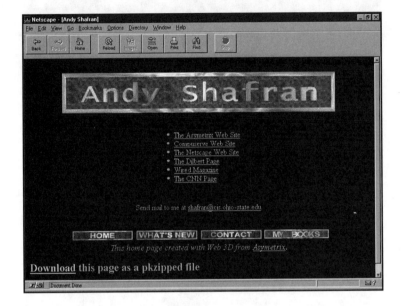

Caution

Creating these images is fun, but during busy periods it can take a long time. The first day I tried using the demo, I was online waiting for over an hour. I gave up and tried again the following morning, and there was no wait at all—I had my images made for me instantly.

Buying Web 3D for Yourself

As I said before, Web 3D is a commercial product that is available in most software stores and directly from the company. Purchasing it costs about $99—but if you're serious about creating images for your Web pages, look no further.

Explore the demo and feel free to use the graphics on the CD-ROM. From my own personal experience, within ten minutes of installing Web 3D on my computer, I had created several cool images and icons for my Web pages. In fact, most of the graphics and images used in this book were created from Web 3D—and I am not a professional desktop publisher.

In addition, Web 3D can be used to build animations as well. These are stored in Windows AVI format, with Web 3D doing all the work for you.

For more information or to order, call Asymetrix at 1-800-448-6543 (or 206-637-1600 for international readers). Or visit their Web site at **http://www.asymetrix.com**.

Using WebScript

Besides the online Web 3D demo, another fantastic site on the Web to create your own customized graphics is **http://webscript.giftlink.com**. This site demonstrates an image-creating software package that builds images and graphics on-the-fly.

The graphics aren't three-dimensional, but you can create whichever ones you'd like quickly and easily. This site lets you create some extremely classy images that are simple and have a small file size. Here, you are limited to creating images with text only, but you can choose from a wide variety of fonts, sizes, and colors when making them. Figure 7.9 shows this home page from WebScript.

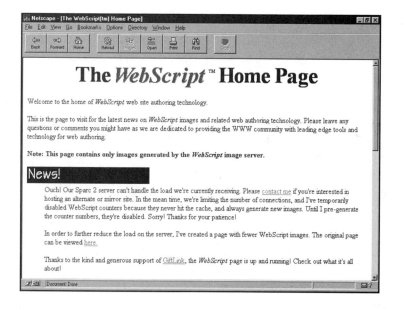

Fig. 7.9
WebScript images come in any size, format, or color.

WebScript lets you create your own customized images from any textual phrase. Using an interactive browser, WebScript works in much the same way as Web 3D does. Click the link marked WebScript Browser to bring up figure 7.10.

Fig. 7.10
Decide on the type of image you want to create.

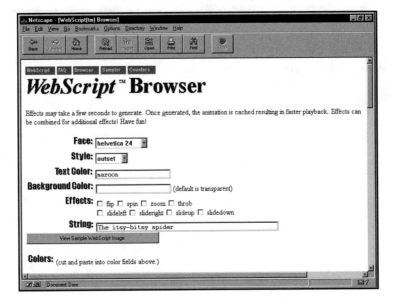

From here, you can choose from several default font types and sizes. Then you can choose from over 500 different colors in which your text should appear (the list of colors is at the bottom of the WebScript Browser page).

You can also select whether you'd like your text to appear animated—such as sliding onto your Web page, or throbbing. Finally, in the String box, type the textual string of the image you want to create. Once you're finished, click the View Sample WebScript Image button to see your results. Figure 7.11 shows the image that appears when I use the settings shown in figure 7.10.

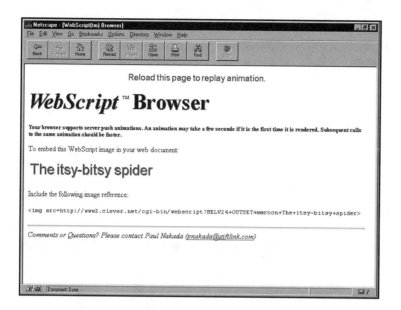

Fig. 7.11
Here's the final
results—not bad if
I say so myself.

Once you've created an image, you can use your right mouse button to save
the image on your PC and use it on your Web page. Alternatively, you can
add a hypertext link to your Web page which points to the image located on
WebScript's server. For my simple image, the HTML tag I would add to my
Web page would be the following:

```
<img src=http://www2.clever.net/cgi-bin/
webscript?HELV24+OUTSET+maroon+The+itsy-bitsy+spider>
```

You can add it just like a normal <IMG> tag; only every time someone stops by
your Web page, they are linked to WebScript and can download the customized image.

Caution

Because of the popularity of this site, WebScript is sometimes unreliable. It's probably
not a good idea to link your Web page to WebScript because it adds an unnecessary
load to their servers. The owner recommends using WebScript to create sample
images. You can run the WebScript program on your own Web server and dynamically create images by downloading the package from its home page. Contact your
Web provider for more information.

II

Livening Your Web Page

Other Software: Using Paint Shop Pro

Besides the two interactive sites mentioned previously, many professional graphics programs exist that let you create, change, and manipulate images for your Web pages.

On the CD

One of my favorites is Paint Shop Pro. A shareware version is included on the CD-ROM accompanying this book, letting you test its impressive array of capabilities. You can create new images from scratch, modify existing ones, or combine text and images. In addition, Paint Shop Pro lets you convert your images into virtually every graphical file type you'll ever need (GIF, JPEG, and PNG included). Figure 7.12 shows me in action working with another image for my Web page.

Fig. 7.12
Paint Shop Pro is the best of the tools out there for creating and manipulating images.

Tip

For the latest edition of Paint Shop Pro, you can always stop by **http://www.jasc.com** to download the newest shareware version.

Current Scanner Quality and Detail

When you want to include personal pictures and drawings on your Web page, sometimes the only way is to use a digital scanner. Scanners come in all different price ranges and quality. You can find an affordable black-and-white scanner for $79, but high-end color scanners can run $999 or more, depending on the quality you are looking for.

Scanners are rated according to *resolution*. Resolution is the number of itsy-bitsy dots that a scanner observes when digitizing your photographs and drawings. Resolution is important because the better resolution your scanner uses, the more detailed your digitized images appear.

When looking for a scanner, you should get at least a 300×300 dpi resolution. This means that for every inch scanned, 90,000 dots are picked up by the scanner. That may sound like a lot, but a standard fax machine uses 200×200 dpi resolution—and you're probably familiar with how blurry faxes can sometimes be. Often, a scanner comes with software that enhances the resolution of scanned images significantly.

High resolution scanners often cost a premium, and can be overkill if you are simply scanning pictures in for your Web page. Oftentimes, 300×300 or 600×600 dpi is enough resolution for casual users.

> **Note**
>
> I use a Logitech PageScan Color scanner. For about $400, it has a 400×600 dpi resolution and comes with all the necessary software to scan color and black-and-white images, and can even make photocopies and send faxes. All of the photographs on my Web page were scanned at this level, so you can visit my page to get a good idea of the type of resolution you might want when buying a scanner.

> **Tip**
>
> As I mentioned in *Creating Your Own Netscape Web Pages*, one great place to scan your own images without buying a scanner is your local Kinko's or other copy store. They usually have scanning equipment available to rent for just a few dollars; this is much cheaper than buying your own scanner. Along the same lines, many local public libraries also have multimedia equipment as well—and those are free!

Optimizing Your Images

So far in this chapter, I've talked about a lot of general details and tactics that are useful when generating and building your own Web page images. There are, however, some technical specifications that you should be aware of when creating and embedding GIF and JPEG graphics into your Web pages.

By taking advantage of several possible enhancements, you can:

- Make your images look better on your Web pages
- Speed up the way images are displayed
- Work with newer compression techniques to make JPEG images smaller and quicker to download

This section explains the changes you can make to your images and shows how to make them.

Transparent GIF Images

One of the advantages of using GIFs instead of JPGs on Web pages is that you can customize GIFs so that their backgrounds appear *transparent*. Transparent backgrounds make GIFs appear like they are floating when placed on a Web page because the color of their background naturally fits in, regardless of Netscape's current background colors.

Figure 7.13 shows an example of what I'm talking about. Here, the Xs have a transparent background, but the Os don't.

Fig. 7.13
The Xs fit in much more nicely with the screen than the Os do.

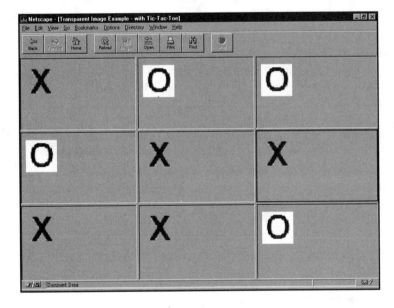

Both images are the same size and have the same color background (white). I used Paint Shop Pro to create both of them. The only difference is that when I created the X image, I told Paint Shop Pro to make the background transparent.

This has the same effect as using an overhead machine when giving presentations. When you put a transparency on top of the overhead machine, the text of the transparency is displayed, but the rest of the paper is transparent and doesn't block or change the light as it shines through.

Making your GIFs transparent improves the way images appear on your Web page. Non-transparent images sometimes look awkward and out of place because they display the background image or color around the shape of the whole image as a square—not the image's actual shape.

Most graphics packages give you the opportunity to create GIFs with transparent backgrounds. With Paint Shop Pro, there is a special checkbox that you can select when saving your image.

Interlacing GIFs

Another technique that makes GIFs more usable is *interlacing* them. Interlaced GIFs are saved and displayed in a recurring manner.

When Netscape loads a non-interlaced GIF, it starts at the very top of the picture and slowly displays the image until it reaches the bottom. Interlaced GIFs work differently. Netscape uses several complete passes to load the image on-screen. The first pass renders a blurry image in which the details of the picture are difficult to make out. Then Netscape goes back and makes a second pass, rendering the image significantly clearer, but still not finished. Finally, Netscape makes it to the last pass and you see the complete image in sharp focus.

The visual effect is much like sitting in an optometrist's office. You look through a viewer and see blurry letters at the end of the room. The optometrist changes your focus and the letters clear up a bit—you can make out the top level, but not much more. Once several more lenses have been flipped, you can see the whole image clearly.

Visit the Que home page at **http://www.mcp.com/que** to see a great example of an interlaced image. Figure 7.14 shows the image halfway through the loading process, and figure 7.15 shows the completed image.

Fig. 7.14
The main Que image uses interlacing so that you don't have to wait for the whole thing to load to move on.

Fig. 7.15
Patience is a virtue. Here's the reward for waiting for the image to load completely.

Downloading interlaced and non-interlaced images takes the same amount of time, but interlaced images offer one distinct advantage. Usually, you can make out what an image looks like one or two passes before it's finished being shown on-screen, and you know whether or not you want to wait around to see the entire image.

This feature is nice because it enables you to place larger images on your Web pages and still leave control in the hands of the people browsing it. They'll quickly get a good idea whether or not they want to stick around and wait for the entire image to load.

Any GIF can be converted into interlaced format. Paint Shop Pro takes care of this conversion automatically if you set that option when you save the file.

When prompted to save a GIF file, you usually are given three options. Here's a quick guide to the differences between them:

- **Version 87a—Non-Interlaced**—Established in 1987, this format was the first widely used edition of GIF, and many older GIFs are stored in this format.

- **Version 89a—Interlaced**—This option is what I encourage you to use. Established in 1989, this version of GIF has better compression techniques than its 1987 sibling, and is interlaced as well.

- **Version 89a—Non-Interlaced**—This format was made available in 1989 for the rare occasions when you do not want to save an image in interlaced format.

> **Tip**
>
> Although any GIF image can be interlaced, don't waste your time unless the file is 10K or larger. Images below 10K are usually loaded on-screen before visitors even get a chance to read the opening text of your page.

Progressive JPEG

Not to be outdone, JPEG images also have features that can optimize how they are displayed within Netscape. Progressive JPEGs are an enhancement on the way JPEG files are stored and thus displayed. More or less, progressive JPEGs are the same thing as interlaced GIFs. Progressive JPEGs load over several passes, each one making an image clearer to see—just like in the example I gave for interlaced GIFS.

To make an existing JPEG into a progressive one, you can download a free conversion program for your computer at **http://www.cis.ohio-state.edu/hypertext/faq/usenet/jpeg-faq/part2/faq.html**. The current edition of Paint Shop Pro doesn't support progressive JPEGs, but it will in a future release.

On the CD

In general, progressive JPEG images are about the same file size as regular ones and take the same amount of time. The main benefit is that visitors can get a good grasp of an image while they are downloading it.

Unfortunately, older versions of Netscape and other WWW browsers don't support the new progressive JPEG format. So visitors using these other browsers won't see your images.

Using *LOWSRC*

One of the new Netscape enhancements gaining popularity is the LOWSRC keyword that you can add to the <IMG> tag. LOWSRC tells Netscape that you want to display two separate images in the same area on-screen.

Typically, LOWSRC tells Netscape to display a low-resolution image that can be downloaded quickly when you first visit a Web page. Once the lower-resolution image is downloaded, Netscape then downloads the regular image specified within the tag. Consider the following example:

```
<IMG SRC="COMICS.GIF" LOWSRC="COMICSBW.GIF">
```

First Netscape displays COMICSBW.GIF, a black-and-white version of my image. Because the image is saved in a gray scale (as opposed to color) format, COMICSBW.GIF is significantly smaller than COMICS.GIF. Once the first image finishes loading, Netscape starts displaying COMICS.GIF on top of it. In my example, the colorized version is around 38K. The black-and-white version is only 7K. Users get to see the general image almost immediately when I use LOWSRC.

This technique is another useful alternative when dealing with larger images. You can create a colorless version of an image and let the visitor to your Web page decide whether they want to wait to see the full-color version. An excellent example of the LOWSRC tag in action can be found on the Disney home page at **http://www.disney.com**. This professional page is optimized so visitors don't have to wait around for a long time to see neat images.

Tip

Again, you can use Paint Shop Pro to quickly convert a color image into a black-and-white one. All you have to do is load the image, and choose Colors, Gray Scale. The image is converted instantly. Make sure that you save the image to a different filename so you don't overwrite your original color image.

New Image Horizons: the PNG Format

Recently, a new type of image has gained in popularity. Billed as the replacement for GIFs, Portable Network Graphics (PNG, pronounced *ping*) images soon will be supported by Netscape.

PNG graphics are very similar to GIFs but are more efficient and can better handle a vast array of colors. Soon, we'll probably start phasing out GIF images to use PNG instead. Although Netscape doesn't support PNG images yet, other popular browsers such as Mosaic 95 already do.

PNG graphics can be displayed as transparent images, and you can choose to save them in interlaced or non-interlaced format.

For more information on the PNG graphics type, visit my favorite PNG information center at **http://quest.jpl.nasa.gov/PNG/**. It's good to know that Paint Shop Pro also can convert images into PNG format if that's what you want.

Note

Rather than bore you with all the details, I'll quickly summarize why PNG exists. Several years ago, CompuServe (an online services company) created GIF as its international image standard, and many people adopted it as their standard as well.

A few years ago, Unisys realized that CompuServe had used some of its patented computer code when developing the GIF format, and decided to enforce its patent. Not wanting to be dependent on another company's patent, CompuServe (along with other developers on the Internet) introduced PNG to be the community-wide graphics format standard. PNG has started to develop significant popularity because of its advantages over the GIF file format—such as not having to tussle with Unisys over who owns the PNG format.

Chapter 8
Image Map Education

The last chapter introduced some important issues regarding the use of images on your Web pages. You learned that using images on your Web page improves its appearance by leaps and bounds. In this chapter, I'll show you how to take your images one step further and put them to work for you.

Using *image maps*, you can link different areas of a single image to different HTML files. This lets visitors to your Web page navigate from page to page by using their mouse to select different areas of an image.

This chapter discusses the ins and outs of adding image maps to your Web pages, taking advantage of new Netscape 2.0 technology that makes creating image maps easier than ever. Anyone can add an image map, called a *client-side image map*, to their Web page in a matter of minutes.

Specifically, this chapter teaches you how to:

- Understand how image maps work
- Tell the difference between client-side and server-side image maps
- Build a simple image map for your Web page
- Decipher the new HTML tags that support client-side image maps
- Link various sections of an image to different HTML files on the Web

How Do Image Maps Work?

You probably already know how to link an image to another HTML file. By embedding the <IMG> tag inside of a Hypertext reference, you can create links from images, just as you would from text. Look at the following HTML example:

```
<A HREF="ROME.HTML"> <IMG SRC="ROME.GIF"> </A>
```

Shown in figure 8.1, this example adds an image of the Colosseum in Rome to my Web page. When visitors click the image, Netscape automatically loads the file ROME.HTML.

Fig. 8.1
Linking an image to an HTML page is easy to do.

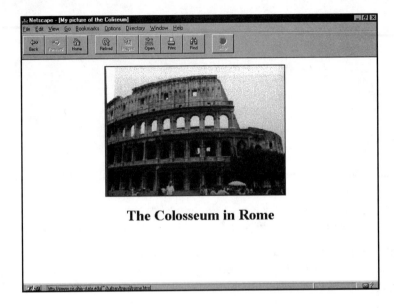

No matter where on the picture you click, Netscape always links to ROME.HTML. This is where an image map could come into play. Using an image map, you can link *different* areas of an image to *different* HTML files, based on what section of the image is clicked.

This is an extremely useful technique because it lets visitors to your Web page get accustomed to a single image, and navigate from page to page by clicking different sections of that image.

Look at the Magnavox home page (**http://www.magnavox.com**) for an excellent example of an image map (see fig. 8.2). Here, the developers have included a picture of a remote control with several buttons drawn on it. Each section of the image brings you to a different spot on the Magnavox Web site. For example, clicking Company Info brings up information about Magnavox, while you can easily imagine what kind of stuff appears when you click Fun & Games.

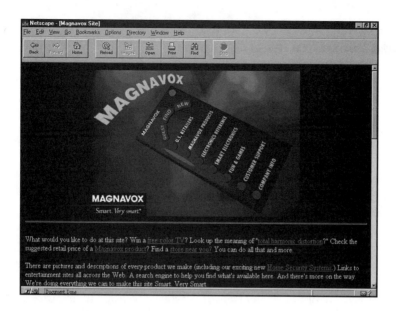

Fig. 8.2
Magnavox's image
map is smart...
very smart.

Image Maps are not New Technology

Clickable image maps have been around for a long time. You have always
been able to add one to your Web page if you knew the right steps to follow—I even discussed them in *Creating Your Own Netscape Web Pages*. With
the release of Netscape 2.0, adding image maps to your Web page has become
significantly simpler and less complicated.

Previously, to add a clickable image map to your Web page, you were dependent on your Web server software. Your server software controls all access to
Web pages at a particular Internet site. To add an image map to your page,
you had to find the right image, decide how each part of the image would
link to a different HTML file, and then set up and customize your server properly. This was quite a hassle, even for those people who could understand every step—and some Web servers don't permit image maps to run on them.
Therefore, using image maps on Web pages was effectively limited to professional Web developers and larger companies; few individuals used image
maps on personal Web pages.

Today, though, creating image maps is much easier. A new development
called *client-side image maps* makes it easier for individual Web page developers—like you—to add a clickable image map to a Web page. More image maps
are being created every day because of their relative ease of use.

II

Livening Your Web Page

Differences between Server-Side and Client-Side Image Maps

As I previously mentioned, *server-side image maps* have been around for a couple of years, but are awkward to use. In this section, I'll explain exactly how server-side image maps run, and why they're being pushed aside for newer technology.

Here's how a server-side image map works. Someone visits your home page and sees a neat image. After looking at the image for a while, they click one area (like one of the buttons on the Magnavox remote control), presumably to take them to a corresponding page of HTML. Netscape stores the coordinates that the user clicked and sends that information to the Web server. The server takes those coordinates and runs a separate program that translates those coordinates into a URL—the filename of the linked area clicked. Then the Web server sends that filename back to Netscape, which goes and loads the file. As you probably can gather, server-side image maps aren't extremely efficient because of how many steps are involved in using them. Also, if you have a Web server that is extremely popular, it spends all its time running the special program that translates pixel coordinates into an HTML file. This puts a heavier load on the Web server, and slows access for everyone reading pages at that particular Web site.

Client-side image maps (called CSIM for short) are significantly simpler. As far as users can tell, the same image appears on-screen, but what happens when they click the image is different. Instead of exchanging information with the Web server, Netscape automatically knows which HTML file to link to—and takes you there automatically. This process is significantly quicker to process (you don't have to wait for the Web server) and easier for Netscape to interpret.

Client-side image maps are more efficient, easier to create, and better for users who visit your Web pages. Eventually, client-side image maps will entirely replace image maps that are dependent on the Web server.

Note

You always can tell whether you are using a server-side image map or a client-side one. Take a look at the status bar at the bottom of the Netscape screen while you move your mouse over an image map. If you see scrolling numbers, then you know it's a server-side image map (those pixel coordinates are sent to the server when you click). If you see a filename instead of coordinates, then you're using a client-side image map.

Who Supports Client-Side Image Maps?

Because they are such a significant advancement, client-side image maps have quickly become supported by all major Web browsers, including the following:

- Netscape 2.0
- Microsoft Internet Explorer
- Mosaic 95
- Arena

This means you won't have to worry about people who visit your Web page not being able to use your new client-side image map. These were introduced with HTML 3.0, and virtually everyone on the Web uses a browser that supports them. Of course, modern browsers also support the older server-side image maps.

Creating a Client-Side Image Map

Now that you understand the difference between the two types of image map technologies, I'm going to show you how you can quickly build an image map on your Web page. I'll step you through building and adding a client-side image map.

In this section, we'll create an actual image map from start to finish. You'll learn how to select the right kinds of images, link the different areas to separate HTML files, and add the correct tags to your Web page.

Finding a Good Image

When creating image maps, the first step is selecting a good image to use. You want to make sure that visitors who see the image understand that there are several different areas on the picture that they can select to link to different items. You need to select definitive images that have different regions easily delineated on-screen, and that make sense to visitors.

Figure 8.3 shows the image I'm going to use for this example, a client-side image map for the ACME Block Company.

Image maps can be created from virtually any graphic that you can add to your Web page. Icons, buttons, bars, pictures, and images of all types can be sectioned out and presented as an image map for visitors. Not all images, however, make sense for use as image maps. In general, pictures become difficult image maps because they often lack clearly defined areas for the user to click. Recall my picture of the Colosseum earlier in the chapter (refer to fig. 8.1). That image wouldn't be a good image map because there aren't any well-defined areas other than the large image of the Colosseum.

II

Livening Your Web Page

Fig. 8.3
These big blocks make it easy for users to identify the different regions of the image map.

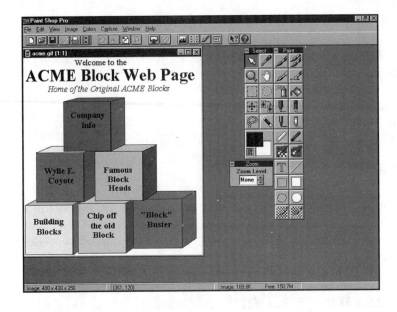

People and animals aren't *always* bad candidates for image maps, but you need to make sure that users will understand they can access different Web pages by clicking different parts of the image (for instance, body parts). Visit **http://www.cs.brown.edu/people/art035/Bin/skeleton.html** for a prime example of how a picture of a person (in this case, a skeleton) can be used as an image map (see fig. 8.4).

Fig. 8.4
Now, where's that funny bone?

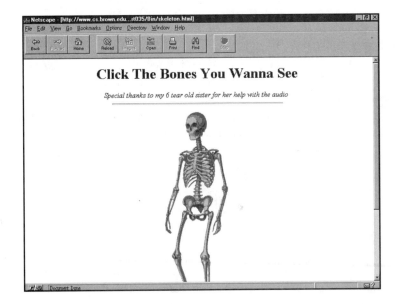

Planning the Map

Once you've selected an image, the next step is to logically divide it into different regions, and define how you want the image map to work.

For my ACME block example, I want each block to be linked to a different Web page (see fig. 8.5).

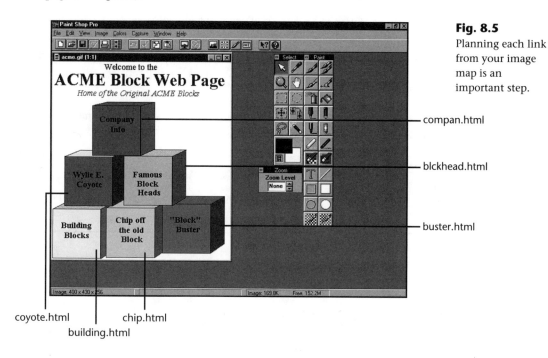

Fig. 8.5
Planning each link from your image map is an important step.

compan.html

blckhead.html

buster.html

coyote.html

building.html

chip.html

Once you have a good idea of how to divide your image map, you're ready to move to the next step—adding the necessary HTML tags to your Web page.

> **Caution**
>
> Make sure that each HTML file your image links to exists. It's easy to forget to create one or more of the HTML files if you create your image map when they don't all exist.

Adding the Image to Your Web Page

With the correct image selected, it's time to start learning the new HTML tags that support client-side image maps. Adding image maps is similar to adding regular images except that you need a new keyword and a couple of new tags.

II

Livening Your Web Page

Fortunately, you won't have to learn all the complicated HTML if you don't want—in a moment, we'll look at a new tool that avoids all that.

If you're going to add the proper HTML yourself, you first need to embed the image into your Web page using the `<IMG>` tag with the `USEMAP` keyword:

```
<IMG SRC="BLOCKS.GIF" USEMAP="#ACME Block Image Map">
```

This tag tells Netscape to display `BLOCKS.GIF` on the Web page. `USEMAP` tells Netscape that the image is a client-side clickable image map, and to look for a section named `ACME Block Image Map` in this HTML file. This named section of HTML tells Netscape how to interpret clicks on different coordinates of the image.

The # is very important because that's how Netscape recognizes named references within a file.

Note

Netscape makes you name each set of image map coordinates so that you can have multiple client-side image maps within a single page.

Now, you're ready for the fun stuff. The next section teaches you how to tell Netscape which portions of an image link to which particular HTML files.

Mapping Your Image

With the image embedded in your Web page, your next step is to define each region on the image graphically. Think of each image as a large piece of graph paper where you have to identify the exact X and Y coordinates for each section that links to an HTML file. For images, coordinates are measured in pixels (the dot resolution of your computer monitor). You have to specify the pixel dimensions of each section.

On the CD

Fortunately, several easy-to-use tools exist that make it easy for you to specify each distinct section for the image map. One of the best, Map This!, is included on the CD-ROM accompanying this book. With Map This!, you use your mouse to draw each section on the image, and thereby create a link to an HTML file.

I'll step you through using Map This! to create a complete image map.

1. Start Map This!. You can run the program directly from the CD-ROM or copy it to your personal computer. (Appendix C shows you how to use the CD-ROM and programs stored on it.) A blank screen appears.

2. Choose File, New to create a new image map from scratch. The Make New Image Map dialog box appears (see fig. 8.6).

Fig. 8.6
First you need to tell Map This! which image you're mapping.

3. Click Let's go find one! to reach the Open existing Image file dialog box where you can specify the image you want to map (see fig. 8.7).

Fig. 8.7
Select your mapped image in this dialog box.

4. Select the image you want to edit (Map This! currently supports only GIF and JPEG image formats—not PNG) and then click Open to bring up the mapping window shown in figure 8.8.

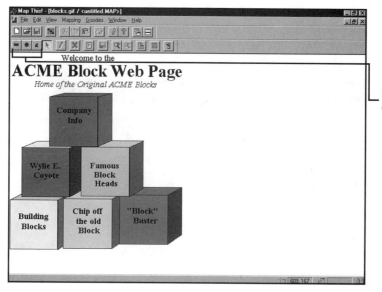

Fig. 8.8
From here, you can map the image with your mouse.

Use these icons to draw shapes

5. Once the image is opened, you can draw three types of shapes to indicate sections on your image: rectangles, circles, and polygons.

6. Draw as many different shapes and sections on your image as you need. For my ACME Block image, I have six different sections, one for each of the blocks. Figure 8.9 shows my image with the six sections marked.

Fig. 8.9
Notice the six rectangles drawn around the significant blocks on the image.

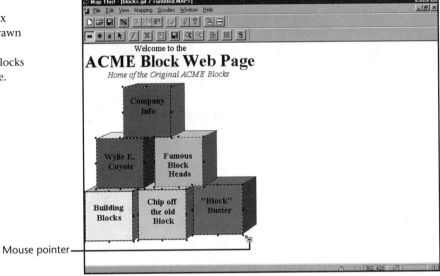

Mouse pointer

7. Now, click the Show/Hide Area List icon on the toolbar to bring up the Area List dialog box (see fig. 8.10).

8. Select a listed area, and then click Edit to bring up the Settings dialog box (see fig. 8.11). Here, type the URL of the file you want linked to this region. Click OK after you've typed the URL.

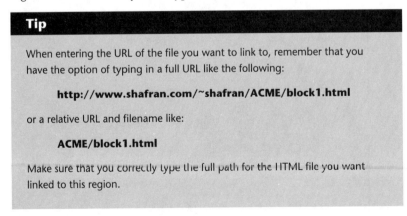

Tip

When entering the URL of the file you want to link to, remember that you have the option of typing in a full URL like the following:

http://www.shafran.com/~shafran/ACME/block1.html

or a relative URL and filename like:

ACME/block1.html

Make sure that you correctly type the full path for the HTML file you want linked to this region.

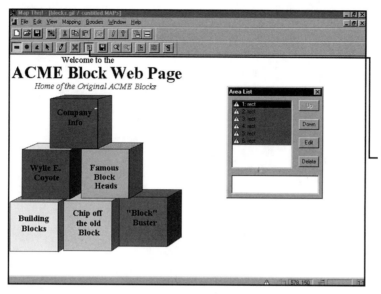

Fig. 8.10
From the Area List dialog box, you can link regions on the image to specific HTML files.

Show/Hide Area List icon

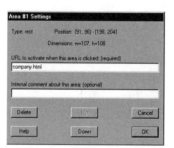

Fig. 8.11
For each area, you've got to tell Map This! what you're mapping.

9. Repeat step 8 for every region defined on your image. After you finish, your Area List dialog box lists each region along with the corresponding linked file (see fig. 8.12).

10. Choose File, Save from the menu bar to bring up the Info about this Mapfile dialog box (see fig. 8.13).

11. Enter the map's title, and make sure that the CSIM radio button is selected as the Map file format. (Remember that CSIM stands for client-side image map.) You also can type in a default URL to link this image to if users click a part of the image outside of the regions you've defined.

Fig. 8.12
My finished Area List dialog box—every region on the image map is now properly linked.

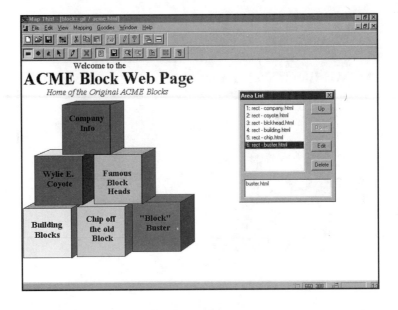

Fig. 8.13
Set your image map options here, and you're nearly finished.

Caution

For your image map to work properly, make sure that the title you type in the Info about this Mapfile dialog box corresponds exactly to what you entered following the USEMAP keyword earlier.

12. When you finish setting your image map options, click OK; Map This! prompts you to save the client-side image map to an HTML file.

Here's a copy of my finished file:

```
<BODY>
<MAP NAME="ACME Block Image Map">
<!— #$-:Image Map file created by Map THIS! —>
<!— #$-:Map THIS! free image map editor by Todd C. Wilson —>
<!— #$-:Please do not edit lines starting with "#$" —>
<!— #$VERSION:1.20 —>
<!— #$DESCRIPTION:The client-side Image Map for ACME Block Com-
pany. —>
<!— #$AUTHOR:Andy Shafran —>
<!— #$DATE:Mon Mar 29 21:38:26 1996 —>
<!— #$PATH:C:\ —>
<!— #$GIF:blocks.gif —>
<AREA SHAPE=RECT COORDS="91,96,198,204" HREF=company.html>
<AREA SHAPE=RECT COORDS="29,206,136,314" HREF=coyote.html>
<AREA SHAPE=RECT COORDS="2,322,110,428" HREF=blckhead.html>
<AREA SHAPE=RECT COORDS="124,319,230,426" HREF=building.html>
<AREA SHAPE=RECT COORDS="161,205,269,311" HREF=chip.html>
<AREA SHAPE=RECT COORDS="247,310,355,416" HREF=buster.html>
</MAP>
```

Now that you've successfully created your image map definition, all you have to do is add it to your HTML document (preferably just below the <IMG> tag), and you're all done. You've just created your own personalized client-side image map.

Figure 8.14 shows what the example image map looks like in Netscape 2.0. Notice how the status bar at the bottom of the screen indicates which HTML file will be linked to as the mouse hovers over a particular block.

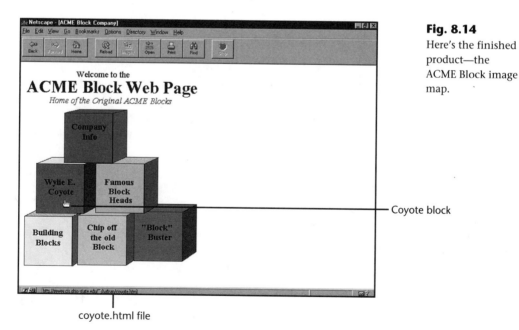

coyote.html file

Fig. 8.14
Here's the finished product—the ACME Block image map.

Coyote block

Understanding the Image Map Shapes

Although you'll probably only create an image map with Map This! or a similar program, this section describes the different aspects of creating an image map definition from scratch, so you can understand all the tags used in the file in the last section.

Once I've added the image tag to my Web page, the next step is to add the <MAP> and </MAP> tags:

```
<MAP NAME="ACME Block Image Map">
</MAP>
```

These are new HTML tags used to tell Netscape where each region of the image is linked. Make sure that the value following NAME corresponds *exactly* to the value used with USEMAP earlier. Otherwise, Netscape cannot interpret the image map links correctly.

The <MAP> tag tells Netscape that this section of your HTML file describes how each region of the image map should work.

Within the <MAP> tag pair, you need to add an individual <AREA> tag for each section of the image you want mapped to another HTML file. You can have three different shapes: rectangles, circles, and polygons.

Rectangles

To create a rectangular section on an image, you need to know the actual pixel coordinates of the upper left and lower right corners of the rectangle.

Pixel coordinates come in pairs, with the upper left corner of an image always identified as 0,0. The first number is the horizontal measurement from left to right, and the second number is the vertical measurement from top to bottom. For example, let's say you want to create a rectangular section like that shown in figure 8.15.

Fig. 8.15
Let's use these coordinates to create this exact rectangle.

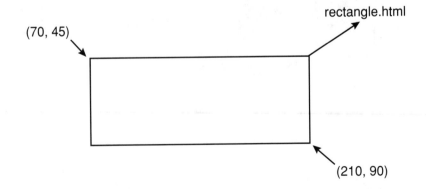

(70, 45)

rectangle.html

(210, 90)

I've labeled the pixel coordinates on this image. To add this section to your HTML file, your <AREA> tag would look like this:

```
<AREA SHAPE=RECT COORDS="70,45,210,90" HREF=rectangle.html>
```

The SHAPE keyword tells Netscape that you've defined a rectangular shape. The COORDS keyword requires four values: X and Y coordinates for the upper left and lower right corners of the rectangle. Finally, the HREF keyword tells Netscape which HTML file you want loaded when the user clicks this particular area—it's that easy!

> **Tip**
>
> In case you have forgotten, squares are rectangles with four equilateral sides. To add a square shape to your image map, therefore, you still use AREA=RECT.

Circles

Mapping circular shapes is almost as easy as rectangles, but there are a few differences. To map the shape of a circle, you only need three coordinates (as opposed to four for a rectangle). You need the X and Y coordinates of the circle's center, and the length of the circle's radius (see fig. 8.16).

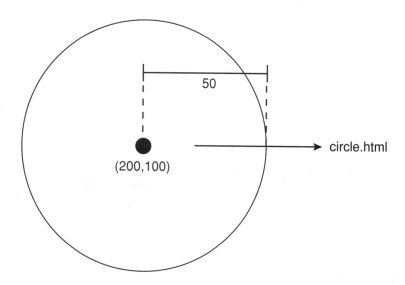

Fig. 8.16
Use these coordinates and the length of the radius to create this circle.

As you can see, the center of the circle is located at 200, 100 and the circle has a radius of 50 pixels. The corresponding <AREA> tag looks like this:

```
<AREA SHAPE=CIRCLE COORDS="200,100,50" HREF="circle.html">
```

Polygons

The final shape you can define on an image map is a polygon. By specifying a polygon, you can identify a shape of any size with any number of sides. Simply tell Netscape the coordinates of every corner of the shape. Take a look at the five-cornered polygon shown in figure 8.17.

Fig. 8.17
Tell Netscape these coordinates to draw this polygon.

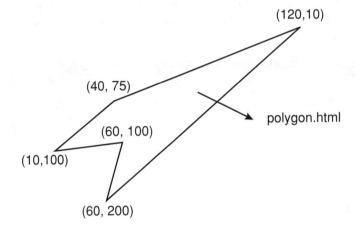

Adding the appropriate <AREA> tag is simple; the only difference is that you need to list a pair of coordinates for each corner of the polygon. Thus, for this example, we have six pairs of X,Y coordinates:

```
<AREA SHAPE=POLY COORDS="40,75,10,100,60,100,60,200,120,10,40,75"
HREF="polygon.html">
```

The key to creating polygon regions on an image map is that the first and last pair of coordinates must be the same, so that Netscape can close the region. While there are six sets of coordinates in this example, notice that the first and last sets are identical.

Caution

Map This! only supports up to 64 sets of corners for a polygon when you draw the shape with your mouse.

How Do Overlapping Regions Work?

When creating image maps, you may have two or more different areas that overlap (see fig. 8.18).

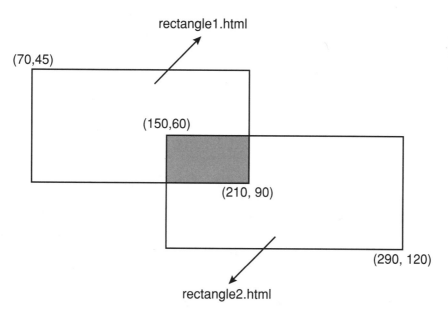

Fig. 8.18
Notice the over-
lapping region in
this drawing.

In this example, there is a small overlapping region for my two rectangles. How does Netscape interpret a click in the overlapping region? The answer is simple—it links to the first region listed in the <MAP> tag. Our example is coded this way:

```
<MAP NAME="Overlap Example">
<AREA SHAPE=RECT COORDS="70,45,210,90" HREF=rectangle1.html>
<AREA SHAPE=RECT COORDS="150,60,290,120" HREF=rectangle2.html>
</MAP>
```

Therefore, Netscape brings you to `rectangle1.html` if the overlapping region is clicked.

Note

Why does Netscape assume that you want a click in an overlapping area to bring you to the first area listed? It's because when Netscape registers a click on an image map, it starts logically reading through the <MAP> tag. It checks each area in turn to see if the coordinates that have been clicked fit within that shape. As soon as it finds a match, it whisks you away to the linked page, not bothering to look at the rest of the areas in the <MAP> tag.

Adding a Default Link

Another concern besides overlapping regions is the issue of what happens when a user clicks outside of all established regions on your image map? You can specify a *default link* that is activated in this type of situation. Default links are nice because they make sure that visitors to your Web page are always linked to *some* page, regardless of where they click on the image.

To add a default link to your image map, all you have to do is add one final region to your image map—a rectangle that spans the entire width and height of your image. For example, my ACME Block Company image is 300 pixels wide and 400 pixels tall, so I'm going to add the following line to the end of my image map definition:

```
<AREA SHAPE=RECT COORDS="0,0,299,399" HREF=default.html>
```

Tip

I use 299 and 399 because the pixel count starts at 0,0. Thus, the 300th pixel across the screen is actually at X coordinate 299.

Caution

Make sure that this default area is the last item in your <MAP> tag. Otherwise, it will supersede any areas that follow.

Of course, you might want nothing to happen when a user clicks outside of your designated areas. In that case, you still should add an all-image <AREA> tag, but use the NOHREF keyword:

```
<AREA SHAPE=RECT COORDS="0,0,299,399" NOHREF>
```

This informs Netscape that any clicks outside of the other defined regions should be ignored. This tag isn't really necessary; it just makes your image map definition more complete.

Test the Image Map with Netscape

Once you're finished creating the image map, make sure that you test it thoroughly with Netscape. Use Netscape to test every region, one at a time, to make sure that your links have been created properly.

Many people overlook this step, assuming that there won't be any mistakes as long as they have followed the above steps exactly; however, typos, incorrect filenames, and other mistakes can easily create flaws in your image map.

Providing a Textual Alternative

Although virtually all new Web browsers support client-side image maps, it's always a good idea to provide some sort of textual alternative. This accommodates visitors to your page who are using a browser that doesn't read client-side image maps, or who don't want to wait for the entire image to download before selecting a region on the image map.

Figure 8.19 shows how I updated the ACME Block home page to have textual links as well as graphical ones. I used a two-column table with the left-hand column displaying the main image map, and the right-hand column showing a simple list of links.

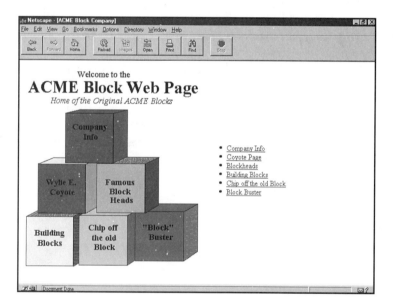

Fig. 8.19
This simple table provides an alternative to using my image map.

Image Map Design Considerations

In this section, I've consolidated several important tips you should keep in mind when you begin using client-side image maps in your Web pages. Some of them are repeated information from throughout this chapter, and others aren't. Basically, this is a last-minute checklist you should run through before you let everyone on the Web have access to your image maps:

- **Choose the right type of image map**—Make sure that you understand the differences between client-side and server-side image maps. Although client-side maps may be more efficient, there are some situations where you don't want to use them—particularly, if you are afraid many visitors to your Web page won't use a browser with client-side capability.

- **Be careful of file size**—Images that are mapped tend to have larger file sizes because they usually appear larger on-screen. Make sure that your image's file size isn't outrageous (for instance, above 100K); otherwise, visitors to your Web page will become impatient.

- **Use interlaced images**—*Interlaced images* are those that load in multiple levels, starting out fuzzy and slowly becoming more detailed. Interlaced images are ideal for image maps because as soon as visitors recognize which area they want to click, they don't have to wait for the whole image to appear. Learn more about interlaced images in Chapter 7, "Advanced Graphics Issues."

- **Define mapped areas clearly**—Make sure that you use an image that makes it easy for visitors to know which sections are mapped to other HTML files. It's easy for visitors to overlook small areas (or illogical areas) on an image map.

- **Test your image twice**—I can't stress this enough. I've seen too many image maps that haven't been tested thoroughly. Usually, some regions link properly to files, but other regions don't. Nobody enjoys using an untested image map. ❖

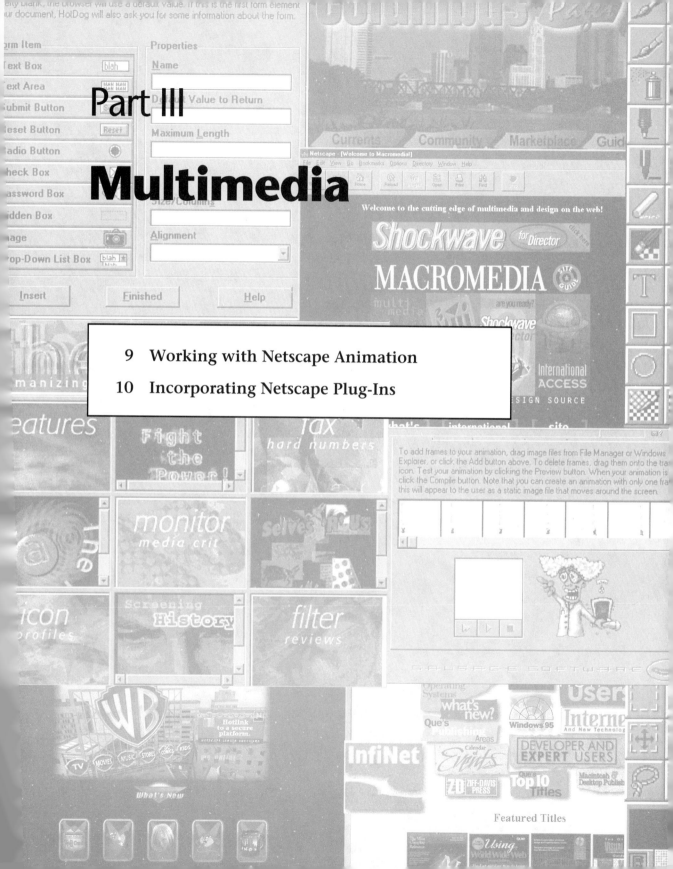

Part III
Multimedia

## Chapter 9

Working with Netscape Animation

One of the most impressive ways to enhance your Web page is by building and incorporating animated or interactive sequences of images for visitors to experience. With Netscape, several types of animation are available to you when creating Web pages. Some of them are easy to add, and others require significant development effort, but they all have one thing in common—they're really cool and make a Web page stand out. Like almost no other existing technology, animation adds excitement, life, and action to Web pages when used properly.

This chapter shows you how you can add animation and animated special effects to your Web page. We'll look at several common types of animation, and step through the process of including animation on your Web page. You'll learn various ways to create and incorporate animation on the Web.

Specifically, this chapter teaches you how to do the following:

- Understand the difference between Server Push and Client Pull animation
- Create a complete set of animation images
- Build and include animation sequences in your Web page
- Work with other animation special effects on the Web
- Use Macromedia Shockwave for impressive integrated animation

Animating Your Web Pages

A key concept of the Web is *multimedia*, the mixing together of text, graphics, and other forms of media. This is the reason that the Web and Netscape have become so popular. So far, you've learned several different strategies for creating Web pages that use both text and images in a creative manner.

You know how to add images to your Web page, create usable image maps, and even coordinate and control all the colors of text, links, and Netscape's background. If you have read *Creating Your Own Netscape Web Pages*, you know how to link audio and video clips to a Web page.

It's time now to add a new dimension—animation. *Animation* is when text, graphics, and information on a Web page automatically move to create special effects within the Web page. With Netscape and the WWW, animation comes in many different shapes and flavors. Here are the different types of animation you can use on your Web page, each of which is discussed in greater detail later in the chapter:

- **Server Push/Client Pull**—This method is the most stable type of animation, as well as the easiest to create. Server Push/Client Pull animation dynamically displays a series of images and graphics in a specific order. Remember as a child when you took a pad of paper and drew a slightly different picture on each page, then flipped through the whole pad quickly? The overall effect was a stilted animation because it made the image look like it was moving by fooling the eye. That's how Server Push/Client Pull animation works. You create a set of images and tell Netscape to display them as quickly as possible (which isn't very quick, but is good enough for most purposes), creating an illusion of animation.

- **Macromedia Shockwave**—A recent innovation, Shockwave is software that "plugs into" Netscape and adds a whole new level of true animation to Web pages. With Shockwave, you can make text move across the screen, create dazzling interactive presentations, build games for your Web page, and make your pages literally come "alive." Anyone who uses Netscape can experience these stunning interactive animations. Unfortunately, creating such animations can be difficult, expensive, and time-consuming. I'll show you how you can experience these neat animations, and then outline the steps necessary to make them yourself.

- **Embedded video clips**—Although not quite animation, new Netscape developments allow you to incorporate video sequences within your Web page. Instead of using separate helper applications that show video clips in a different window, you now can display video clips as part of your Web page. You can create your own video clips from scratch, or make a digital movie with a video camera or VCR, and then include those animated sequences in your Web page.

- **Java applications**—Java is the exciting new programming language that works seamlessly with Netscape. Although writing Java programs is complicated, one payoff is the ability to create animated sequences of text and images that are part of your Web page. For example, a Java animation could display a cartoon image of a man leaping back and forth across the screen. I'll show you one way you can build a Java animation easily by using an existing tool. Chapter 13, "Making Some of Your Own Java," talks more about Java, a related scripting language called JavaScript, and how to use these technologies in your Web pages.

- **Marquee text**—In Chapter 5, "The New Generation of HTML Tags," you learned about some new HTML tags introduced by Microsoft. One pair of them was `<MARQUEE>` and `</MARQUEE>`. Using these tags, you can designate text to scroll back and forth across the screen. Although not supported by Netscape at the time this book was written, Microsoft's Internet Explorer supports this new tag pair, and Netscape undoubtedly will soon.

Why Add Animation?

As you'll quickly learn, working with animation in Web pages can be a daunting task. It is difficult to create the necessary files, hard to organize them correctly, and can be a challenge to add them to your Web pages properly. All that said, many people choose to avoid using animation on their Web pages rather than deal with the hassle.

Many times though, you'll find that animated Web pages are often worth the trouble. A Web page that has animation built in is very attractive, fun to visit, and resonates in visitors minds to make them want to come back again. Animation is one way you can distinguish your Web page from the millions of others out there.

III

> **Note**
>
> Personally, I like to experiment with the different animation methods because it's another way I can expand the breadth of my site. By adding various animated sequences using the methods described in this chapter, visitors often send e-mail and come back to visit several times—simply because there aren't many people who know how to add it to their Web page and, consequently, few animated Web sites.

Multimedia

Working with Netscape Animation

Beginning with Netscape 1.1, you can incorporate dynamically loaded HTML documents directly into your Web pages. Using new "meta" tags, you can easily tell the Netscape browser to automatically load one HTML file after another. Within each HTML file, you can specify images to be displayed. The overall effect is that images are dynamically loaded into your Netscape window one after another. By loading a sequence of images, you can emulate animation. This *dynamic animation* is built into Netscape and comes in two distinct flavors, Server Push and Client Pull. Using either of these two methods, Netscape automatically loads subsequent images without requiring visitors to your Web page to click any additional links, buttons, or images.

> **Note**
>
> Before I talk about these two methods, I want to explain what I mean by "server" and "client." You're probably already familiar with how the Web works. On your personal machine, you run Netscape and connect to many different Web sites across the Internet. The version of Netscape running on your personal machine is called a *client*. There are literally millions of individual clients out there, because everyone who uses Netscape (or another WWW browser) on their PC is considered an additional client.
>
> On the other hand, there are significantly fewer servers. A *server* is a different type of program, one that maintains a Web site and communicates with the various clients that talk to it. Web servers are in charge of all the Web pages at a particular site. Netscape sends a message to the server and requests to see a particular HTML file. The server interprets the request and, if possible, sends the requested file back to the client. This type of communicating happens all the time between Netscape and the server software; you generally don't notice it, because it happens in the background.
>
> Here's an example of how this client/server relationship works. Use Netscape to visit the Walt Disney Web server at **http://www.disney.com**. Netscape sends a message across the Internet to the Disney server that basically says, "Hey, I want to access your Web page. Please send me the files so I can display them on my personal machine." The server proceeds to send the files to your client version of Netscape, which displays them on your screen. In a single session, the client can send lots of requests to servers all across the Internet, and that's what you and I call *Web browsing* (or *surfing*).
>
> When you start creating Server Push and Client Pull animation, you need to understand the client/server nature of the Web, because you are sending additional instructions back and forth between Netscape and the server that tell Netscape which images to load in an animated sequence.

Client Pull

Pretend that you're extremely wealthy and have a butler serving you. You lie back in your chair and ring a little bell whenever you want the butler to bring something to you. The butler only comes when you ring the bell, waits for your explicit instruction, and then brings exactly what you've requested. Essentially, this is how Client Pull animation works. You order a particular Web server to load a certain set of HTML files one at a time.

First, you point Netscape to a particular HTML document. As Netscape interprets all the tags in the file, it notices a new *meta tag*. This meta tag contains instructions that Netscape sends to the Web server, which automatically requests a second HTML file. This process repeats many times, because a new meta tag in each HTML file tells Netscape to request additional HTML files. In this manner, you are creating dynamic animation. Without any additional clicks or commands, Netscape automatically loads one HTML file after another. To create animation, you have to ensure that each HTML file points to a particular image to be displayed within Netscape.

For example, let's say that I have three separate images that show a boat sailing across the screen (see fig. 9.1 through fig. 9.3). Each image moves the boat a bit further across the screen.

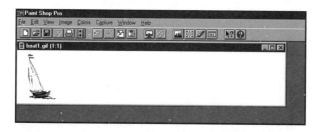

Fig. 9.1
My sailboat starts here.

Fig. 9.2
It quickly starts sailing across the screen (it caught a good wind).

III

Multimedia

Fig. 9.3

This is the end of the sailboat's journey.

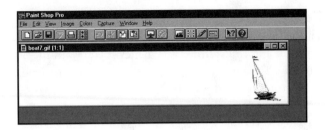

You want Netscape to automatically load all three images, one after another, to create an animated sequence that makes the boat appear to move across the screen. Using Client Pull, Netscape loads the image shown in figure 9.1. As soon as the entire image has been downloaded, it immediately starts to display the image shown in figure 9.2. Once that image is completed, Netscape displays the image shown in figure 9.3, the final image in this simple animated sequence.

The entire time, your client version of Netscape is in control. It tells the server what image to display next, and when to display it. The server is simply the client's butler, bringing it the requested images.

Creating animation sequences using this method is straightforward and easy to accomplish. In a moment, I'll step you through the entire process of creating a Client Pull animation sequence.

Server Push

Conversely, Server Push animation gives control of the animation to the server. In Client Pull, the Netscape client sends messages to the server, telling it which image it wants to display next. Let's imagine a butler at a dinner party who is supposed to automatically bring out the next course of a meal every 30 minutes. Regardless of whether everyone is finished, the butler's instructions are to keep serving. In this case, the butler is acting like the WWW server and is constantly sending down information at a regular interval. Instead of waiting for the guest (client) to signal that it is ready for the next course, the butler keeps serving automatically.

This is how Server Push animation works—all the work is done by the WWW server and the client just waits for another file or image to be sent down the pipeline, having no control over the matter.

The biggest difference between Client Pull and Server Push animation is the length of time during which the client and server talk to each other. With Client Pull, Netscape only sends a brief message to the server (rings a bell) that tells the server what image it wants to retrieve. During Server Push, the client and server are constantly communicating. The server focuses on the client, and spends a lot of time exchanging information with the client.

This distinction is important because a Web server that uses Server Push animation often suffers from performance problems. Since it has to be in constant communication with each client it is communicating with, it can only talk to a certain number of clients at once. A single butler can only serve so many guests at a time before getting overwhelmed. You can imagine how easily a Web server becomes overloaded if it has to keep track of many different Netscape clients simultaneously. With Client Pull animation, the Web server just responds to various commands sent to it by Netscape clients, and doesn't have to focus its attention on a specific client.

Server Push animation is significantly more complicated than Client Pull. With Server Push, you need to use a programming language (such as C) to write a program that tells the Web server when to send images down to the client. Because of the relative complexity and the significant strain that it puts on Web servers, Server Push animation is not used very often. I only describe Client Pull animation in this chapter because that's the type most Web sites use. For a complete example of Server Push animation, and a sample program you can use, visit **http://home.netscape.com/assist/ net_sites/pushpull.html**. Additionally, some Web providers don't even permit Server Push animation sequences because of the load placed on the WWW server. It's best to check with your Web provider before trying to build your own Server Push animation.

Building an Animated Example

Now that you understand exactly how Netscape animation works, you'll now learn how to build an animated sequence for your own Web page. In this example, I'll show you how to animate a boat sailing across the top of a Web page. Get the basics with this example, and apply your own creativity later.

The next few sections describe how to create the necessary images, what new HTML tags you should be familiar with, and how to build and test the sequence of animation.

Deciding on the Animation

The first step in animating your Web page is thinking up a neat animation sequence. With animation, you have virtually no limitations. To help your creative juices flow, here are a few ways I've used animation on my Web pages:

- Headlines that move or slide into place
- Your name spinning in 3D at the top of the screen
- Photographs showing a progressive sequence of events, such as a dog catching a Frisbee
- Animals or vehicles traveling across the screen

Once you have decided what animation you want to create, the next step is planning how many different images you want to use to depict this particular animation. For the boat example, I've decided to use seven different images showing the boat sailing across the screen.

Caution

Don't choose a huge number (like 25 or more)! Visitors to your Web page automatically start downloading each image in your sequence, and having a large number means that it feels like it takes forever to see the whole sequence. Try to stay between five and ten unless you have a particularly special animation to create.

Tip

If you can't decide how many images to use, don't worry. You can always add additional images or take some away later, once you evaluate the whole sequence in action.

Creating the Images

Once you've decided on a sequence and know the number of images you want to use, the next step is to create each image individually. Creating a sequence of images can be difficult and extremely time-consuming, because each image must be created and saved separately. For this example, I had to create seven different images of a boat sailing across the screen (see fig. 9.4 for four of those images).

There are several tools that you can use to create sequences of images. I used Paint Shop Pro for this example. First, I created a blank background, pasted the sailboat from a clip art package onto the image, and saved the file as boat1.gif. I next used cut-and-paste operations within Paint Shop Pro to move the boat slightly to the right of its original position, and saved that new image as boat2.gif. I repeated those steps five more times until I had seven images. By the final image, my sailboat had almost made it to the right hand edge of the screen. As you can imagine, it was a lengthy process to get all seven images just the way I wanted them.

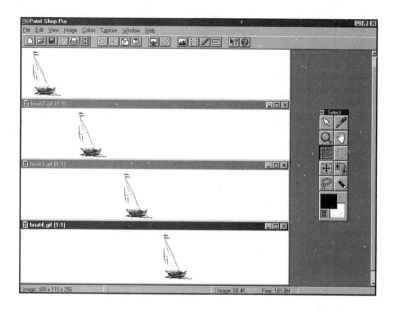

Fig. 9.4
A seven-step sequence shows my boat sailing.

When I saved my images, I tried GIF and JPEG formats. Each of these formats has advantages over the other for various types of images. In the example, my boat pictures are black and white (gray scale), and are much better suited for the GIF format. Each image is only about 2K because GIF optimizes itself for black-and-white images. The same pictures saved in JPEG format averaged about 6K each—quite a difference. Based on those numbers, I chose GIF over JPEG. If I had been using color images, I most likely would have found JPEG to be better.

It's also good to note that, in general, you want all of your images to be the same height and width in pixel dimensions. Otherwise, your animation may look stilted and disjointed because the subsequent images won't line up correctly.

Note

You can use virtually any paint program that saves images into GIF or JPEG format. Several advanced programs exist to make it easier for you to create sequential image files. For example, Asymetrix's Web 3D (see Chapter 7, "Advanced Graphics Issues," for more information) will build an animated video for you, then allow you to save each frame of the animation as an individual GIF file.

> **Tip**
>
> Make sure that you name each image in your sequence in a logical manner (like
> `boat1.gif` through `boat7.gif`). This helps you keep track of the whole sequence
> and display it later in the correct order.

Making the HTML Files

Once all of your images are created, the next step is to build the corresponding set of HTML files that tells Netscape how to display the animation. Using
a new HTML meta tag, you direct Netscape to load one HTML file after another. Here's an example of my first HTML file, named `boat1.htm`:

```
<HEAD>
<META HTTP-EQUIV="Refresh" CONTENT="1; URL=boat2.htm">
<TITLE> Boat Animation Example Frame 1</TITLE>
</HEAD>
<IMG SRC="boat1.gif">
<BR>
<CENTER My boat starts sailing</CENTER>
```

That's the entire file. Notice that it has only a couple of parts. The first important line is the one that contains the `<META>` tag. This tag tells Netscape that it
is about to start working with animation. Notice the `CONTENT=` keyword. This
keyword tells Netscape to wait for one second after the current file is loaded,
and then read `boat2.htm`. You can change the waiting time by increasing `1` to
any value you prefer (including `0`, which tells Netscape not to wait at all before loading the next file).

The rest of my `boat1.htm` file should look familiar to you. It displays a
message that appears in the title bar, and then tells Netscape to display the
`boat1.gif` image on-screen. Figure 9.5 shows how Netscape displays this first
step of my dynamic Client Pull animated sequence.

Fig. 9.5

Here's the first
image in my
animation
sequence.

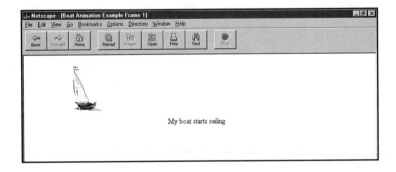

Caution

To make sure that the animation works properly, you should include the <META> tag within the <HEAD> and </HEAD> tag pair, and above the title (denoted by the <TITLE> and </TITLE> tag pair).

Once `boat1.htm` is finished, it's time to create `boat2.htm`. This file is extremely similar to the first one:

```
<HEAD>
<META HTTP-EQUIV="Refresh" CONTENT="1; URL=boat3.htm">
<TITLE> Boat Animation Example Frame 2</TITLE>
</HEAD>
<IMG SRC="boat2.gif">
<BR>
<CENTER The boat catches a breeze and takes off!</CENTER>
```

As you can see, there are just a few changes. This file tells Netscape to display `boat2.gif` on-screen (see fig. 9.6), wait one second, and then load the next HTML file, which is `boat3.htm`. You need to create a new HTML file for each step in your sequence of animation, telling Netscape what to display on-screen, how long to wait, and which HTML file to load next.

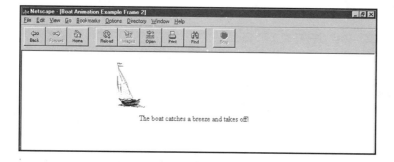

Fig. 9.6
The boat is swiftly sailing to the right.

Of course, the last file in the sequence must look a little different. Since the boat in our example is going to reach the right edge of the screen and move no further, `boat7.htm` must tell Netscape not to load another HTML file (see fig. 9.7):

```
<HEAD>
<TITLE> Boat Animation Example Frame 7</TITLE>
</HEAD>
<IMG SRC="boat7.gif">
<BR>
<CENTER>It's the end of the road... sea for this boat.</CENTER>
<HR>
<A HREF="boat1.htm">See the animation again!</A>
```

III

Multimedia

Fig. 9.7
This boat's sailing
days are over.

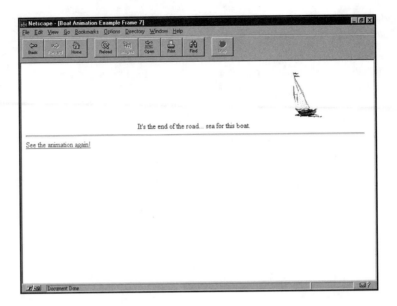

For the last file, I have simply removed the <META> tag. Netscape loads this HTML page in the standard manner, and waits for the next command from the visitor. You can find the complete boat example on the CD-ROM accompanying this book.

Note

You might have realized that the key to Client Pull animation is that Netscape loads one HTML file after another, regardless of what tags and instructions are in each file. To emulate animation, I load a different image from each HTML file, but that's only the tip of the iceberg. I can use Client Pull animation for many other practical purposes.

One example would be to create an automated presentation. Each HTML file could have several images and a bunch of text, and Netscape could step through the sequence, spending 60 seconds on each page. This would give the visitor a chance to see each screen before it disappeared, but would not make the visitor responsible for moving the presentation along. Client Pull animation is a powerful tool whose usefulness extends far beyond simple animation examples.

Unfortunately, performance is the main opponent of Netscape animation. In my boat example, the figures are each about 2K. With seven of them, people have to download 14K to see this animation. Imagine if I had a color image that was slightly larger. It'd be easy to have a set of files that were 10K each—and that takes a while to download—which is longer than most people are willing to wait.

Framing Your Animation

One popular way to use animation on a Web page is to incorporate that technology with frames. Frames allow you to have one section of your screen not changing—with static text—while another frame has the animation sequence running.

For many Web sites, this is the ideal solution for incorporating an animated sequence with sets of HTML files that aren't animated. Figure 9.8 shows the same animation running in two frames.

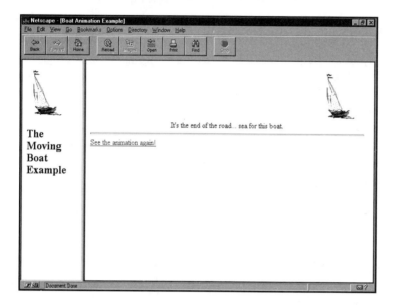

Fig. 9.8
Frames and animation work very well together.

Testing the New Animation

With all your images and HTML files set, you're practically done with your Client Pull animation. The final step is to test your animation. This is an extremely important step that's easy to forget. To test your animation sequence, open the first file (in the example, it's boat1.htm) in Netscape. Your sequence of images should start automatically displaying, and Netscape should load each subsequent HTML file.

Use the following checklist to ensure that your animation works properly:

- **It reaches the end of the sequence**—Make sure that Netscape goes through the entire sequence and stops loading new files once it gets to the end. Although you can create infinite loops of animation, it is strongly recommended that you have a clear beginning and ending point.

- **Performance is acceptable**—Time the total duration for Netscape cycling through the sequence of HTML files. Make sure that each image is small and reasonable, and that there aren't too many images in the sequence.

- **Sequence of images makes sense**—Each subsequent image in the animation should logically belong after the one that preceded it. If my boat started on the left, then jumped to the right, and ended up in the middle of the screen, it might not make sense. Each image in an animation should be the logical next step to accomplish a good special effect.

> **Note**
>
> As you can tell, creating a dynamic sequence of images that emulates animation does have some drawbacks. First, there is no true animation—only a sequence of images that load automatically. Second, you can't add sound effects. If I want to play "Come Sail Away" (by Styx) in the background while my ship cruises across the screen, I'm out of luck. Other types of embedded video and animation, like Shockwave and video clips, might better suit my needs by incorporating audio with a sequence of images. Dynamic Client Pull animation is best suited for presentations and extremely small, gradual animations.

Another Animation Example

On the CD

For another look at an animated sequence, use Netscape to visit the CD-ROM accompanying this book. There you find a new sequence of animations that shows my name spinning in three-dimensional space. Using Web 3D, I made a simple step-by-step cycle of my name spinning. Figure 9.9 shows the whole sequence of images.

Each image was created individually and saved to a separate file. Then I created the corresponding HTML files. In each file, I pointed to an image specifically, and then, using the <META> tag, I pointed to the next file in the sequence. In this sequence of 14 images, I had to create 14 separate HTML files—one for each image.

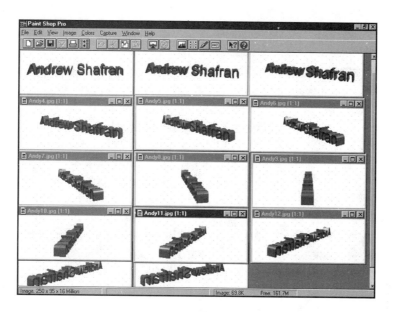

Fig. 9.9
Here's another
type of animation.

A New Kind of Animation: Working with Shockwave

Although built-in Netscape Client Pull/Server Push animation is nice, it isn't true animation, and there's no level of interaction between your Web page and the people who stop by. Netscape automatically starts loading the sequence of HTML files that you specify—that's it.

A new program, Shockwave, has taken the Web by storm and has added incredible levels of true animation and interactivity to Web pages. By combining Shockwave and Netscape, you can build truly animated images, banners, and logos into your Web page while using files of a reasonable size. In addition, you can build interactive games, presentations, and demonstrations that react to the visitor's mouse or keyboard commands.

Shockwave is a new Netscape plug-in from Macromedia (**http:// www.macromedia.com**), whose home page is shown in figure 9.10. Netscape plug-ins are programs that integrate completely with your Netscape window, allowing you to view and experience unique types of information without using a separate helper application. I'll talk more about various Netscape plug-ins in the next chapter, but for now I want you to get "shocked" with Shockwave.

III

Multimedia

Fig. 9.10

You can learn about Shockwave at the Macromedia home page.

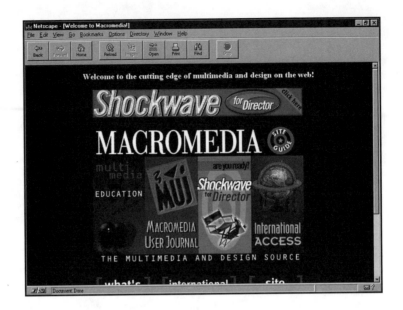

Understanding Shockwave

Shockwave is available for free to anyone on the Web. To use Shockwave, you must visit the Macromedia Shockwave download page (**http://www.macromedia.com/Tools/Shockwave/sdc/Plugin/index.htm**) and select the correct version for your computer (Windows, UNIX, or Macintosh). In addition, you have to use Netscape 2.0 or later.

Once you've downloaded and installed Shockwave, you can experience *shocked sites*. Whenever Netscape finds a Shockwave animation, it displays it automatically in your Netscape window. Figure 9.11 shows a simple Shockwave animation in action.

For a fantastic set of Shockwave experiences, including games, animated banners, and more, visit the Shockwave Gallery at **http://www.macromedia.com/Tools/Shockwave/Gallery/index.html**. Many sites on the Web will start using Shockwave soon to create fantastic interactive sites. Already, you can find Shockwave examples at locations such as the CompuServe site (**http://www.compuserve.com**).

Figure 9.12 shows me playing Asteroids with Shockwave (**http://www.macromedia.com/Gallery/Shockwave/Games/Stroids/index.html**).

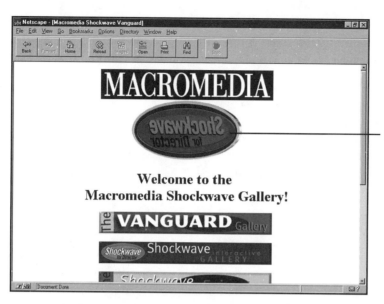

Fig. 9.11
This image shows
the Shockwave
logo spinning.

Spinning logo

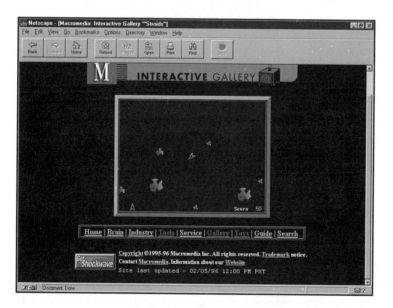

Fig. 9.12
Watch out for that
asteroid on the left!

III

Multimedia

Making Some Shocking Examples

While using Shockwave interactive presentations is fun, creating them isn't
quite as easy. Shockwave lets you view animations created with another
Macromedia product, Director. Director is a multimedia authoring tool that is

on the cutting edge of integrated multimedia, animation, and sound technology. Unfortunately, Director is not free (it costs around $500), so creating multimedia experiences for your Web page can be costly.

Director lets you build customized images from scratch and then specify interactions with different parts of the images. For example, in the Asteroids game, Shockwave lets you create several different objects—the spacecraft, asteroids, and bullets. Once each object is created, you can specify how the objects should work with one another. So, in Asteroids, a space rock moves across the screen until it gets bumped by a bullet, and so on.

A great feature of Director is the ability to incorporate animation and sound together in one package. This makes multimedia examples more useful and fun.

Be aware that creating Director animations is no walk in the park. Director is a professional level software package and can be difficult to use for the uninitiated. Personally, after using Director for several hours to try to create a simple, but cool, animation, I was miserably unsuccessful. Patience and experience are a must to create a worthwhile multimedia example.

Java Animation with Egor

Another technology new to Netscape 2.0 allows you to create Java based animations to embed directly in your Web page. Java is a programming language created by Sun Microsystems that allows tremendous flexibility in how your Web page looks and acts, including the ability to use animation.

Figure 9.13 shows the Java logo steaming at **http://java.sun.com**.

Creating Java applets on your own can be a rigorous process. I'll introduce you to Java in Chapter 13, "Making Some of Your Own Java."

On the CD

But there are other ways to build Java based animation without learning anything about Java or knowing a thing about programming. One such tool is called Egor the Animator by Sausage Software (the same people who put together HotDog and HotDog Pro). I've included a shareware version of Egor on the CD-ROM with this book, or you can download it directly from **http://www.sausage.com**.

All you have to do is create your sequence of animated images (like my set of seven boat images earlier in the chapter) and then load Egor (see fig. 9.14).

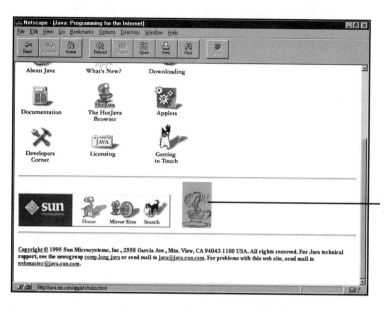

Fig. 9.13
The Java coffee cup is animated with a Java applet.

Steaming animated cup of coffee

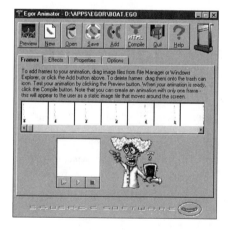

Fig. 9.14
Egor is a zany tool that builds Java-powered animations.

III

Multimedia

Once you have the set of images created, click the <u>A</u>dd button from Egor. Choose your images that depict your sequence of events and add them to Egor's list. I added all seven of my boat pictures to build a Java animation of my boat sailing.

Once you've added the set of images, click the <u>P</u>review button and Egor shows you how the animation appears in Netscape. It's really amazing how easy it is. In Netscape, you see a true animation—not the stilted Server Push or Client Pull effect. My boat fluidly moves across the screen.

Egor has several additional options for your Java animation. You can add a soundtrack to play along with the animation, choose a default background color, choose how many times to repeat your animation, and more. Egor is truly a powerful tool for anyone who wants to build fantastic animated examples for Web pages.

Unfortunately, Egor is shareware, and you can only use it to build sample animations on your personal computer. To get these Java animations to work on your Web page, you have to register Egor ($49.95). But if you are serious about cool animations, it's worth the money.

Note

Although not free, Egor is likely a better animation choice than any of the others presented in this chapter. Egor is affordable, allows you to build dynamic true animation sequences with sounds, and is a new technology designed specifically for the WWW.

Personally, I registered Egor and use it for all of the special effects on my Web pages.

Other Animation Examples

Besides the other types of animation discussed so far in this chapter, there are several other ways to add animation—or at least moving images and text—to your Web page. This section describes a few other ways to do this.

Some of these methods can be done with Netscape, while others work only with Microsoft's Internet Explorer. I've included information about building animations for both of these browsers because they are both popular and tend to share new features and innovations with one another.

Animated GIF Images

 Probably the newest technology for adding animation to Web pages is using animated GIF images. Animated GIF images are simply a set of GIFs that are all tied together as one image. The GIF image file format allows you to save multiple images as different "frames" of an animation—but tied together as a single image.

With Netscape, you can embed this new type of GIF into your Web page and Netscape 2.0 will automatically parse the separate frames of the GIF and display them subsequently one after another—creating a neat animation effect.

On the CD

Animated GIF technology is new and using it along with Web pages is quickly gaining popularity. Only Netscape 2.0 supports animated GIF but the other browsers are sure to follow suit. Most popular graphics programs (such as Paint Shop Pro) don't allow you to build animated GIF images. That's why I've included a special program on the CD-ROM with this book called GIF Construction Set—it's the only existing tool which lets you build animated GIF images. You can also download GIF Construction Set at **http://www.north.net/alchmey/alchemy.html**.

Check out GIF Construction Set for more information on building animated GIF images, or converting existing images into a single animated one.

Animated GIF images are a good way to add animation to your Web page without much complication. In appearance, they look like Java animations because they are smooth and true animations—unlike Server Push and Client Pull—but unlike Java, you can't add sound to GIF animations. Since they are so new, many sites and individuals have yet to take advantage of this innovative technology.

Marquee Scrolling Text

One of the new HTML tags introduced by Microsoft allows you to add scrolling text and banners to your Web page. Serving as an animated marquee, your text can scroll horizontally across the Web page.

At the time this book went to press, Netscape didn't support the new <MARQUEE> tags, but Microsoft's Internet Explorer did. Perhaps by the time you read this, Netscape also will support these tags.

Netscape Web developers don't have to be left out in the cold when it comes to marqueed text. Another way to emulate marquee text scrolling across your page is by using a simple JavaScript applet that is mentioned in Chapter 13, "Making Some of Your Own Java."

Tip

To keep up-to-date on new Netscape extensions, stop by the Netscape home page (**http://www.netscape.com**) regularly. Alternatively, visit this book's home page, where I keep an online list of new HTML enhancements that work for your Web page (**http://www.shafran.com/enhance/**).

III

Multimedia

Looking at Video Clips

Netscape's Client Pull and Server Push aren't the only ways to add movement to your Web page. Another method that's becoming popular is embedding video clips directly into your Web page. Just like added images, embedded videos are included with a simple HTML tag, and will work as long as visitors to your Web page use the correct Netscape plug-in.

There are several ways you can add video clips to your Web page. The easiest is to create a link to them as described in *Creating Your Own Web Pages*:

```
<A HREF="mymovie.qt">Experience my personal Video</A>
```

After you add this line of HTML to your Web page, you are linked to a Quicktime movie. Visitors to your Web page can download the Quicktime helper application from Apple (**http://www.apple.com**) and watch the video.

Soon, Quicktime will be available as a Netscape plug-in and can be directly viewed as part of a Web page. See Chapter 10, "Incorporating Netscape Plug-Ins," for more information on how plug-ins work and how they can be added to Web pages.

If you are using Internet Explorer, you can embed video clips in your Web page using new Microsoft tags. I talk about these dynamic video tags in more detail in Chapter 5, "The New Generation of HTML Tags." ❖

Chapter 10
Incorporating Netscape Plug-Ins

Before the release of Netscape 2.0, one of the biggest criticisms for Netscape and the WWW is that only a few types of files can be viewed from directly within the Netscape Navigator. You're generally limited to plain text and HTML files, and only a handful of image file types—GIF and JPEG (and sometimes PNG).

However, there are many different types of files that people want to embed directly into their Web pages. Files such as video and sound clips, Microsoft Word documents, and images in a plethora of different common formats were limited in usefulness on the WWW until Netscape 2.0 was released.

With new open-ended technology, Netscape now allows software developers across the world to create plug-ins and lets users experience many different types of files alongside standard HTML files. Now at your fingertips, you can "plug in" many different types of common files directly into your Web page, and let visitors experience a true multimedia showcase.

In this chapter, I introduce you to Netscape plug-ins and show you how you can use them to enhance your Web pages. I profile several popular plug-ins that are useful to Web page developers. You'll learn how to plug in multimedia presentations, audio sound clips, video clips, Microsoft Word and Adobe Acrobat documents, and a variety of common image file types (including BMP and TIFF) quickly and easily.

Specifically, in this chapter, you'll learn how to do the following:

- Download and install a variety of popular Netscape plug-ins
- Add Live Objects to your Web pages that take advantage of the plug-in technology

- Decide which types of files can and can't be added to Web pages with plug-ins
- Configure your WWW server to permit Netscape plug-ins to run on your Web pages

Understanding Netscape's Open-Endedness

The biggest enhancement Netscape 2.0 offers over other WWW browsers is the ability to incorporate many different file types directly into a single Web page. Netscape calls this technology *Live Objects* because you can add dynamic and interactive content—such as VRML worlds and multimedia clips into a regular Web page with a single new HTML tag.

The advantage of Live Objects technology is that Web page developers can now "plug-in" virtually any file type they want to and allow visitors to experience their Web pages in a new light. Many different software companies have announced various plug-ins that work directly with Netscape 2.0 and better. For a complete list of all the available plug-ins, visit **http://home.netscape.com/comprod/products/navigator/version_2.0/plugins/index.html** (see fig. 10.1). Netscape tries to keep this list current with new plug-ins that have been released or are currently being beta-tested.

Fig. 10.1

Netscape tracks most of the popular plug-ins from here.

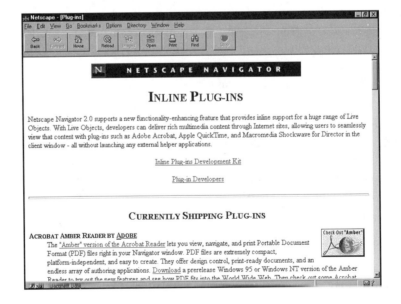

Using Plug-Ins

Anyone who uses Netscape 2.0 can experience plug-ins for themselves. Simply visit the company listed in Netscape's plug-in index and follow the instructions there for downloading and installing the plug-in onto your own machine.

Once it is installed, you'll never even know a plug-in exists until you visit a Web page that uses that specific file type. When Netscape comes across a special plug-in file, it automatically loads the correct program required to view the plug-in. So, once you've installed a plug-in, you can forget about it because Netscape takes care of running it whenever it's needed.

At any time you can check which Netscape plug-ins are installed. Simply choose Help, About Plug-ins and you'll see a list of supported plug-in file types (see fig. 10.2).

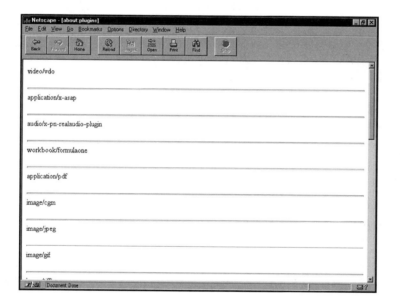

Fig. 10.2
I have quite a few plug-ins installed on my machine.

You can find a recent version of most of the plug-ins I talk about in this chapter on the accompanying CD-ROM in the back of this book. This prevents hours being spent downloading the various plug-ins from WWW sites. Invariably, new editions of plug-ins are constantly being introduced. For each plug-in that you use, make sure you stop by the home page I have listed to see if you've got the most current version. Be aware that new plug-ins are constantly being developed and that keeping on top of them can be a difficult task.

On the CD

III

Multimedia

Learn About Plug-In Gimmicks

You'll quickly notice that virtually all of the plug-ins you come across are free. Anyone on the WWW can download and install them on his or her own machine without many complications. Don't be overwhelmed by corporate America's generosity too quickly, though. Plug-in developers give away free plug-in players to anyone who wants them, but creating the special file types that work with the plug-ins can be expensive.

It's as if a camera company started freely giving away tons of a new kind of film. Anyone could use their own camera and take pictures with the film, and not pay a cent. But here's the catch. That company may have a special film development process that only it can do—for a premium price. So although you get the actual film for free, it's just a gimmick, because you end up paying just as much for developing it as you would using normal Kodak film.

Take the new Macromedia Shockwave plug-in (**http:// www.macromedia.com**) as a prime example. Shockwave is a cool plug-in that adds animation and special multimedia sound effects to your Web page (I talked about Shockwave in the last chapter). But to create these cool presentations, you need to purchase Macromedia Director, which costs several hundred dollars. Subsequently, most people will download and install the Shockwave plug-in, but few Web page developers will be able to create their own for their Web pages.

Not all plug-ins work like this. In fact, some of the most useful ones for enhancing Web pages work with other popular file types including Word documents and popular graphic formats. Most plug-in developers that work like Macromedia also let you test out their complete software packages for free—for a limited time. This lets you evaluate using the plug-in and creating special files for the plug-in to see if it's worth your money to buy it.

In this chapter I try to discuss only plug-ins that are useful to people creating Web pages. I mention all the free plug-ins, and the ones that let you test drive their entire software packages, to help steer you around the plug-in developers that are just out to make a buck.

Plug-In Limitations

Unfortunately, several plug-in disadvantages also come into play. Each different file type you want to add to your Web page requires visitors to have downloaded and installed a different plug-in in order to work properly. So if you embedded a sound clip, a video clip, a Microsoft Word document, and a small TIFF image in one Web page, visitors have to be using Netscape 2.0 (the only browser that currently supports plug-ins) and four separate plug-in programs which have to be downloaded and installed individually.

This can be an inconvenience because some plug-ins can take quite a while to download (because of their file size). In addition, that's now five pieces of software you need to keep track of when new versions are released.

Eventually, this problem will erase itself. Most people on the WWW will download and use a standard set of popular and common plug-ins—possibly downloaded along with Netscape. Until then, be aware that using plugged-in files on your Web page means that visitors will most likely have to download the corresponding plug-in first. So, the moral of the story is to not overload your Web page with too many plug-in specific files.

Note

As a general rule, whenever you use a plug-in on your Web pages, make sure you always have a link to the Web site where visitors can download and install that plug-in for themselves. Otherwise, visitors won't be able to experience the new files and objects you painstakingly added to your Web page because they may not know where to go to find the right plug-in.

Creating Your Own Plug-Ins

Netscape encourages software developers to create their own unique and customized plug-ins. By releasing a Software Development Kit (SDK) for Windows and the Macintosh, Netscape gives away all the tools necessary to create your own plug-in from scratch. This is different than using plug-ins—you can actually create new programs that act as any of the plug-ins discussed in this chapter.

In general, only software developers will be interested in this information, but if you're eager to learn some advanced details about how Netscape works, stop by this Web page. Figure 10.3 shows the online documentation Netscape provides for creating your own custom plug-in from scratch (**http:// home.netscape.com/eng/mozilla/2.0/handbook/plugins/ index.html**).

III

Multimedia

Fig. 10.3
Start here when creating your own plug-ins.

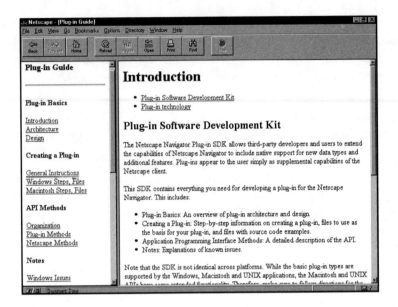

Adding Plug-Ins to Your Web Page

Now that you're familiar with what plug-ins are and how you can use them, this section shows you how to add plug-in files to your Web page.

There are pieces of information that are important to adding plug-ins to Web pages. First, you need to learn the new HTML tag <EMBED> and the corresponding keywords that go with it. Second, you need to configure your WWW server (or have your site administrator configure it) to allow Netscape plug-ins to work properly.

The HTML Tags

Netscape plug-ins use the newly introduced tag <EMBED>. By embedding specific files within a Web page, Netscape automatically knows that it should load the corresponding plug-in. Take the following example:

```
<EMBED SRC="resume.doc">
```

This simple line of HTML adds the file resume.doc to my Web page. The file extension .DOC signifies that my embedded file is a Microsoft Word file. When Netscape sees this line of HTML, it knows that it's supposed to load the corresponding plug-in which can be used to view Word documents. (I talk about this plug-in later on. It is the Word Viewer by Inso.) All plug-ins use a different file extension to identify the files they're associated with.

In addition to using the SRC keyword, you've also got to mention the height and width of the plug-in window:

```
<EMBED SRC="resume.doc" HEIGHT=200 WIDTH=400>
```

The HEIGHT and WIDTH keywords specify the size in pixels of the window containing the Netscape plug-in. Figure 10.4 shows a sample plugged-in Word document at the Inso home page.

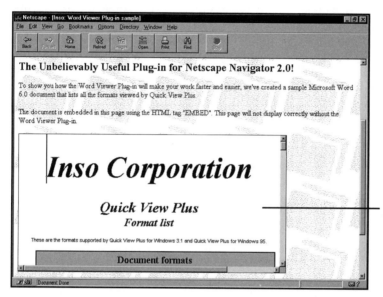

Fig. 10.4
Embedded files can appear in any height or width.

Embedded Word document

Each plug-in has its own unique keywords that pertain specifically to that type of file. For example, embedded video clips allow you to fast forward, stop, and rewind the clips as they play if you add the proper keywords to your HTML tag.

Note

If you want to reference embedded files on the entire screen, you don't have to even worry about using the <EMBED> tag. All you need to do is build a hypertext link to your file:

```
<A HREF="resume.doc">See my resume in Word</A>
```

Netscape recognizes the .DOC file extension and loads the proper plug-in automatically on the entire screen.

III

Multimedia

Configuring Your WWW Server

When Netscape communicates with a WWW server and requests a specific HTML page, they exchange lots of information. One part of this exchange occurs when the server tells Netscape what type of file it's going to send to the browser—usually an HTML file. Netscape automatically knows how to display HTML files and format the tags saved inside of them. Netscape tells the server that it recognizes HTML files before they get sent—after all, that's Netscape's main job. All this communication goes on automatically in the background without users or Web developers worrying about how Netscape and WWW servers talk to one another.

Netscape and the WWW server know how to recognize several different types of files besides HTML, including GIFs, JPEGs, and regular text. In the case of plug-ins, the WWW server is often sending back and forth new and different types of files besides those that it recognizes by default. For the previous example, the WWW server is sending back a Microsoft Word document.

You've already learned how Netscape recognizes these new file types—you download a plug-in. Then when you visit a Web page that has a plug-in, Netscape loads the corresponding program for that file type. If you want to add embedded files to your Web page, you've also got to customize your WWW server.

The WWW server uses MIME standards to recognize many different file types. MIME standards are the worldwide way for documents to be branded electronically. Thus, a file that ends with .HTM or .HTML is branded an HTML file. Each WWW server has its own listing of all the MIME file types it recognizes. Each WWW server has its own customized way of configuring MIME file types. If you run your own WWW server, consult your user's manual—you're most likely looking for a file named MIME.TYPES.

If you're like most people, and don't run your own WWW server, you need to send a message to your system administrator asking him or her to add MIME support for the plug-in you want to add to your Web page.

Caution

Before you send mail off to your system administrator, check out the Web Providers home page. Many Web providers have an online listing of all the MIME types they're configured to support. This prevents system administrators from getting many duplicates of the same question.

For each plug-in I describe, I'll tell you the specific MIME addition you need to make in order to add this type of file to your Web page. It's up to you to configure your WWW server, or send an e-mail to your system administrator requesting his or her support—without it, your embedded files won't work properly.

The following is a sample of what a MIME definition looks like. This MIME definition is used for the VoxWare video plug-in (described later). It identifies all files with the .voc extension as special VoxWare files:

```
audio/voxware vox
```

> **Note**
>
> Unfortunately, if you use a large online service provider like Prodigy, AOL, or CompuServe, you aren't likely to have MIME support for VoxWare or any other unique file type required for Netscape plug-ins to work when added to your Web page.

Document Plug-Ins

Adding formatted documents has long been a desire of many Web page developers. Frustrated by the formatting limitations of HTML, Web developers longed to be able to use tools that they are already familiar with to create Web pages.

Several new plug-ins allow you to add formatted documents to Web pages. This section introduces you to the Inso Word Viewer and Adobe Amber— both useful and important plug-ins for any Web page developer.

The Word Viewer by Inso

Probably one of the most useful plug-ins that exists, the Word Viewer lets you embed Microsoft Word documents *directly* into your Web page. This free plug-in displays documents just as they'd appear on your personal computer in Microsoft Word.

On the CD

This unbelievably useful plug-in adds an entire new dimension to what you can do with your Web page. Many people use Microsoft Word (version 6.0 or 7.0) to create all sorts of word processed files. Word is the most popular word processor in the entire world. Although it's so powerful, you haven't been able to add these documents to Web pages because they weren't in HTML format. You would lose all font control, text attributes, and paragraph formatting features that you set in a Word document unless you added the appropriate HTML tags.

III

Multimedia

Now, you can embed your documents directly into your Web page, and people with the Inso Word Viewer automatically see the document as it was meant to be seen in Word. Resumes, letters, papers, the actual chapters in this book, and any Word documents are now fair game for Web pages.

Downloading and Using the Word Viewer

You can find and download the Inso Word Viewer at **http:// www.inso.com/plug.htm** (see fig. 10.5). The file viewer is available for Windows 95, Windows 3.1, and the Macintosh platforms.

Fig. 10.5

Make sure you download the right version of the Word Viewer for your own computer.

Use Windows Explorer or File Manager to double-click the downloaded file and then run the setup.exe program to start the installation process.

Once the viewer is installed, you are ready to view any Word documents on the Web. Visit **http://www.inso.com/plugsamp.htm** to see how a document appears when embedded as part of the HTML file. Notice how in figure 10.6 it only takes up part of the window? That's because of the HEIGHT and WIDTH keywords used when adding the document to the Web page. Click the text marked "here" right below the sample Word file to see the same document taking up the entire Netscape window instead of just a portion (see fig. 10.7).

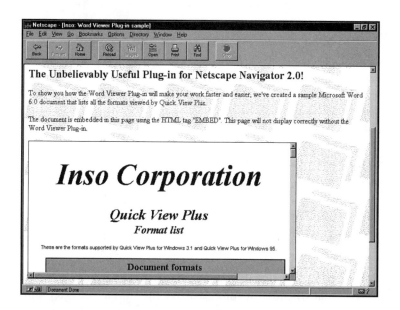

Fig. 10.6
You can scroll through the embedded file using the mini-scroll bars.

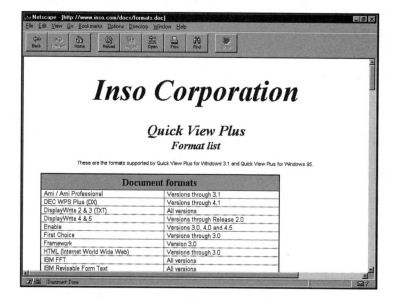

Fig. 10.7
Here's the Word document displayed full-screen.

III

Multimedia

> **Note**
>
> When looking at a document displayed full-screen, you can print it directly to your printer, or choose File, Save As from the Netscape menu bar and save the Word file onto your computer. The file is saved in Word format and you can edit and make changes to it just like any other Word file.

Setting Up Your WWW Server

Now that you've seen how easy the Word Viewer is to use, you're probably all ready to add some Word documents to your Web page. I described the process earlier in the chapter. The MIME type that you need to add to your WWW server is the following:

```
application/msword doc
```

Basically, by adding this line to your MIME.TYPES file, you are telling your WWW server that whenever it comes across a file with a .DOC extension it should send a special message to Netscape telling it to load the Inso plug-in. If you run your own server, you can add the line yourself, or just drop some e-mail off to your system administrator letting them know you'd like this new MIME type added.

Adding Word Documents to Your Web Page

Once your WWW server recognizes Microsoft Word's DOC format, you can now add Word files to your Web page. Like most of the other Netscape plug-ins, you have two options for adding Word documents—full or partial screen.

To add a link to a Word document and have it appear in the entire Netscape screen, use the following tag:

```
<A HREF="mydoc.doc">Read my Document </A>
```

It's just like linking to any other file in your Web page. Remember, you can also point to files in subdirectories so that you can better organize your Web site:

```
<A HREF="docs/mydoc2.doc">Read my Second Document </A>
```

The above tag adds a link to the file named mydoc2.doc, which is located in the docs subdirectory.

The other way to add Word documents to your Web page is to embed them directly into another page of HTML using the <EMBED> tag:

```
<EMBED SRC="mydoc.doc" ALT="Get the Word Viewer Plug-In to see this
file" WIDTH="400" HEIGHT="200">
```

This tag tells Netscape to embed your Word document in a window that is 400 pixels wide and 200 pixels tall. You can specify any dimensions here. The Word Viewer automatically adds scroll bars to the window so that visitors can read through the entire Word document if your window isn't large enough.

Notice how I used the ALT keyword within the <EMBED> tag. This is in case people who don't have the plug-in installed stop by my home page. They'll see the alternative text instead of getting an error. Just as when you use images, it's always a good idea to specify alternative text on your Web page when you can.

You can add as many different Word documents to a single Web page as you'd like. Remember that Netscape must download the entire Word file before it can display it in the plug-in window, so try to keep your files small and to the point. Many people add their resumes, frequently asked questions, or other small amounts of information to their Web page in Word format so they don't have to retype that information with HTML tags.

Adobe Amber

Adobe Acrobat has become the most popular way to publish documents electronically. Acrobat is a program that lets you view documents in their original format, regardless of what application you created them with. Excel spreadsheets, Word files, colorful images, newspapers, and presentations created in virtually any application on almost every computer platform imaginable can be saved in a universal Adobe Acrobat format.

The advantages of this are easy to see. Macintosh users can create impressive color presentations, save them in Acrobat format, and then immediately distribute them to anyone on the WWW regardless of the type of computer they use—Mac, Windows, DOS, or UNIX. From Acrobat, users can save, print, or edit the files without worrying about the original program they were created from. Acrobat saves and reads files with the PDF (Portable Document Format) extension.

Adobe (**http://www.adobe.com**) created Amber, which is a simplified version of Acrobat that works as a plug-in directly from your Web pages. Amber only allows you to read and look at PDF documents—not create them. It's an amazing plug-in. Figure 10.8 shows Hamlet by William Shakespeare loaded as a sample Acrobat file displayed from within Netscape (**http://www.adobe.com/cgi-bin/byteserver3/Amber/Hamlet.pdf**). Notice how all the Netscape buttons and commands appear, as well as the Amber maneuvering buttons, which let you scroll from page to page and zoom in and out of a document.

III

Multimedia

Fig. 10.8
To be or not to be... that is this Amber question.

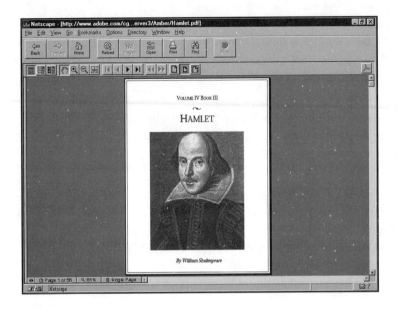

You'll find Acrobat extremely useful for exchanging documents with people all across the WWW and retaining all of the formatting and text characteristics. Unfortunately, Amber is only a reader. You cannot create PDF files with Amber; instead, you must purchase Adobe Acrobat—but more on that later.

> **Note**
>
> For as amazing as Amber is to use, it's really a simple concept. Amber files are saved like snapshots, only electronically. Amber knows how to paint the screen so it appears just like the original document. This technology is based on PostScript, the revolutionary language that high quality printers use to achieve amazing quality and resolution.

Finding and Installing Amber

You can find and download Amber on the WWW at **http://www.adobe.com/Amber/Index.html** or check out the CD-ROM that comes with this book (see fig. 10.9).

Amber installs itself as a Netscape plug-in automatically. Note that you can also run Amber independently of Netscape if you want to read a PDF file without loading up your WWW browser first. To do this, simply click the Adobe Amber icon that appears when Amber is installed.

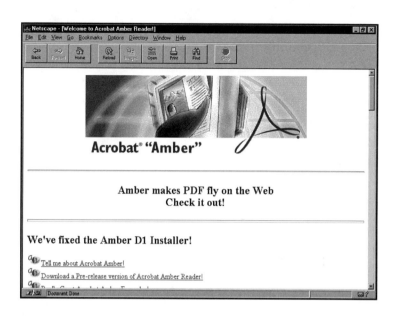

Fig. 10.9
You can download
Amber for virtually
every platform
from here.

Setting Up Your WWW Server for Amber

Now that you've seen how easy Amber is to use, you're probably all ready to add some PDF files to your Web page. I described the process earlier in the chapter to modify your WWW server to handle these new file types. The MIME type that you need to add to your WWW server is the following:

```
application/pdf pdf
```

If you run your own server, you can add the line yourself, or just drop some e-mail off to your system administrator letting him or her know you'd like this new MIME type added.

Using Amber in Your Web Pages

As I alluded to before, adding PDF files to your Web page isn't a free process. You must first purchase Adobe Acrobat and install it on your computer. Adobe Acrobat and Adobe Acrobat Pro are separate packages that you can get at any local computer store. They are used to create PDF files from any other program on your computer.

This isn't the only plug-in that I refer to in this chapter that will cost you money to create files for your Web page—but it's likely one of the most useful. Purchasing Acrobat can cost you around $100—but, in my opinion, it's worth every penny. Acrobat adds an entire new dimension to electronic publishing. In addition to enabling you to plug directly into Netscape, PDF files let you share preformatted info worldwide.

III

Multimedia

Personally, I purchased Acrobat to add some innovative flyers and documents to my Web page. Creating the PDF files was done in a matter of minutes because of the way Acrobat works with any existing application on your computer. Several great Acrobat examples can be found at **http://www.adobe.com/Amber/amexamp.html**.

Once you purchase Acrobat, you can add PDF files to your home page easily. Instead of embedding them into a Web page, simply create a link to the proper PDF file.

To add a link to a Word document and have it appear in the entire Netscape screen, use the following tag:

```
<A HREF="acrobat/paper.pdf">Read my PDF file </A>
```

FIGleaf Inline

My favorite plug-in is called FIGleaf Inline, by Carberry Technology. Before this plug-in, you could only insert GIF and JPEG images into your Web page. FIGleaf changed all that. Virtually every popular graphic and image file type can now be embedded directly into your Web page.

When Netscape recognizes an embedded graphic, it automatically loads FIGleaf and displays the image as it is meant to be seen. You can even zoom in and out of a picture being viewed with FIGleaf Inline.

You can download this plug-in at **http://www.ct.ebt.com/figinline/download.html**. It is available for Windows 95, Windows 3.1, and Macintosh users. The following table is a complete list of all the different image file types that you can embed and view from within Netscape. I've listed the name of each image type and the common file extension associated with each of them.

Image Type	File Extension
Computer Graphics Metafile	CGM
Tagged Image File Format	TIFF/TIF
Encapsulated PostScript	EPSI/EPSF/EPS
CCITT Group 4 Type I	G4
CCITT Group 4 Type II	TG4
Microsoft Windows Bitmap	BMP
Microsoft Windows Metafile	WMF
Portable Network Graphic	PNG
Portable Pixmap	PPM

Image Type	File Extension
Portable Greymap	PGM
Portable Bitmap	PBM
Sun Raster files	SUN
Graphics Interchange Format	GIF
Joint Photographic Experts Group	JPEG/JPG

No longer will you need to convert images that are stored in other formats into GIF and JPG format—which can sometimes lose detail, be inconvenient, and take up a lot of time. You can include new images in your Web page by using the standard <EMBED> tag:

```
<EMBED SRC="pictures/mypic.cgm" HEIGHT=40 WIDTH=40>
```

All you need to do is create a hypertext link to your CGM, TIF, or other graphics file. This tag points to the file named mypic.cgm, which is located in the pictures subdirectory from my HTML file. When Netscape loads the page, you won't notice anything different; the new images appear like other GIF and JPG pictures. You can also add the BORDER keyword to specify a colored line that appears around the entire image. This is similar to the BORDER keyword used when adding regular images to your Web page with the <IMG> tag.

Figure 10.10 shows an example of several CGM files on the Carberry home page.

Fig. 10.10
FIGleaf Inline adds unparalleled flexibility and ease of use to imaging on your Web pages.

III

Multimedia

Caution

One reason GIF and JPG images are the international standard is because they are good compromises between image file size and picture quality. Other file types such as TIF and CGM may offer better detail for images, but their file sizes often make them prohibitively large (excess of 400K each) to use with the WWW. Make sure embedded images are of a reasonable file size, otherwise you may want to convert them to GIF or JPG format for that reason alone (use Paint Shop Pro on the CD-ROM to accomplish these conversions).

Note

If you want to reference an image to appear across the entire Netscape window, instead of your specific pixel coordinates, use the following tag:

```
<A HREF="pictures/mypic.cgm">View my picture</A>
```

Setting Up Your WWW Server for FIGLeaf

FIGleaf Inline is a great product—but setting up your WWW server to work with all these different image formats can be challenging. You need to customize your MIME.TYPES file for every image file format you want to be able to add to your Web page.

If you run your own server, you can add the line yourself, or just send some e-mail to your system administrator letting him or her know you'd like this new MIME type added. The MIME.TYPES list was not available at the time this book went to press. If you are interested, visit the Carberry Technologies Web page.

Presentation Plug-Ins

You can also add graphical and interactive presentations to your Web pages. These presentations typically consist of a set of slides that you want to appear one after another. You can tell Netscape to display the slides automatically, or one at a time—they're perfect for creating informative presentations.

WebShow by SPC

Have you ever had to give an informative presentation? You start building a set of slides or transparencies to use as your visual aid, and then you go through them one at a time. Using the new WebShow plug-in, you can embed slide-show presentations right into your Web page.

When people visit, the presentation will automatically begin and people will be able to read slide-by-slide without using their mouse or keyboard. WebShow is a nice plug-in because it adds colorful and simple-to-create presentations. Like most other plug-ins, WebShow only displays the presentations; it doesn't create them. You create your own presentations by using a trial version of WordPower, a professional presentation package.

What makes WebShow and WordPower so attractive is the fantastically small file size of their presentations. A single presentation that's 30 pages long can be as small as 11–15K. A similar presentation in Microsoft's PowerPoint couldn't even begin to compare to that type of file size. You can recognize WordPower presentations because they always end with the file extension .ASP.

Downloading and Using WebShow

The WebShow plug-in is free and can be downloaded by anyone who has Netscape 2.0 installed on his or her machine. Visit **http://www.spco.com/asap/asapwebs.htm** to download the latest version of WebShow, or check out the CD-ROM accompanying this book. Figure 10.11 shows the WebShow main download page.

On the CD

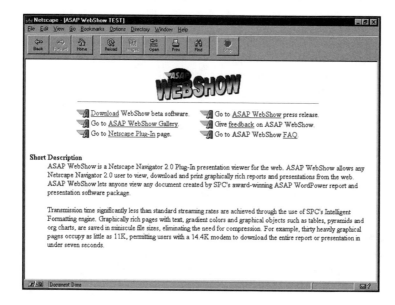

Fig. 10.11
Find the WebShow plug-in here.

III

Multimedia

Once you've downloaded and installed WebShow on your machine, you can experience all sorts of interactive presentations. Stop by the PC World presentation at **http://www.pcworld.com/resources/promos/asap-presentation.html** (see fig. 10.12). You'll get a good grasp of the kinds of simple, yet effective, presentations that you can view and add to your Web pages.

Fig. 10.12
Here's a PC World presentation that plays itself automatically.

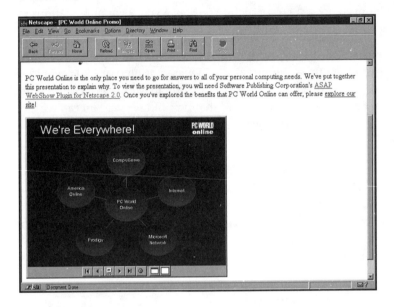

Setting Up Your WWW Server
Now that you've seen how impressive WebShow presentations are, you're probably all ready to add one to your Web page. I described earlier in the chapter the process to modify your WWW server to handle these new file types. The MIME type that you need to add to your WWW server is:

```
application/x-asap asp
```

If you run your own server, you can add the line yourself, or just drop some e-mail off to your system administrator letting him or her know you'd like this new MIME type added.

Creating and Adding WebShow Presentations to Your Web Page
As with so many of the other plug-ins, only the viewer for these presentations is free. To create the colorful presentations I alluded to earlier, you need to purchase a product called WordPower, which will set you back about $99.

However, the nice people at SPC allow anyone on the WWW to download and test drive WordPower for two weeks. This means you can use WordPower and create some of your own presentations, and then decide whether or not it's worth the $99. You can download WordPower directly from ASAP at **http://www.spco.com**. Remember that you only have 14 days to evaluate WordPower. To use it after your two weeks are up, you must purchase it. Figure 10.13 shows a WordPower presentation being created.

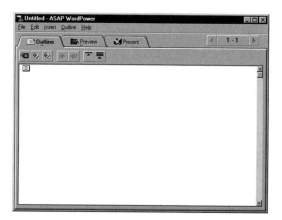

Fig. 10.13
WordPower is easy and intuitive to use.

I'm not going to go into any detail about how to use WordPower—that's for you to explore. It's a pretty easy program to use, and I was able to create a good presentation in under an hour. Once your presentation is complete, you can add it to your Web page using the <EMBED> tag:

```
<EMBED SRC="mypresent.asp" HEIGHT=200 WIDTH=400>
```

In addition, several other keywords can be used with the <EMBED> tag to add further control to how your presentation appears. The following are several of my favorite (and most useful) keywords. Visit **http://www.spco.com/asap/webparam.htm** for a complete list of the keywords you can use when embedding a presentation on your Web page:

■ AutoPlay=—You can set this keyword to TRUE if you want the presentation to automatically scroll through each slide, or FALSE if you want to make visitors use the keyboard arrows and mouse buttons to step through it.

■ NavBar=—Set this keyword to ON if you want to add a Navigation bar that lets visitors step through a presentation using a mouse. OFF removes the navigation bar.

III

Multimedia

- Effect=—If you want WebShow to move from page to page in a special manner, set this value to be one of several possible values. Stop by **http://www.spco.com/asap/webparam.htm** for more information on this and other keywords.

To add a link to a presentation using several of the optional keyword tags, here's how the HTML would look:

```
<EMBED SRC="mypresent.asp" HEIGHT=200 WIDTH=400 AUTOPLAY=ON NAVBAR=ON>
```

The same presentation is added to the Web page, but now Netscape automatically plays through the presentation and the navigation bar is now viewable.

Macromedia's Shockwave

Shockwave is the truly multimedia presentation package. Using Shockwave, you can experience animated presentations that have their own musical soundtracks right from your Web page.

If you want to create killer animated presentations, check out Chapter 9, "Working with Netscape Animation," where I discuss Shockwave in more detail and show you how you can create animations yourself.

Shockwave can be found on the CD-ROM in the back of the book or at **http://www.macromedia.com**.

Audio Plug-Ins

Adding music and sound to Web pages has always been a popular choice. Visitors enjoy hearing background music, or being able to select from interesting songs or sound effects.

Several new Netscape plug-ins allow you to build audio sounds into your Web page. This section outlines the best audio plug-ins and shows you how you can add some plugged-in sounds to your pages.

RealAudio

RealAudio lets you receive and play live feeds of radio and audio sounds directly from Netscape. As long as you have a 14.4 connection or better and the RealAudio plug-in installed, you can listen to audio feeds come from various WWW servers—such as a radio and news stations. Previously, Netscape would download an entire sound clip, then play it on your computer. RealAudio works differently. It plays audio clips as they're being downloaded, provided you have a 14.4 baud connection or better. You don't have to wait for the whole file to download and then listen.

At 14.4 baud, the RealAudio player is about equivalent to AM sound quality. 28.8 gives you full FM quality—that's pretty impressive. The file size is also impressive. RA (RealAudio) files are about 1K per second—or 3.6 megs to digitize an entire hour—now that's compression. FM quality files are about double that in file size.

Downloading and Using RealAudio

The RealAudio plug-in is a free download to everyone. Visit the RealAudio home page at **http://www.realaudio.com** (see fig. 10.14).

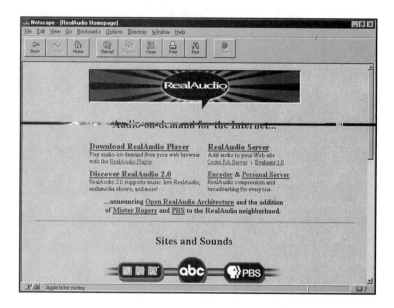

Fig. 10.14
Here's the center of audio examples for the Web.

You'll quickly notice that there are several different RealAudio players. Version 1.0 is optimized for individuals who have only a 14.4 baud connection to the WWW, while 2.0 is for those of you who have a 28.8 baud or better connection. There's no rule for using one or the other, but if you try using version 2.0 with only a 14.4 baud modem, your audio sounds will be choppy and possibly unintelligible. RealAudio has separate versions for Windows 95, Windows 3.1, Macintosh, and UNIX operating systems.

Note

Before becoming a Netscape 2.0 plug-in, RealAudio was the most popular helper application on the Internet. You could listen to audio sounds using the RealAudio player, but instead of being embedded in your Web page, the player was a Netscape helper application.

III

Multimedia

From the RealAudio site, there are many different places you can learn how RealAudio sounds work. Most of these locations don't use RealAudio as a plug-in, just a helper application. Figure 10.15, though, shows a great example of RealAudio sounds that can plug into your Web page (**http://www.realaudio.com/products/ra2.0/pn.htm**).

Fig. 10.15
This RealAudio example shows what plugged in sounds will soon look like.

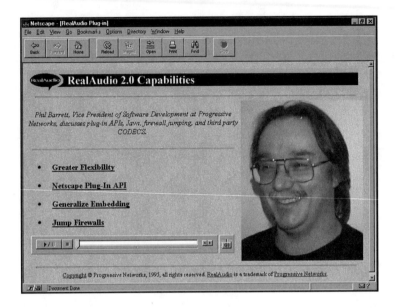

Notice that there are several controls to give you flexibility on starting and stopping sounds and the volume.

Setting Up Your WWW Server

After seeing RealAudio in action, of course you'll want to customize your WWW server to be able to add RealAudio sounds to your Web page. The MIME type that you need to add to your WWW server is the following:

```
audio/x-pn-realaudio-plugin rpm
```

If you run your own server, you can add the line yourself, or just send some e-mail to your system administrator letting him or her know you'd like this new MIME type added.

Creating and Adding RealAudio Sounds to Your Web Page

Unfortunately, adding RealAudio files isn't as easy as listening to them. Since RealAudio files are a continuous feed of sound that is sent to visitors, a separate piece of software called the RealAudio Server must be installed at each and every Web site that produces RealAudio sounds.

RealAudio Servers come in two basic varieties—professional and personal. The professional RealAudio Server starts at about $1,500 for a basic edition, and allows you to simultaneously feed ten people audio sounds from a single server. The prices only go up from there. Most people won't be adding a professional server to their Web site unless they are part of a large company, or rely on audio sounds to do business (such as a radio station). You can download a free version of the professional RealAudio Server to evaluate for about a month. This lets you try it before you buy it to make sure you want to invest in this fascinating technology.

Individual users can download and install the personal version for free (although RealAudio might start charging a nominal fee soon). The personal Server allows you to have two simultaneous feeds of RA sounds running from your own Web server at once. It's a great option if you aren't part of a large company. The only drawback to running the personal edition of the RealAudio Server is that it only works on WWW servers that run on Windows NT or the Macintosh. Check with your system administrator for more information on your Web server and more detailed help for getting the RealAudio Server to work with your account.

Once you've downloaded and installed a RealAudio Server at your page, your next step is to use the RealAudio Encoder. The Encoder lets you create new audio sounds from scratch and save them in RA/RPM format, or you can convert other popular sound files to use on your Web page. The RealAudio Encoder is free and is extremely easy to use. Use the following table as a guide.

RealAudio Product	URL
Professional Server	http://www.realaudio.com/prognet/serrel.html
Personal Server	http://www.realaudio.com/persserv/
Encoder	http://www.realaudio.com/products/encoder/

Once you've gotten the RealAudio Server running and you have encoded several files, adding them to your Web page is the easy part. All you have to do is use the <EMBED> tag like every other plug-in uses. Additionally, several other keywords can be added to your <EMBED> tag. For a detailed list, visit **http://www.realaudio.com/products/ra2.0/plug_ins/**.

III

Multimedia

Toolvox by Voxware

Another program that embeds sounds into your Web page, Toolvox is a more attractive alternative to individuals who want to create cool multimedia pages. Toolvox compresses audio files up to an astounding 53 to 1 ratio. An entire minute of a Toolvox'd audio file is only 18K!

Toolvox is optimized for sounds that have one voice, multiple voices, or for singing—one person at a time. With other types of sounds, you won't find the quality that RealAudio offers; although, with a 53 to 1 compression ratio, you won't miss anything else from RealAudio.

Playing Sounds

There are two pieces to using Toolvox: the player and the encoder. The player is just like any other Netscape plug-in. You've got to download it from the Toolvox Web page (**http://www.voxware.com/download.htm**) and install it on your personal machine.

Once properly installed, you can listen to any Toolvox audio clips. One perfect clip would be JFK's inaugural speech, sponsored and put online by Voxware itself (**http://www.voxware.com/voxintro.htm**) (see fig. 10.16).

Fig. 10.16
We can all listen to JFK's patriotic inaugural speech.

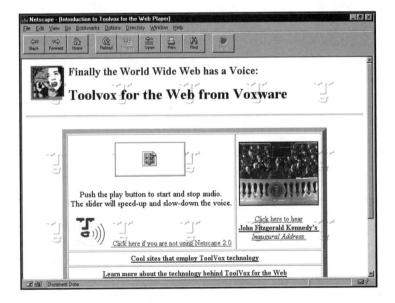

Configure the WWW Server

Now that you've heard how impressive Toolvox sounds are, you're probably all ready to add one to your Web page. I described earlier in the chapter the process to modify your WWW server to handle these new file types. The MIME type that you need to add to your WWW server is:

```
audio/voxware vox
```

If you run your own server, you can add the line yourself, or just drop some e-mail off to your system administrator letting him or her know you'd like this new MIME type added.

Creating ToolVox Sounds

Once you've got the player installed and working correctly, it's time to learn how to build and add vox'd audio clips to your Web page. For free, you can download the Voxware audio encoder, which converts sound files from Windows WAV (and AIF) format into VOX format. Download the Toolvox encoder at **http://www.voxware.com/download.htm**.

With Toolvox for the Web, you can embed a file to directly play as a Netscape plug-in. Since Toolvox files are so small (each minute is only about 18 KB), visitors will experience very rapid response. The Voxware plug-in will start playing the file as soon as a small buffer is created, usually within a few seconds.

For example, to use the file JFK.VOX, you would enter the following HTML tag:

```
<EMBED SRC="jfk.vox" PLAYMODE=auto VISUALMODE=embed >
```

Notice the two additional keywords that Toolvox uses from the `<EMBED>` tag. The PLAYMODE keyword tells Netscape to start playing the audio clip as soon as it can, and VISUALMODE adds a toolbar to the audio clip so you can start and stop the sound clip. The following lists the separate values you can assign the PLAYMODE keyword when using vox'd sounds on your Web page:

- User—Visitors must click either the Vox icon or the player window's Start button on the Web page to start the sounds.
- Auto—The sound begins to play automatically when the Web page appears.
- Cache—Visitors download the sound file and don't hear it at all—it is saved on their personal computer.

The VISUALMODE keyword determines how the Web Player appears on the page. The following lists the separate values you can assign the VISUALMODE keyword when using vox'd sounds on your Web page:

III

Multimedia

- `Icon`—A face icon appears on the Web page that appears red when sound is playing.
- `Background`—There are no controls to the sound file; it plays automatically with no way to turn it off.
- `Embed`—The Web Player window appears on the Web page giving visitors more control over how the sounds are heard.
- `Float`—The Web Player appears in a floating window with the same controls as `Embed`.

Video Clips

Multimediaplug-ins wouldn't be complete without looking at the new ones that are optimized for viewing video clips on the Web. Several new plug-ins make it significantly easier to experience embedded multimedia right from your Netscape Web page.

> **Note**
>
> These new plug-ins allow for truly embedded video—similar to the new Microsoft video tags covered in Chapter 3 that only work for Internet Explorer.

QuickTime

QuickTime is the Video file format pioneered by Apple (**http://www.apple.com**). QuickTime works on multiple file platforms, is extremely efficient, and offers unparalleled quality and ease of use.

Soon, a new Quicktime plug-in is expected from Apple—but it wasn't released by the time this book was written. Keep your eyes posted on the Netscape Plug-in Home Page for further announcements on how you will be able to dynamically embed QuickTime video clips in your Web pages.

PreVu MPEG Plug-In

On important video plug-in that you may want to take advantage of is PreVu. PreVu is an MPEG video player that displays video clips as they are being downloaded. MPEG videos are quite large and can take a long time to download. PreVu lets you start watching the video clips instantly so you immediately know whether you want to wait for the entire clip to download.

Stop by **http://www.intervu.com/download.html** to learn more about installing and using PreVu optimized videos on your Web page. PreVu offers a step-by-step installation process for setting up PreVu on your computer and getting it to run.

VDOLive

VDOLive is another video based Netscape plug-in that lets you watch video clips directly inside your Web page as they are downloaded. People who use video clips on their Web pages will want to investigate VDOLive because of the significant increase in performance that visitors enjoy when stopping by your Web page. Videos that took hours to download before you could watch them are now watched on-the-fly.

VDOLive must be downloaded and installed just like all of the other Netscape plug-ins. You can download the free VDOLive player at **http://www.vdolive.com/newplug.htm** (see fig. 10.17).

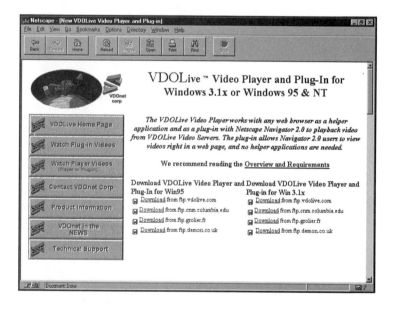

Fig. 10.17
VDOLive is an interesting alternative for Web pages that use many video clips.

Later this year, VDOLive promises to release a program that will automatically convert videos in other file formats into the .VDO format. You'll be able to convert Windows AVI, Apple's QuickTime, and the MPEG video format with a single program. Then visitors won't have to worry about using many different video file formats. If you're a video junkie, stop by its home page to see if its encoder is ready for action!

Multimedia

III

VRML

On the cutting edge of technology, Virtual Reality Modeling Language (VRML) lets you create entirely new three-dimensional worlds that can be explored. VRML (pronounced *ver-mull*) is the next generation of a truly interactive WWW.

Many new Netscape 2.0 plug-ins focus on allowing you to dynamically incorporate VRML worlds and objects directly into your Web pages. In the Netscape plug-in registry, you'll find a half-dozen plug-ins specifically focused on incorporating VRML worlds inside standard Web pages.

While browsing through VRML worlds is fun and easy to do, creating VRML spots for your Web pages is exceedingly difficult. VRML is similar to HTML in that it is a text-based language that tells a browser how things will appear on-screen. Unlike HTML, VRML is much more complex and must compensate for every three-dimensional object and wall, and decide how to make all the pieces of these new worlds interact with one another. Creating VRML worlds is beyond the limited scope of this book—but it is quickly becoming a popular topic.

If you are interested in learning more about building VRML worlds for yourself, stop by **http://vrml.wired.com** or **http://www.vrml.org**—two of the main VRML resources on the Web.

Alternatively, take a look at Que's *Special Edition Using VRML*. This book provides an in-depth guide to understanding and building your own virtual reality worlds and steps you through creating some of your own examples. ❖

Part IV

Working with CGI Scripts, Forms, and Java

Chapter 11

Understanding and Using CGI Scripts

Welcome to Part IV of this book. This is where you'll start learning some advanced ways to customize your Web page. While so far you've learned all about new HTML tags and features, now I'll show you how you can write your own programs from scratch and add them to your Web page.

While exploring the WWW, you've probably encountered things called CGI scripts or maybe you've filled out an online form or two at various Web sites. If you're like most people (including me), you've shied away from using these things in your Web page because they appear to be complicated and difficult to use. Many people assume that they need some sort of programming background to understand how to add neat and interactive CGI scripts to their Web pages.

They're wrong. Creating and adding CGI scripts is easy. Anybody can include interactive scripts and forms just by learning a few tidbits of information. That's what you'll learn in this chapter. I'll introduce and explain to you all about CGI scripts and then we'll build some simple ones together. Once you realize how easy scripts are to use, I'll profile several popular scripts and show you how to add them to your Web page in a few minutes.

Specifically, in this chapter, you'll learn how to do the following:

- Recognize CGI scripts and how they're used on Web pages
- Build several simple scripts from scratch
- Add CGI scripts to your Web pages
- Use existing scripts, such as counting visitors and displaying random images with only a few modifications

What are CGI Scripts?

CGI, short for *Common Gateway Interface*, is the standard which allows WWW browsers to interactively communicate with WWW servers. You can write programs, called CGI scripts, that are run on a WWW server whenever pointed to by a browser.

Note

You may wonder why we don't just refer to them as CGI *programs* instead of *scripts*. There's an important difference between scripts and programs. When you create a program, you write many lines in a computer language such as C or Pascal, and then you've got to *compile* the program. Once it's compiled, then it can be run.

Scripts, on the other hand, don't need to be compiled. When you run a script, the computer just reads each line in the file and runs the command you've told it to. Just like an actor reads directly from his movie script and then acts his part, a computer performs the actions of the script while reading through it. Scripts aren't as powerful as programs, but they tend to be easier to create.

With the WWW, you can create either scripts or programs—they both work the same. But the initial CGI programs were scripts so the name just stuck. I usually stick with creating scripts because they are much easier to make and don't require previous programming knowledge, but you'll hear the terms CGI scripts and CGI programs used interchangeably.

CGI scripts are stored on a WWW server just like HTML files. Whenever a browser points to a script, the program starts running, and then sends the results of the program back to the WWW server, so it can then send that info back to Netscape. Common Gateway Interface is the international translator that all WWW servers, browsers, and scripts are familiar with—it lets them communicate with one another.

Imagine if you worked in a large company that had offices all around the world. Realizing that everyone won't know different languages, your company makes you stick to a very strict format for sending messages back and forth. Translators in each country recognize the different messages and translate them into the corresponding foreign language. That's how CGI works. When you write a CGI program, you must adhere to a strict message format, so that WWW browsers and servers across the world will be able to translate your message.

You'll learn how to create and write your own CGI scripts, and how to communicate with your WWW server in the correct manner. For more information on the basic concepts of CGI scripting, visit the CGI home page at **http://hoohoo.ncsa.uiuc.edu/docs/cgi/overview.html**.

Server Side Includes

Similar to CGI scripts, another mechanism discussed in this chapter is called Server Side Includes (*SSI* for short). Normally, CGI scripts are triggered by adding a hypertext link to a Web page. Once that link is clicked, the CGI script then runs. Server Side Includes are scripts that are triggered whenever a Web page is loaded. Server Side Includes affect when a CGI script is triggered—not what it does or how it runs. You can trigger CGI scripts via hypertext links and Server Side Includes interchangeably.

Here's an Example—a Counter

One extremely popular CGI script counts how many people have visited a particular Web page. Many people want to track the number of visitors they have for their own posterity, or to know how popular their site is. Counting visitors must be done with a CGI script. All you have to do is add a Server Side Include command to this script directly in your Web page:

```
<!--#exec cgi="http:/cgi-bin/counter.cgi"-->
```

All this simple line of HTML does is tell the WWW server to execute the program `counter.cgi` that's located in the subdirectory called `cgi-bin` every time this page is loaded.

When someone stops by, Netscape sends a message to the WWW server telling it to execute the CGI counter script. The counter script is simple. All it does is increment the number of people who've stopped by. Then it sends the new number back to Netscape so it can be displayed on-screen. Figure 11.1 shows how Netscape displays the counter—it's pretty simple.

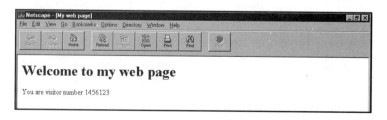

Fig. 11.1
Wow, a lot of people have visited this page!

That's it. All you have to do is write the `counter.cgi` program (I'll show you how later on in this chapter). Take a look at figure 11.2 to see how the script works in a visual sense.

Fig. 11.2
Here's how a CGI script communicates with the WWW server and browser (Netscape).

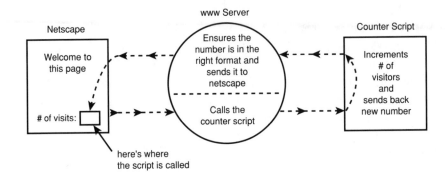

Forms Require Scripts

You may have also noticed interactive forms when you visit different pages on the Web. These forms request different pieces of information from people as they visit Web pages. Figure 11.3 shows an example of how The Case uses forms to let people sign up and receive a free mystery e-mail every week (**http://www.thecase.com/**).

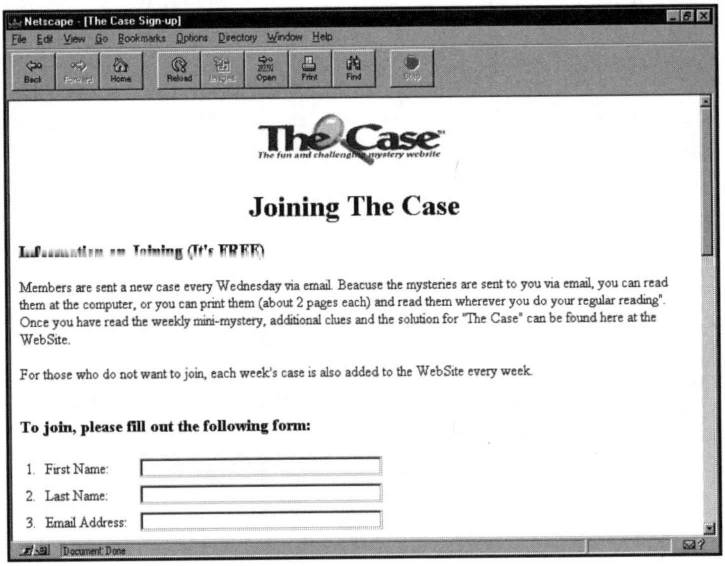

Fig. 11.3
Enter the requested information for each field on the form.

Adding forms to Web pages is just a matter of learning new HTML tags, but CGI scripts are needed to process the information submitted from each form. Read Chapter 12, "Figuring Out Where Forms Fit In," for a more thorough explanation of forms, and I'll show you how CGI scripts are a vital part of that process.

Where To Get More CGI Information

CGI scripting is virtually an unlimited topic. While this chapter introduces you to several popular and common scripts and programs for your Web page, it is by no means a definitive source of everything about the Common Gateway Interface. If, after reading this chapter, you want to learn more about CGI scripts, check out *Special Edition Using CGI* or *Special Edition Using Perl*, both large and useful references from Que on this advanced topic.

Alternatively, take a look at the following WWW sites. These sites offer introductions and references to advanced CGI materials and are a logical next step once you've finished this chapter:

- Yahoo page:

   http://www.yahoo.com/Computers_and_Internet/ Internet/World_Wide_Web/ CGI__Common_Gateway_Interface/

- CGI Programmer's Reference:

   http://www.best.com/~hedlund/cgi-faq/

- CGI Script Tutorial:

   http://WWW.Stars.com/Seminars/

How Scripts are Built

CGI Scripts come in many shapes, sizes, and formats. As mentioned previously, CGI scripts are actually programs written in a programming language, referenced in your Web page, and ready to run.

Before you can start writing scripts, you've got to choose a scripting or programming language, and ensure that your WWW server permits CGI scripts to be executed.

Scripting Languages

You can write CGI scripts in just about any programming language. The following are some of the common CGI languages that you'll probably run into when creating your own scripts:

- **UNIX Shell scripts**—Installed on every UNIX machine, this simple scripting language issues a series of commands one after another and has several popular constructs from other languages. It's also the most basic and easiest way to create scripts from scratch. I use UNIX shell scripts for many of the examples in this chapter.

- **Perl**—The most popular CGI language, Perl is a straightforward script language that programmers and non-programmers alike use. Visit **http://www.perl.com** for more information.

- **C**—C is the most common programming language and has a vast following. Experienced programmers often choose to create CGI scripts with C because of its flexibility and familiarity. I tend to stay away from C programs because it is really optimized for programmers, and I'm not a top-notch C programmer.

- **Visual Basic**—You can create visual basic applications that run when you are using a Windows 95 or Windows NT Web server.

- **Applescript**—This easy-to-use scripting language available for Mac servers is an excellent choice if available.

To create CGI programs, you've got to have the particular programming language installed on your WWW server. Most WWW sites support shell scripts and Perl. Check with your WWW administrator to make sure.

Note

One new programming language you might want to check out is Cmm. This new language advertises itself as "a lazy man's C" with all the benefits of creating scripts in C, but none of the drawbacks, limitations, and complexities. If you are interested, visit **http://www.nombas.com** (*nombas* stands for "No MBAs"—a true engineering and enterprising company). Cmm is a completely free language, and there are several unique, entertaining, and interesting scripts available for free (including a game—hangman).

On the CD

I've also included a version of Cmm on the CD-ROM in the back of this book for many different operating systems. For people interested in creating powerful, effective, and simple scripts, Cmm is definitely worth evaluating.

Configuring Your WWW Server

Once you've selected a scripting language, the next step is to make sure that the WWW server that hosts your Web page allows scripts to run. Since CGI

scripts are actual programs that run on a WWW server, Web providers sometimes restrict or forbid access to running them on their Web server:

- **Security**—Unfortunately, some bad apples on the Internet and WWW
  exist. These individuals roam around WWW pages looking for CGI
  scripts that have small security loopholes which can be exploited. These
  loopholes center around the fact that CGI scripts are programs that run
  on a WWW server. Although security problems don't run rampant,
  some Web providers don't permit CGI scripts to run on their servers. If
  you would like more information about security and CGI scripting, visit
  the following sites. They are both tremendous sources of information
  and have been well written.

  WWW Security FAQ: **http://www-genome.wi.mit.edu/WWW/
  faqs/www-security-faq.txt**

  CGI Security FAQ: **http://www.cerf.net/~paulp/cgi-security/**

- **Performance**—Imagine if ten people accessed your Web page at the
  exact same time. Ten separate copies of the CGI script are run simultaneously. Think about running multiple programs on your own personal
  computer. Even running multiple small programs can bring the most
  powerful PowerPC or Pentium to its knees in a matter of moments.
  Although Web servers are better equipped for this situation, it's easy
  to imagine a scenario where CGI scripts can overwhelm a server—
  especially if a lot of people visit your Web page. Some WWW servers
  don't allow you to run CGI scripts for this reason, or will ask you to
  limit the length of your CGI scripts.

Make sure that your Web provider permits CGI scripts to be run. Also remember the earlier discussion of Server Side Includes. You may need to ask your
Web provider to permit Server Side Includes to run as well if you plan on using CGI scripts in this fashion on your Web pages. In most situations, there
will be a specific subdirectory that you must add your CGI scripts to, usually
named cgi-bin. All scripts must be saved within that subdirectory, otherwise
they won't work properly.

Check with your Web provider for specific information on your situation.
Usually it has a set of instructions that explain how to add CGI scripts to
your Web page.

> **Note**
>
> Most commercial Web providers allow CGI scripting, with two large and notable exceptions—AOL and CompuServe. If you use either of these two large services to house your Web page, you're out of luck when it comes to CGI scripts. If you want to add interaction to your Web page, check out Chapter 13, "Making Some of Your Own Java," and you can learn how to add JavaScript commands which will work.
>
> Personally, my old Web provider (The Ohio State University) didn't let CGI scripts run, so I checked out other low cost providers and moved my home page there.

The Two Parts of Every Script

Each CGI script has two important and distinct sections to it—the MIME content header and the actual program. It's important to discern between these two sections of the script.

The first part of a CGI script is usually simple—it's only a single line. It tells the WWW server what kind of information the script is sending back to Netscape. Remember Chapter 10, "Incorporating Netscape Plug-Ins," when I talked about MIME types? This is the exact same issue. Both your WWW server and WWW browser want to know exactly what kind of information to expect. For most cases, CGI scripts only return text, or HTML files.

To let your WWW server know you are sending an HTML file back, you'd use the following line:

```
Content-type: text/html
```

It's that simple. Once you've got the Content return type defined, the rest of the CGI script is up to you—it's the program you want to run.

Building Some Basic Scripts

So far, you've picked a language and made sure your Web provider supports CGI. Let's start building some scripts. In this section, I've described how to build four separate scripts from scratch. In each of them, I use the UNIX shell scripting language.

On the CD

The scripts are listed in order of complexity, with the first few being extremely simple and straightforward. In each of them, you'll learn an important CGI concept. You can actually use these four scripts directly in your Web page if you'd like—they're on the CD-ROM located in the back of the book.

Once you're familiar with these simple scripts and the concepts I've demonstrated, you'll move on to using some more in-depth scripts and learn how to add them to your Web page.

For each of these scripts, you've got to save them as a separate file in the `cgi-bin` subdirectory. To trigger the script, add a link to your Web page that points to the separate script file. For example, to use the first script below, save it as a separate file named `script1.cgi` in the `cgi-bin` subdirectory of your Web site. To trigger it, add the following link to your Web page:

```
<A HREF="cgi-bin/script.cgi">Run Script 1</A>
```

This adds a hypertext link to your Web page. By clicking the text marked `Run Script 1`, Netscape goes out and runs the particular CGI script pointed to in this HTML tag. You can add all of these sample scripts to your Web pages in this fashion.

Note

For your UNIX server to know that it's supposed to execute the script, you've got to set some special file attributes. Normally, a script file is a regular text file. You need to tell UNIX that this file has a set of commands that should run when called upon by Netscape. You've got to issue a specific command at the UNIX prompt.

Set your script file to be executable with the `chmod` command. For example, if your script file name is `myscript.cgi`, you'd use `chmod` like this:

```
chmod a+x myscript.cgi
```

If your Web server isn't a flavor of UNIX, check with your system administrator to learn how to make your CGI script file executable.

As Basic as It Gets—Text Only

The first script is really simple—there are only a few lines to it:

```
#!/bin/sh
echo "Content-type: text/plain";
echo;
echo "Here's the simplest script that displays a sentence.";
```

As you noticed, this script has only four lines to it. The first line identifies it as a UNIX shell script and tells your WWW server where to find the shell script language, so it can interpret the rest of the program. Most likely your shell script definition is in the `/bin/sh` subdirectory like mine.

The second and third lines go together. They are extremely important because they tell Netscape and the WWW server what kind of information this script is sending back. For this script, we're sending back just a line of plain text, as specified by text/plain. For your script to work properly, you've got to have the extra echo command in there (line 3).

The fourth and final line to my simple script prints the sentence Here's the simplest script that displays a sentence. surrounded by quotes.

I've named this script sample1.cgi and placed it within the cgi-bin subdirectory on my Web site. To reference it from my Web page, add the following line of HTML:

```
<A HREF="cgi-bin/sample1.cgi"> Test out script one</A>
```

Now your Web page is linked to this sample script (see fig. 11.4). Once the hot text is clicked, the sample1.cgi program is run. This script sends back the content type information (which doesn't appear in Netscape) and then the line of text specified. Figure 11.5 shows how Netscape looks after clicking the script.

Fig. 11.4
My script is ready to run.

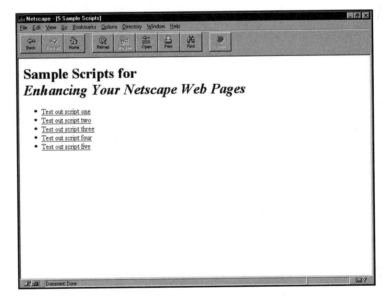

Fig. 11.5
There's not much to this script, but it's a start.

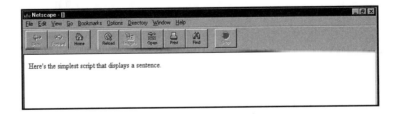

> **Note**
>
> You may have noticed that the content type described for the CGI script resembles the way MIME types were described in the last chapter. MIME is the standard that describes how electronic information should be identified and encoded. There are separate MIME types for text, HTML, GIF, JPEG, and virtually every other type of information that can be sent and received electronically.

Made for Web Pages—Text and HTML

You can also send back bits and pieces of HTML and have Netscape display text formatted on-screen. The major differences between this and the previous script is that I am using a different content type, and I have HTML tags embedded in the text that gets sent back to Netscape:

```
#!/bin/sh
echo "Content-type: text/html";
echo;
echo "<HTML>";
echo "<TITLE>";
echo "The results from this script";
echo "</TITLE>";
echo "<H1> Thanks for clicking on Script 2</H1>";
echo "<HR>";
echo "<BODY>";
echo "You've just clicked on script 2 and";
echo "the results are that Netscape runs this script";
echo "and reads this HTML file and formats it correctly";
echo "<P>";
echo "<A HREF="scripts.htm">Back to the Scripts page</A>";
echo "</BODY>";
```

Although this script is longer, it isn't any more complicated than the first one. Since Netscape knows that it is receiving an HTML file, it automatically interprets the tags and displays the results of the script.

Notice how I embedded several different kinds of HTML tags, including a reference to another document. You can add literally any tags and amount of information that you'd like to appear when this script is run.

> **Note**
>
> Thus far, these two scripts have been absolutely nothing special. You could have accomplished the same thing by linking your Web page to another HTML file which had the same text in it as the CGI script did.
>
> That's why you won't use CGI scripts in this manner very often. The next two examples are better for describing actual situations where CGI scripts are used in Web pages for adding dynamic—that is, constantly changing—text to Web pages.

Adding Dynamic Content to Your Script— Inserting the Date and Monthly Calendar

So far, you've learned how to create two simple CGI scripts that always print out the same information every time they're executed. That's not very much fun, and doesn't add a lot of value to your Web page—you could just as easily add the line of text or HTML to your own page without writing a script.

Now let's learn how to add some dynamic content to your Web page. Using the UNIX shell script, we're going to run two UNIX commands—date, which displays the current date and time on the WWW server, and cal, which prints out a calendar of the current date. These two programs can display different information each time they run depending on the date and month. Take a look at the following script:

```
#!/bin/sh
echo "Content-type: text/html";
echo;
echo "<HTML>";
echo "<TITLE>";
echo "The results from script 3";
echo "</TITLE>";
echo "<H1> Thanks for clicking on Script 3</H1>";
echo "<HR>";
echo "<BODY>";
echo "Today's date is";
date
echo "<P>";
echo "Here's the monthly calendar: <PRE>";
cal
echo "</PRE><P>";
echo "<A HREF="scripts.htm">Back to the Scripts page</A>";
echo "</BODY></HTML>";
```

You'll notice that this script is very similar to the previous one, except for the lines that say only date and cal. These two lines execute UNIX system commands and insert information inside of the script. You can run any UNIX command (the script displays the output from running that command) or even execute other scripts. This makes the results from this script unique every time it runs.

Note

Several other UNIX commands that you may want to experiment with in Web pages are banner, finger, mail, man, and grep. These commands are standard UNIX programs that can be run independently at a UNIX prompt. By embedding them into a CGI script, you are adding new functionality to what happens when a script is run. Consult your WWW administrator or a UNIX manual for more details on these UNIX commands and how they are normally used. Just like date and cal in the previous script, they can be used as part of a CGI script.

Tip

See how I used the <PRE> and </PRE> tags to surround the output of the cal command? That's so Netscape displays the information as it appears when the command is executed and keeps the same formatting.

Interactive Scripts—Using Server Variables

By printing the date every time the script runs, you've created a dynamic script—one whose results change every time it runs. There are other ways you can customize scripts to create dynamic and interactive content.

One way is to capture information about the WWW browser that's running the script. Your WWW server automatically keeps track of certain pieces of information for every individual that stops by, including the WWW browser he or she uses, his or her home domain, the last page he or she visited, and much more. This example shows you how you can use some of that info in a CGI script:

```
#!/bin/sh
echo "Content-type: text/html";
echo;
echo "<HTML>";
echo "<TITLE>";
echo "The results from script 4";
echo "</TITLE>";
echo "<BODY>";
echo "<H1>Welcome to the Twilight Zone. </H1>";
echo "We know all about you_ Want some proof? <P>";
echo "<B>Your WWW browser is: </B>";
echo $HTTP_USER_AGENT;
echo "<P>"
echo "<B>Your Web Provider is: </B>";
echo $REMOTE_HOST;
echo "<P>";
echo "<B>The last web page you visited was: </B>";
echo $HTTP_REFERER;
echo "<P>"
echo "</BODY></HTML>";
```

Every time someone executes this script, different values are returned. There are three variables that I use in this script. $HTTP_USER_AGENT prints out the name of the WWW browser that you are using, $REMOTE_HOST prints out the domain name you are connecting from, and $HTTP_REFERER displays the URL of the last page you visited.

> **Note**
>
> Most Web sites keep track of this information and store it for later use. That's how they know if their advertisements are working. For example, let's say they advertised their Web site at Yahoo (**http://www.yahoo.com**). They keep a log of the $HTTP_REFERER address to know how many people saw the ad at Yahoo and then visited their Web page.

Advancing CGI Scripts

CGI scripts don't have to always perform the same specific actions such as returning a line of HTML or displaying a visitor's Web server. You can also use common programming constructs such as if-then-else, do-while, and repeat-until.

If-then-else commands allow a CGI script to logically decide which branch of a script to run. For example, you could build a script that displays one message to Netscape 2.0 users and a different message to non-Netscape users. Similarly, do-while and repeat-until commands are common programming tools that let you repeat an action for a set amount of time.

Adding Cool Scripts to Your Web Page

In the last section, I showed you four different CGI scripts that all worked a little differently. Each one of them was useful for showing you how to build your own scripts from scratch. Now you're going to learn how most people use CGI scripts—they borrow them.

Many, many CGI scripts already are in existence on the WWW. Scripts that count visitors, create a guestbook where people can sign in, process forms of information, and more are all available for free on the Internet. Why reinvent the wheel when all you have to do is download these scripts and add them to your Web page?

The Visitor Counter Script

This script is by far the most popular type of CGI script on the WWW. Many people want to track the number of individuals who visit their home page. They like to know how popular their page is, and whether or not anyone ever stops by. Personally, I like knowing whether my page is ever seen by outsiders, or just sits alone in some corner of cyberspace.

This counter script is written in Perl. Remember that you've got to have a Perl compiler installed on your WWW server in order to run it. The following is the entire script:

```perl
#!/usr/bin/perl
#
#       COUNTER.CGI
#
print "Content-type: text/html\n\n";
($PAGE = $ENV{'DOCUMENT_URI'}) =~ s/\//_/g;
if (!(-e $PAGE))
  {
    open(NEW,"> $PAGE");
    print NEW "0";
    close(NEW);
    exit(0);
  }
open(COUNTER,"+< $PAGE");
flock(COUNTER,2);
$_=<COUNTER>;
seek(COUNTER,0,0);
$_++;  print;  print COUNTER;
flock(COUNTER,8);
close(COUNTER);
```

It's not very long and is rather simple and elegant. This script can be called by as many different Web pages as you want to use it on. Basically, this script checks to see if a special counter file exists for the HTML document that is tracking the number of visitors. If not, it creates one for you automatically. Then, it opens the special counter file, retrieves the number stored within it, adds one to that number, saves the new number in the counter file, and sends the new number back to Netscape.

The only trick to this simple script is the `flock` command. Short for filelock, `flock` ensures that if two people visit your Web page simultaneously, they won't both try to increment your counter file at the same time—one is locked out until the other request has been processed.

Name your script `counter.cgi` and then place it in your `cgi-bin` subdirectory. Don't forget to issue the appropriate `chmod` command that I talked about in the beginning of the chapter, which is the following:

```
chmod a+x counter.cgi
```

Now all you have to do is add a single line of HTML to your Web page:

```
You are visitor number:<!--#exec cgi="cgi-bin/counter.cgi"-->
```

Whenever someone visits your home page, the `counter.cgi` is run every time and displays a newly incremented number—it's really that easy. Figure 11.6 shows an example of how the counter works when added to a Web page. This script is called in a slightly different way than the other scripts described in this chapter because it is a Server Side Include (SSI). This won't affect how the script runs, just when it is called. In this example, it is triggered when the page is loaded (the `<!--#exec>` tag) as opposed to building a link to this separate file.

Fig. 11.6
Not many people have visited so far.

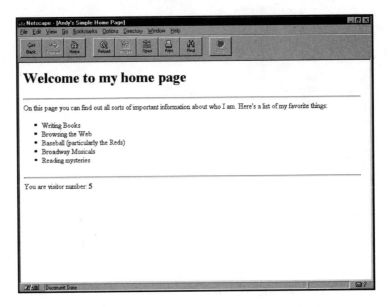

This script is part of an impressive collection of public domain CGI scripts written by Matt Kruse. I've included this and several other CGI scripts on the CD-ROM in the back of the book. You can see Matt's new scripts by visiting **http://web.sau.edu/~mkruse/www/scripts/index.html**.

On the CD

> **Note**
>
> If you don't want or don't have access to creating CGI scripts, there are several public domain counters that you can add to your Web page with no CGI scripting—just a simple URL. The best one can be found at **http://www.digits.com**. This site will step you through adding a counter to your Web page in just moments.

The Random Image Script

Another one of my favorite CGI scripts is the random image generator. This script is useful for displaying one of a set of images at random on a Web page. For example, I have three different pictures of myself that I like to use on my

Web page. This script loads one of those three images at random when the page is visited. It's neat because every time someone visits my page, they might see a different image:

```perl
#! /usr/bin/perl
# Random Image Displayer Version 1.2
#
# Necessary Variables
  $basedir = "http://www.shafran.com";
  @files = ("me.gif, meandliz.gif, me2.gif");

# Options
  $uselog = 0; # 1 = YES; 0 = NO
       $logfile = "piclog";

  srand;
  $num = rand(@files); # Pick a Random Number

# Print Out Header With Random Filename and Base Directory
  print "Location: $basedir$files[$num]\n\n";

# Log Image
  if ($uselog eq '1') {
     open (LOG, ">>$logfile");
     print LOG "$files[$num]\n";
     close (LOG);
  }
exit;
```

You can customize this script to work for you if you have a set of images you'd like displayed at random. All you have to do is store all of the images in a single directory, and set the two variables at the top of the script. Type in the URL of the directory containing the images in the line beginning with $basedir (replace my URL), and then type in each filename individually (separated by commas) on the next line. That's all the changes you need to make.

On the CD

Basically, all this script does is count the total number of images it has to choose from. Then, from that number, it picks one of them at random to be displayed.

To use it in your Web pages, it works inside of the <IMG> tag. So to display a random image on your Web page, make sure the script is saved (I call it randimg.pl), and in the cgi-bin subdirectory:

```html
<IMG SRC="cgi-bin/randimg.pl">
```

So instead of pointing to a specific GIF or JPEG, your <IMG> tag points to this script instead which, in turn, picks one picture at random to display.

You can also use this script when defining a background image for your Web page. Every time visitors stop by, you can have a different style of background by specifying background images instead and using the following tag:

```
<BODY BACKGROUND="cgi-bin/randimg.pl">
```

On the CD

This script is part of another impressive collection of public domain CGI scripts written. Written by Matt Wright, you'll find this and several of his other world famous CGI scripts ready for you to use on the CD-ROM in the back of the book. You can see Matt's new scripts by visiting his script page at **http://worldwidemart.com/scripts/**.

Finding and Building Other CGI Scripts

Besides the two CGI scripts that I described in detail previously, I've included several other popular scripts on the CD-ROM in the back of this book. The following sections list some of the ones ready for you to use.

Each of these scripts comes with instructions for installing them on your Web page. You'll find most of them similar to the steps mentioned previously to add the counter and random image scripts to your pages.

Matt Wright's Scripts

Matt Wright is a professional CGI script writer and an author of Que's *Special Edition Using CGI*. His scripts are used worldwide. You'll find this impressive collection of scripts on the accompanying CD-ROM along with instructions on using them. The following are just a sampling:

- **Guestbook**—This is a guestbook script that was written for users to add their entry automatically.
- **Free for All Link Page**—This is a script that allows users to freely add links to your page.
- **WWWBoard**—This allows for threaded discussions and acts as a message system.
- **Simple Search**—This allows you to implement a simple search of files in your directory on your Web page.
- **FormMail**—This is a formatting interactive form response.
- **Animation**—Put some animation into your pages using Server Push animation (see Chapter 9, "Working with Netscape Animation," for more information).
- **Countdown**—Countdown to the date of your choice!

Matt Kruse's Scripts

Some of the following scripts are free; others are shareware. See their information file on the CD-ROM for more information:

- **Image Indexer**—A very simple script which takes your images in any directory and makes an index HTML document containing them.
- **Indexer**—A robust way to index and search your HTML documents.
- **Comments Page**—Easily and quickly create a comments page for visitors to your Web page (like a guestbook).
- **WWW Access Statistics**—Find out how many accesses Web pages are getting, who is going there, and other related information.
- **Table Generator**—This script creates tables interactively. You specify the size of the table, fill in the cells, and check some options and the table (along with the HTML source) will be automatically generated!
- **Mail Links Generator**—Do you get lots of mail? Do your mail messages contain WWW sites that you want to check out later? If so, this script will automatically pull them out and update your own personal hotlist so you can easily go to them later.

Other places you may want to explore that have useful CGI scripts that you can use for free include the following:

- Selena Sol's Public Domain Script Archive—This is another good sampling of CGI scripts you can pluck right off the WWW:

  http://www.eff.org/~erict/Scripts/
- Shareware CGI scripts—You'll find many useful and usable scripts written in C and AppleScript:

  http://128.172.69.106:8080/cgi-bin/cgis.html
- The CGI newsgroup—Ask your questions to the CGI experts and gurus worldwide. Virtually every CGI question gets posted and answered, here:

  news:comp.infosystems.www.authoring.cgi

Chapter 12
Figuring Out Where Forms Fit In

Filling out forms is a necessary part of life. They're probably one of the most widely used ways people communicate information, facts about themselves, and their opinions. Credit card applications, income taxes, surveys, and questionnaires are all important and vital parts of keeping track of information. Some are easy to fill out, while others ask difficult questions and require thoughtful responses (we all wish income tax forms would fall in the first category).

Regardless of how they're used, all forms have one thing in common: they are just a standardized way to get a lot of information in a short amount of space. Forms ask everyone the same questions and give everyone the same choices when selecting an answer. This makes it easier for us to compile and look at the info that we learn from filled out forms.

Not wanting to be outdone by its paper counterpart, the WWW lets you create your own customized electronic forms directly inside of Web pages. By learning a few new HTML tags and building a simple CGI script, you can create virtually any type of form you'd like.

This chapter introduces you to electronic forms and shows you how you can build them into your Web page. I'll show you around the new HTML tags, demonstrate some simple tools for building forms interactively, and then lead you through several examples of adding a form to your Web page.

Specifically, in this chapter, you learn how to:

- Use forms to get visitor feedback
- Recognize and use the common HTML tags that pertain to forms
- Use HotDog to create forms without worrying about HTML details

- Create several different types of form fields including checkboxes, radio buttons, and password boxes.
- Use customized CGI scripts to process and interpret submitted data
- Build a full form example into your Web page

A Forms Overview

On the WWW, filling out forms is just like using them in real life. You have several screenfuls asking you to type in specific pieces of information and answer certain questions. True to life, electronic forms can come in many shapes and sizes. Some ask you only for your name and address, while others drill you for income level, personal buying habits, or ask you to enter your own comments and suggestions as feedback.

Most people use forms to get and store information about people who visit their Web pages. They want to hear from visitors and gauge their opinions of their Web pages or other related issues. For example, figure 12.1 shows the simple feedback form you can fill out when browsing through the Macmillan Computer Publishing home page.

Fig. 12.1

All Macmillan wants is your e-mail address and your personal thoughts and comments—an easy form to fill out.

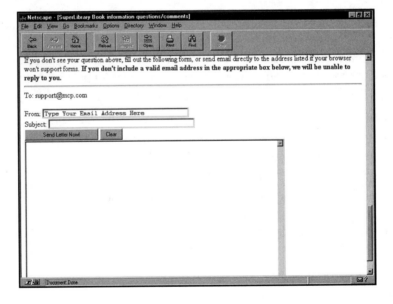

Of course, forms can also ask for significantly more detailed information about you. Take a look at figure 12.2. At the Boardwatch home page, you can order a subscription to *Boardwatch*, the magazine about the Internet, WWW, and BBSes. Here they want to know everything except for your Zodiac sign when filling out this form (**http://www.boardwatch.com/cgi-win/subs/subsnew.exe**).

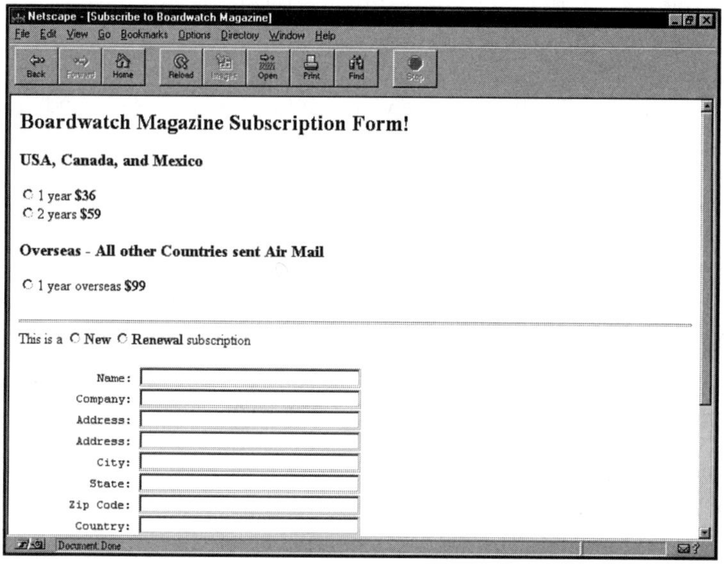

Fig. 12.2
Boardwatch is a good example of an advanced form, which you can subscribe to online.

In the following few sections, you'll learn how to create your own custom forms that suit your own needs.

Using Forms

From the user's point of view, all you have to do is type in the requested information and click a button that sends that form off to some WWW server somewhere. After a few moments, a message is generally sent back thanking you for filling out the form, and then you're ready to keep on surfing the Web.

All that's really happening is that you are running a special CGI script on the WWW server (see Chapter 11, "Understanding and Using CGI Scripts," for a more in-depth explanation of CGI scripts). That script can be customized to do any number of activities including processing the form and sending a thank-you message back to your Web page visitors.

Creating Forms

Creating forms, on the other hand, is much more involved. You've got to decide what kind of information you want to ask visitors, how your questions are formatted on-screen, and what you do with submitted forms. You can automatically send them via e-mail, store them in a file, or do both.

It's important to realize that when adding a form to your Web page, there are two separate and distinct steps—creating the HTML file and creating the CGI processing script. Without the CGI script, your form would be useless because Netscape wouldn't know what to do with the information on the form. And without the HTML file, the CGI file would get lonely because nobody would ever use it.

Making HTML and CGI files isn't difficult, but it can be time-consuming. You're already familiar with all types of HTML tags and codes, so learning a few new ones isn't too difficult—especially when you use a tool such as HotDog. As you learned in the last chapter, CGI scripts are really easy to use and add to Web pages as long as you understand what's going on.

Working with Form Tags

Form tags are an entirely new set of HTML tags that aren't used anywhere else. Each different type of input element has its own unique HTML tag.

On the CD

Keeping track of all these new tags can be difficult, because each input element has its own unique idiosyncrasies and differences. In this section, I'm going to use HotDog to quickly and easily add HTML form tags to your Web page. You'll learn all the pertinent form tags without having to worry about many of the HTML details.

> **Tip**
>
> See Chapter 2, "Getting Familiar with HotDog," for more information on installing and using HotDog's basic and advanced features.

You can add forms to any Web page. In fact you can even have multiple forms within the same Web page—as long as they aren't embedded within each other.

Using <FORM> and </FORM>

The first and most important HTML tag associated with forms is </FORM> and </FORM>, like in the following example:

```
<FORM METHOD=POST ACTION="cgi-bin/formfill.cgi>
</FORM>
```

The `<FORM>` tag has two important keywords that you should be familiar with— `ACTION` and `METHOD`. The `ACTION` keyword tells Netscape what CGI script to run when visitors have finished filling out the form and want to submit it to the WWW server. You'll learn more about this later, but to use forms on your Web page, you must be able to support CGI scripts. In this example, my form is pointing to the script named `formfill.cgi` which is stored within the `cgi-bin` subdirectory.

The other keyword associated with `<FORM>` is `METHOD`. This keyword has two choices, `GET` and `POST`. `METHOD` describes the manner in which Netscape and your WWW server communicate with one another when submitting the finished form. Both methods work fine, but `GET` has some limitations when using it for large forms. Because of this limitation, most people automatically use the `POST` method (as I have above).

Once you've added the `<FORM>` and `</FORM>` tags to your Web page, it's time to start building the different input types with HotDog. Click the Forms icon to bring up the Define Form Elements dialog box (see fig. 12.3).

Form

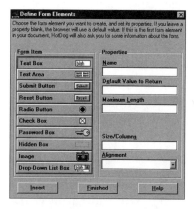

Fig. 12.3
You can add virtually any type of form element from this dialog box.

Caution

The limitation with the GET method is that you can only send 1,024 characters of information from a form to your WWW server. In most cases, 1,024 characters is more than enough. But since both the GET and POST methods work efficiently, Web developers don't want to have to worry about remembering this important detail. I use POST for all of my examples in this chapter.

> **Note**
>
> HotDog automatically asks for this information if you try to add a form element to your HTML file without building the <FORM> tag first.

You've got to name each element in the form differently so you can reference that information directly in the CGI script. That's how Netscape keeps track of the information you type in the form. It tells the server, "Hey, we have a name field on this form and the person typed in a specific value." The server then triggers a CGI script to read through each element on the form.

Text Box

The first form element you'll add is a standard one line text box. This type of form element is useful for getting a single piece of information—such as a name, message subject, or e-mail address.

From the Define Form Element dialog box, click the Text Box button. For this form element, you can specify several different attributes for how it works and displays on-screen. The most important property is Name. Every form element must have a unique name that lets Netscape and your WWW server tell one field of information from another.

It's a good idea to give your form element a relevant name. So, for example, if I'm asking for visitors to type in their first names in this text box, FirstName is a good name for it. Some examples of bad names would be box1, text1, form1, and related names.

You can also specify whether you want Netscape to display any information by default in that field by typing something in the Default Value to Return box.

In addition, you have control over how wide your text box appears across the screen. This property doesn't control how many characters of information people can enter, just how wide the field appears. By default, text boxes are 20 characters wide. You can increase or decrease that number to your liking by typing in a number in the Maximum Length box.

When you've finished typing in your text box properties, click the Insert button at the bottom of the dialog box. Figure 12.4 shows HotDog just before you click this button.

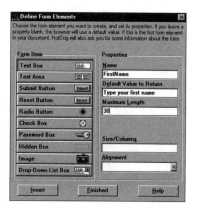

Fig. 12.4
My text box is
ready to ask
people for their
first names.

Here's the HTML string that HotDog adds to my Web page:

```
<INPUT NAME="FirstName" TYPE="TEXT" VALUE="Type your first name"
SIZE="30">
```

Notice how your choices translate into HTML keywords. The `<INPUT>` tag tells
Netscape that this is a form element. The `TYPE=` tag defines the type of form
element being added, and the other keywords match up directly with the values you entered into HotDog.

Tip

Make sure that `<INPUT>` and all the other form-related tags are located between
`<FORM>` and `</FORM>`—otherwise, they won't work properly.

Text Areas

Another common form element is a text area. This element uses the
`<TEXTAREA>` tag to display on-screen. It's similar to a text box because visitors
can type in information, but it allows them to type in their own comments
and questions, often with no limit on the messages they send. Many forms
use text areas as default comment fields. Click the Text Area button in
HotDog from the Define Form Elements dialog box. The keywords for a
text area are similar to a text box.

First, you've got to name the new form element, then you can decide
whether or not you want a default value to appear. In the Maximum Lengths
box, you can specify a limit on the number of characters people type into
your text area—usually this isn't done because the point of a text area is to let
visitors type in their own comments until they're finished.

Text area elements also let you define the height and width of the area on-screen by specifying the number of rows and columns it should take. The default text area coordinates are 1 row and 20 columns (or characters) wide—this is usually not large enough. Specify the height and width of your text area in the Rows and Size/Columns boxes. Figure 12.5 shows a text area being defined that is 50 columns wide and five rows tall.

Fig. 12.5
I'm adding a small text area to this form.

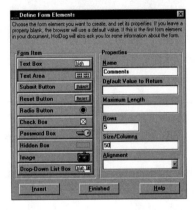

Here's the HTML string that HotDog adds to my Web page:

```
<TEXTAREA NAME="Comments" ROWS=5 COLS=50></TEXTAREA>
```

Check Box

Sometimes you want to provide visitors with several options they can select from. Using the Check Box element, you create a simple checkbox that visitors can check and uncheck easily with their mouse. This element is extremely useful for asking people yes and no questions. It's like an online true and false test. People only have two options to choose from.

To create a checkbox on your Web page, click Check Box from the Define Form Element dialog box. You only have to worry about two attributes—the Name and Default Value to Return (see fig. 12.6). Like before, the Name element is how Netscape and your WWW server identify that particular piece of info on the form.

The Default Value to Return element works differently. This box is the phrase of information sent to your CGI script if this checkbox is selected. Usually, the default value is something like Yes, or True. So when a visitor stops by your Web form and clicks a checkbox, you send a message to your script that basically says "this checkbox has been marked." Your CGI script already recognizes the checkbox from its unique name.

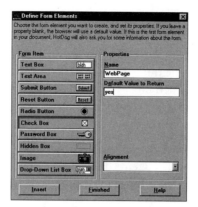

Fig. 12.6
Checkbox
elements are about
the easiest ones to
create.

Here's the HTML string that HotDog adds to my Web page:

```
<INPUT NAME="WebPage" TYPE="CHECKBOX" VALUE="yes">
```

Without any text describing them, a checkbox appears lonely, a simple small box on the page. Make sure you add identifying text that shows what you are asking in that checkbox. Here's my updated HTML, with a good line of identifying text:

```
<INPUT NAME="WebPage" TYPE="CHECKBOX" VALUE="yes"> Did you like my
web page?
```

Figure 12.7 shows this example (and another) in Netscape.

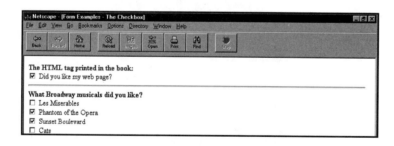

Fig. 12.7
Text boxes come
in many shapes
and forms.

> **Note**
>
> By default, the checkbox is unmarked when it appears in the form. If you want the checkbox to appear marked, add the keyword CHECKED to your tag:
>
> ```
> <INPUT NAME="WebPage" TYPE="CHECKBOX" VALUE="yes" CHECKED> Did you
> like my Web page?
> ```

Radio Button

Similar to Check Box, Radio Button also allows visitors to make choices with their mouse. Radio buttons are a set of options where only one of those options can be marked at one time. In figure 12.7, I created a set of checkboxes that lets visitors select which Broadway musicals they liked—they could choose all or none of them. If I did that same checkbox in radio button form, users could only choose one option from that list.

To create a set of radio buttons on your Web page, click the Radio Button button in the Define Form Elements dialog box. Just like Check Box, there are only two values for you to worry about—Name and Default Value to Return.

Each of these two attributes works slightly different in radio buttons. To group a bunch of selections together, you have to have several radio buttons that all have the same name. Netscape displays all radio buttons with the same name together, and only lets you select one option. Since you have several radio buttons all pointing to the same name, your CGI script needs to have some way to discern between all of the different options. That's where the Default Value to Return option comes into play. Instead of setting it as a "yes" or "true" value, type in a default value that is related to that entry in the radio button list. Figure 12.8 shows the creation of the first radio button.

Fig. 12.8
Although simple, radio buttons work differently than checkboxes.

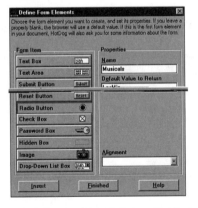

After creating four possible values for my musicals radio button and adding a small title, here's the HTML code for my radio button, which is shown in figure 12.9:

```
<B>What's your favorite musical?</B>
<BR>
<INPUT NAME="Musicals" TYPE="RADIO" VALUE="LesMiz"> Les Miserables
<BR>
<INPUT NAME="Musicals" TYPE="RADIO" VALUE="Phantom"> Phantom of the
```

```
Opera <BR>
<INPUT NAME="Musicals" TYPE="RADIO" VALUE="Sunset"> Sunset
Boulevard <BR>
<INPUT NAME="Musicals" TYPE="RADIO" VALUE="Cats"> Cats
```

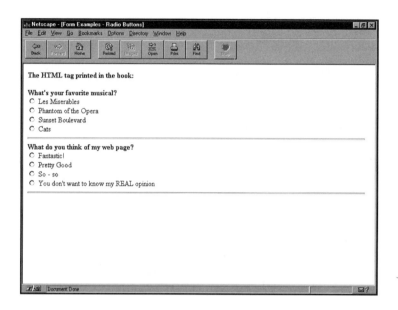

Fig. 12.9
Now you can
only choose one
musical instead
of them all.

IV

CGI Scripts, Forms, and Java

Notice how, in my HTML codes, I have four separate <INPUT> tags. Each one
of them identifies a RADIO button whose NAME is Musicals. But each separate
button has a different value attached. Also, don't forget to add the appropriate text after each button to identify that choice. Without it, you'd just see
four radio buttons (see fig. 12.10).

Fig. 12.10
These radio
buttons are
unusable!

Tip

You can also use the CHECKED keyword with radio buttons to indicate a default value.

Select from a List

The third and most flexible way to list options for visitors on your form is by
creating SELECT buttons. With the <SELECT> tag, you can create a drop-down

or scrollable list box that lets people choose from a set of options. Drop-down and scrollable list boxes are extremely useful for presenting a large set of options without taking up a lot of space on your Web page (see fig. 12.11).

Fig. 12.11

These two form elements let you hide a lot of options in a small area.

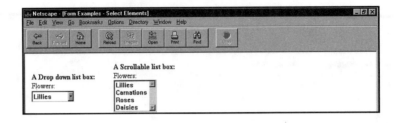

These tags are extremely flexible and can be modified in many ways. Unfortunately, they're also the only form tag that HotDog doesn't build for you entirely.

Click the Drop-Down List Box button from the Define Form Elements dialog box in HotDog to bring up the options shown in figure 12.12.

Fig. 12.12

Drop-down list boxes have many features you can use.

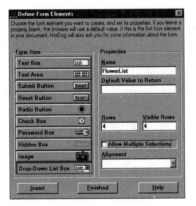

First, you've got to name this form element—you're probably used to this by now. Next you've got to decide how many different selections visitors are going to choose from. For the flower list shown in figure 12.11, I had four flowers to select from—that's enough for me. You can type any number you want in the Rows box.

Then you need to decide whether you want to create a drop-down or scrollable list box. To create a scrollable list box, type in the number of rows you want visitors to be able to see at one time in the Visible Rows box. If you want to create a drop-down box, leave that box blank (or type in 1, or 0).

Finally, you can check the Allow Multiple Selections checkbox if you've created a scrollable list box. This permits visits to choose multiple items, instead of only one.

When you're all finished, click the Insert button, and HotDog adds some HTML that looks like this to your Web page (this is a scrollable list box):

```
<SELECT NAME="FlowerList" SIZE= 4>
<OPTION>
<OPTION>
<OPTION>
<OPTION>
</SELECT>
```

You're almost finished. Regardless of the type of list box you create, all you have to do is add the actual value for each row in your list box. Each option in the list box has to have its own value—just like in creating radio buttons. Modify the <OPTION> tag to add the DEFAULT keyword, and then add a phrase after the tag that will appear in the actual list box, like the following:

```
<OPTION VALUE ="rose">Roses
```

In this tag, Netscape displays Roses in the list box. When Roses is selected, it sends the value rose to the CGI script that processes the form. So, once finished, here's the full HTML for the list boxes you saw earlier in this section. For the drop-down list box, it is the following:

```
Flowers:<BR>
<SELECT NAME="FlowerList">
<OPTION VALUE="lily">Lillies
<OPTION VALUE="carn">Carnations
<OPTION VALUE="rose">Roses
<OPTION VALUE="daisy">Daisies
</SELECT>
```

For the scrollable list box, it is the following:

```
Flowers: <BR>
<SELECT MULTIPLE NAME="FlowerList" SIZE= 4>
<OPTION VALUE="lily">Lillies
<OPTION VALUE="carn">Carnations
<OPTION VALUE="rose">Roses
<OPTION VALUE="daisy">Daisies
</SELECT>
```

Note

To mark an option in a list box as a default value, add the keyword SELECTED to the correct <OPTION> tag. So, to make daisies the default flower in my list box, I'd use the following tag:

```
<OPTION VALUE="daisy" SELECTED> Daisies
```

Submit and Reset Buttons

The last two basic form elements you should be aware of are the Submit and Reset buttons. These two buttons should appear on all of your forms. The Submit button adds a small icon to your form that, when clicked, tells Netscape to send in all the data from the form to the ACTION URL specified in the <FORM> tag. Without including a Submit button on your form, you won't be able to collect any information because visitors will never be able to tell Netscape to send in their data.

Similarly, the Reset button has an important function. An almost identical button, Reset clears all of the values that visitors have typed and sets them back to their original defaults. All text, checkmarks, and selections are lost and reset to the default settings.

To add a Submit button to your form, click Submit Button from the Define Form Elements dialog box (see fig. 12.13). Then click the Insert button. You don't have to define any special traits for this button to work properly. When viewed from Netscape, a button appears that has "Submit Query" written on it. If you'd like your Submit button to display something else, type the text in the Default Value to Return box from HotDog.

Fig. 12.13
Adding submit buttons is extremely simple.

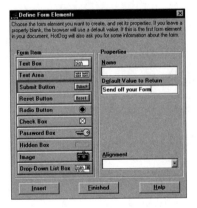

The HTML tags for a standard Submit button is the following:

```
<INPUT TYPE="SUBMIT" >
```

A Submit button with your own text displayed, however, looks like this:

```
<INPUT TYPE="SUBMIT" VALUE="Send off your Form">
```

Figure 12.14 shows both of your Submit buttons on a Web page.

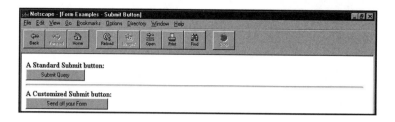

Fig. 12.14
Submit buttons are the most important element of the whole form.

Adding a reset button is virtually the identical process. Only this time, click the Reset Button form item in the Define Form Elements dialog box. You can also change the text of your reset button by typing some text in the Default Value to Return box.

Here's the HTML code of two different reset buttons:

```
<INPUT TYPE="RESET">
<HR>
<INPUT TYPE="RESET" VALUE="Reset the entire form">
```

Figure 12.15 shows how they look in Netscape.

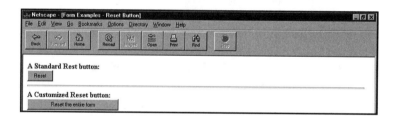

Fig. 12.15
Reset buttons are simple to use and should always be present.

The Other Piece of a Form— Defining the *ACTION*

Now that you know how to add all of the different form elements to your Web page, it's time to figure out what to do with all of the information that visitors submit.

When you originally added the <FORM> tag to your Web page, you also had to specify it with an ACTION. This ACTION consists of a URL that determines what your Web page does whenever someone fills out your form and clicks the Submit button. You have two main choices when filling out the ACTION URL:

- **Sending e-mail**—You can tell your form to package up the results in a single e-mail message and automatically mail it to your e-mail address of choice. So, for example, if my ACTION URL is **ACTION="mailto:johnny@shafran.com**, every time someone

On the CD

clicks the Submit button, Netscape drops off some e-mail with the information the visitor typed in. Unfortunately, the information that is sent to you is often jumbled up and can be difficult to decipher. Many programs exist that will decipher your e-mail message automatically and format and store them. My favorite is WebForms (you can find it on the CD-ROM with this book). E-mail is often a good option if you want to file and keep track of your form responses.

Tip

If your Web provider doesn't allow CGI scripts to run (like AOL or CompuServe), sending form responses via e-mail is your only option for using forms on your Web pages.

- **Running a CGI script**—The more common method of processing forms is to create a customized CGI script that looks at all the data sent back by Netscape, parses it for you, and stores it however you like (it can even e-mail a parsed version that's easy to read directly to your account). If you choose to run a CGI script—the way I do in the following example—you need to have a special Perl file that interprets form responses and makes it easy for you to work with CGI scripts. Visit **ftp://ftp.ncsa.uiuc.edu/Web/http/Unix/ncsa_httpd/cgi/cgi-lib.pl.Z**. The file you download is in UNIX compressed format. Most likely, you will need to uncompress it (type `uncompress cgi-lib.pl.Z` at your UNIX prompt). Contact your system administrator for more details. The `cgi-lib.pl` file must be in the same subdirectory as the CGI script that your form points to.

Build an Example

In this section, I'm going to guide you through building a complete form and corresponding script from scratch. I'm going to create my CGI script in Perl and show you each line individually so you can easily create your own form and script.

Create the Form

To demonstrate how to create a CGI script, let's first make a simple form. All this form does is request a visitor's name, his or her e-mail address, and then asks him or her to fill out a comment. The HTML code for this form is as follows:

```
<FORM METHOD=GET ACTION="cgi-bin/simple.cgi">
<B>Please enter your Name: </B>
<INPUT NAME="VisitorName" TYPE="TEXT" SIZE="50"> <P>
<B>Please Enter your e-mail address:</B>
<INPUT NAME="E-mail" TYPE="TEXT" SIZE="50"> <P>
<B>Type any comments you might have: </B><BR>
<TEXTAREA NAME="Comments" ROWS=6 COLS=50></TEXTAREA>
<INPUT TYPE="SUBMIT"></FORM>
```

Figure 12.16 shows how this simple form appears in Netscape.

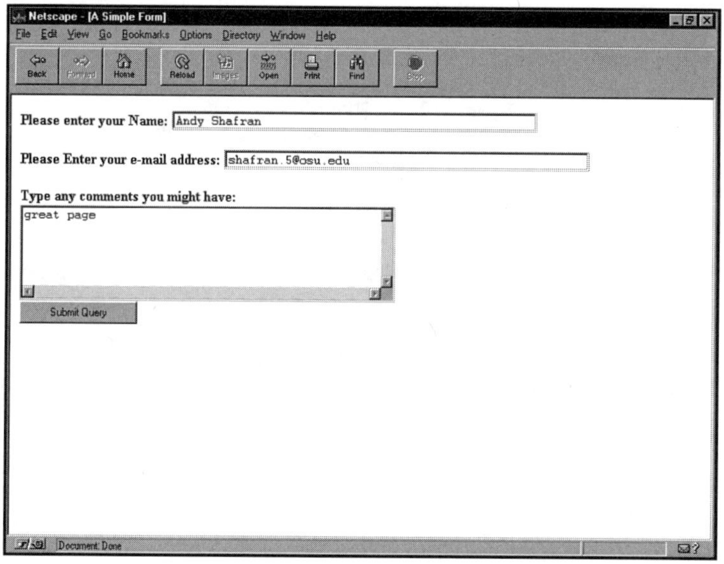

Fig. 12.16
It may not be pretty, but this simple form can be useful.

As you can tell, there are three form elements—two text boxes and one text area. I've defined the ACTION on my form to run the CGI script named simple.cgi which is located in my cgi-bin subdirectory.

Making the CGI Script

Once you've put together that simple form, you can build the corresponding script. The following script has four parts.

First, it points to the Perl files and then initializes cgi-lib.pl—which is required for all CGI scripts that work with forms. Then it reads in the actual data sent by the Submit button:

```
#!/usr/bin/perl
require 'cgi-lib.pl';
&ReadParse(*input);
```

Next, I translate each named form element into a variable name. Variable names must begin with the dollar sign ($). Notice how I have a different field name for each of my form elements:

```
$NameField = $input{'VisitorName'};
$EmailField = $input{'Email'};
$CommentsField = $input{'Comments'};
```

Now, I create a simple piece of output that is sent back to Netscape that basically repeats what the user just submitted. This is important because it gives feedback to the user and tells him or her that the form has been processed:

```
print "Content-type: text/html\n\n";
print "<H1>Thanks For Submitting a Form</H1>";
print "<B>Visitor Name:</B> ",$NameField,"<br>";
print "<B>E-mail Address:</B> ",$EmailField,"<br>";
print "<B>Comments:</B> ",$CommentsField,"<p>";
```

Figure 12.17 shows the output as shown in Netscape.

Fig. 12.17

Here's the output from my script.

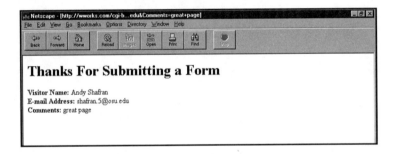

Finally, I write the fields of information submitted into a file named comment.txt. First, I've got to open the file, write the data I want to it, and then close the file:

```
$comnt = "comment.txt";
open(NOTE,">>$comnt");
print NOTE "Name: $NameField\n";
print NOTE "E-mail: $EmailField\n";
print NOTE "Comments: $CommentsField\n\n";
close NOTE;
```

The output of the file looks like the following:

```
Name: Andy Shafran
E-mail: shafran.5@osu.edu
Comments: great page
```

Every time someone clicks the Submit button, his or her name and comments are recorded to this file. Anytime in the future, I can look at this file and see what comments have been sent to me—it's a great way to interact with people who visit your site.

In case you were wondering, here's the whole CGI script in its entirety:

```perl
#!/usr/bin/perl
require 'cgi-lib.pl';
&ReadParse(*input);
$NameField = $input{'VisitorName'};
$EmailField = $input{'Email'};
$CommentsField = $input{'Comments'};

print "Content-type: text/html\n\n";
print "<H1>Thanks For Submitting a Form</H1>";
print "<B>Visitor Name:</B> ",$NameField,"<br>";
print "<B>E-mail Address:</B> ",$EmailField,"<br>";
print "<B>Comments:</B> ",$CommentsField,"<p>";

$comnt = "comment.txt";
open(NOTE,">>$comnt");
print NOTE "Name: $NameField\n";
print NOTE "E-mail: $EmailField\n";
print NOTE "Comments: $CommentsField\n\n";
close NOTE;
```

Now that you've seen a simple script and form in action, you're ready to create your own forms for your Web pages. Feel free to modify this simple script to fit with your own form's field names and specifications.

For more advanced form processing, check out Chapter 11, "Understanding and Using CGI Scripts." In that chapter, I describe several form processing CGI scripts that are included with the CD-ROM in the back of this book, and show you where you can get more information about building and using forms in your Web pages. ❖

Chapter 13
Making Some of Your Own Java

Easily, the most acclaimed recent WWW innovation is the addition of Java and JavaScript to Web pages. These two new innovations allow an unprecedented amount of customization and interaction for WWW users and Web page developers.

Java is a brand-new programming language enabling you to create applications, called applets, that run directly from Netscape. Geared towards advanced developers and experienced programmers, Java breaks new boundaries when it comes to adding animation, interaction, usefulness, and fun to Web pages. On the other hand, JavaScript is a new and easy-to-use scripting language that lets Web developers bring new dimensions to their Web pages without worrying about advanced programming concepts. Related to Java, JavaScript is an easier-to-use and less complex variation of Java.

In this chapter, I'll introduce you to both Java and JavaScript. You'll learn the history behind each of these new technologies, and how they can be used to enhance your Web pages. Additionally, I'll step you through numerous JavaScript examples that can enhance your Web pages in minutes—without you having to be a professional programmer. You'll learn how to spice up your Web page with several fun JavaScript examples that don't take very much time to learn and understand.

JavaScript is probably the most important new WWW enhancement for the very reasons listed above. CGI is often too complicated to work with and build, while Java is mainly for programmers. JavaScript is easy enough for anyone to understand, yet powerful enough to add complete and dynamic information to your Web pages.

Specifically, in this chapter, you'll learn how to do the following:

- Tell the difference between Java and JavaScript
- Create simple JavaScript applets without prior programming knowledge
- Include the example JavaScript applets directly into your Web page
- Control text attributes, forms, and user interaction with JavaScript applets
- Find all the tools necessary to create your own Java applets
- Add existing Java applets to your Web page

Using JavaScript

In the past few chapters, you've learned all about writing your own programs and scripts to interact with your Web pages. These methods required you to create a new program, customize your WWW server, and then link your Web page to your CGI script. While CGI scripting is powerful, it can be complicated and awkward to use.

New to Netscape 2.0 is JavaScript, a dynamic new scripting language that works directly from a page of HTML. JavaScript is an entirely new scripting language that is relatively easy to use and doesn't require any programming knowledge to use many of its features. Netscape released JavaScript to make it easier for Web developers to add true interaction and fun to Web pages—without worrying about the CGI drawbacks and limitations. To get a CGI script working, you had to fiddle with your WWW server, make sure that CGI scripts worked properly, write the script in a programming language, and then link it into your Web page. With JavaScript, you can add the necessary commands directly to your Web page with little to no hassle.

You'll use JavaScript to add a new level of interaction between visitors and your Web page. For example, using only a few lines of JavaScript, you could display a different message to visitors depending on the time of day they visited your Web page, or you could pop up messages whenever a visitor's mouse wanders over a hypertext link.

Besides making Web pages more entertaining and fun, JavaScript can also be used to verify that users have filled out a form properly, or to scroll important text across the bottom of the user's screen (similar to Microsoft's <MARQUEE> HTML extension).

As you'll see in a moment, JavaScript commands are embedded alongside standard HTML tags.

> **Caution**
>
> Although similar in name to Sun Microsystems Java (described later in this chapter), JavaScript is completely different. Java is an actual programming language which must be compiled by Netscape before it can run, while JavaScript works alongside other HTML tags to add dynamic interaction between visitors and your Web page. Java and JavaScript commands actually look similar—to a point—but Java has significantly more features and aspects that are required in a robust programming language.
>
> JavaScript was originally named LiveScript by Netscape. Its name change was a direct result of the popularity of Java (and has caused significant confusion along the way) and collaboration with Java's author—Sun Microsystems.

JavaScript Structure

The first place to start when creating JavaScript applets, or programs, is Netscape's JavaScript Authoring Guide reference. Point Netscape to **http://home.netscape.com/eng/mozilla/Gold/handbook/javascript/index.html** as shown in figure 13.1.

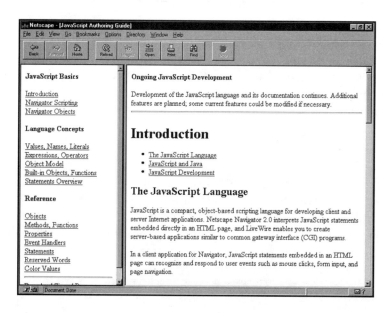

Fig. 13.1
Complete JavaScript technical documentation can be found here.

By browsing through this site, you'll see the complete technical specifications of how JavaScript works. You'll learn that JavaScript is a complete scripting language that has many standard functions and built-in capabilities.

One of the most important technical specifications you'll learn is that JavaScript is case-sensitive. All functions, commands, keywords, and other programming concepts must be referred to in the proper case—otherwise, they won't work properly.

Another quirk about JavaScript comes when you need to use a set of quotation marks within another set of quotation marks. In JavaScript, you've got to switch back and forth between single and double quotation marks when embedding them within one another. For example:

- This "is a 'wrong "example of using 'quote marks.
- This "is a 'better example' because they match up" correctly.

> **Note**
>
> In this chapter, I don't spend much time explaining many of the basic JavaScript programming concepts such as using variables, functions, arrays, structures, keywords, operators, and other typical things associated with scripting and programming languages. Instead, I simply show you how to use JavaScript in several practical examples.

The <*SCRIPT*> tag

You can add JavaScript commands to your Web page in two ways. The easiest is to include JavaScript commands inside of other HTML tags. For example, the following piece of HTML is a hypertext link that points to my Web page, with an additional JavaScript command:

```
<A HREF="http://www.shafran.com/~andy"
onMouseOver="window.status='Wanna visit my home page?'; return
true">Andy Shafran's Home Page</A>
```

Without the JavaScript commands, this tag would simply print Andy Shafran's Home Page and when clicked upon, bring you to the specified location. With the JavaScript commands added, Netscape displays Wanna visit my home page? in the Netscape status bar at the bottom of the screen when the mouse hovers over the text on the Web page (see fig. 13.2).

Fig. 13.2
I've just changed what Netscape displays in the status bar at the bottom of the screen.

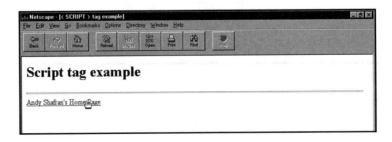

The other way to add JavaScript to your Web page is by using the <SCRIPT> tag. A new set of tags, <SCRIPT> and </SCRIPT>, tells Netscape that you have a set of JavaScript commands to add to your Web page. Inside of the <SCRIPT> tag, you need to tell Netscape which scripting language you're using— JavaScript. Here's an example:

```
<SCRIPT LANGUAGE="JavaScript">
<!--
document.write("<HR>")
    document.write("<B>This document was last changed:</B>")
    document.write(document.lastModified)
    document.write("<HR>")
//-->
</SCRIPT>
```

This snippet of code tells Netscape to display two horizontal lines across the page and, in the middle of them, state the date in which this file was last modified. Figure 13.3 shows how Netscape interprets this set of JavaScript commands.

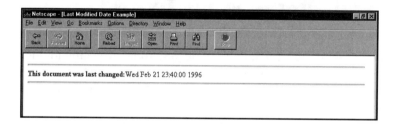

Fig. 13.3
JavaScript calculates the last modified date for you automatically.

Notice how all of my JavaScript code is enclosed within HTML comment tags—<!-- and //-->. This hides your JavaScript commands from other browsers that don't recognize them (such as Netscape 1.2, Mosaic, or Internet Explorer). You'll put all of your JavaScript commands within HTML comment tags when you use the <SCRIPT> tag.

You can also refer to JavaScript applets saved in different files by using the SRC= keyword in the <SCRIPT> tag. This tells Netscape to retrieve the specified file and treat it as if it were embedded within that particular HTML file. This is useful if your JavaScript applet is long, or you want to keep it separate from your HTML files:

```
<SCRIPT LANGUAGE="JAVASCRIPT" SRC="myjavasc.js">
```

This tag tells Netscape to retrieve the file named myjavasc.js because I have my JavaScript commands stored there.

> **Note**
>
> Often, it's a good idea to put the `<SCRIPT>` and `</SCRIPT>` tags at the top of your Web page within your document's heading (`<HEAD>` and `</HEAD>`). This is because Netscape processes JavaScript commands in the order they appear within your HTML file. Called programming functions (snippets of JavaScript code that you refer to later in your Web page but define in the heading) must appear before you can use them. You'll learn more about functions later on.

> **Caution**
>
> Unfortunately, text written via JavaScript is not displayed when you print a page. If you printed the previous page, you would get a blank screen.

Several Simple Ways To Add JavaScript to Your Web Page

Now that I've introduced you to JavaScript and shown you around this new scripting language, I'm going to demonstrate many practical, fun, and useful ways you can use JavaScript in your Web pages. Soon, you'll find yourself interspersing virtually all of your Web pages with various JavaScript commands because they're easy to use, allow uncomparable flexibility and interactivity, and tend to make Web pages more exciting and alive.

As with most new technologies on the WWW, sometimes it's difficult to find practical uses for JavaScript—other than adding special effects to your Web page. Remember that the WWW is all about presentation and interaction, and that JavaScript is another vehicle that lets you interact with visitors and impress them when they stop by your Web site.

Change the Text in Netscape's Status Bar

As I showed you previously, one of the easiest enhancements you can make is by changing the text that appears in the Netscape status bar at the bottom of the screen. When you add hypertext links to your Web page, Netscape normally displays the corresponding URL in the status bar. However, you can change the text that appears there and customize it to whatever you'd like. When a visitor's mouse hovers over the link, instead of displaying the URL, you can display a different textual message.

All you have to do is add the `onMouseOver` JavaScript command to your `<A HREF>` tag:

```
<A HREF="http://www.mcp.com/que" onMouseOver="window.status='Visit
the Que Web page immediately, do not pass GO'; return true">Que
Publishing Web Page</A>
```

This line of HTML adds a single phrase to your Web page—Que Publishing Web Page—but changes the status bar's text. Figure 13.4 shows you this tag from Netscape's point of view.

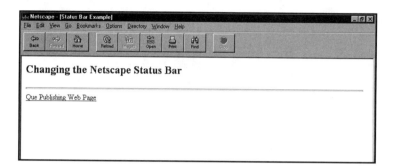

Fig. 13.4

You can add descriptive and humorous words and phrases to the status bar.

Notice how I've actually embedded two separate JavaScript commands. The first one tells Netscape to change the status bar (window.status=). The second (return true) signifies that we're at the end of this snippet of JavaScript—without it, Netscape would display an error.

Caution

Remember that JavaScript is case-sensitive. OnMouseOver is not correct, it must be onMouseOver. Also, don't forget that when embedding quotation marks inside of other quotation marks, you must alternate between double (") and single ('), respectively.

Tip

If you want to include single or double quotation marks in your status bar text, you've got to precede that character with a slash (\)—as in \" or \'. For example, to print out the word *don't* in the status bar, you'd use this tag:

```
onMouseOver="window.status='don\'t'; return true"
```

Show a Message When a Link is Clicked

Another way you can enhance and change the behavior of links on your Web page is by making a window, or small dialog box, appear whenever a visitor clicks on a particular link.

The following is an example of how you can tell Netscape to display a new dialog box when a link is clicked upon:

```
<A HREF="http://www.mcp.com/que" onClick="alert('You\'re leaving my
Web page. Goodbye')">Que Publishing Web Page</A>
```

In this JavaScript example, we are using the onClick event. This tells Netscape that when this link is clicked, it needs to create an Alert dialog box that looks like figure 13.5.

Fig. 13.5

You can add alerts to all of your hypertext links.

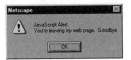

In JavaScript, alert is used to display an important message when an event (such as clicking a link) triggers it.

Tip

Use the Alert box sparingly because it can be extremely bothersome if overused. Visitors don't want to constantly have to dispel an Alert box each and every time they select a hypertext link.

Of course, you can add both the onClick and onMouseOver events to your link if you'd like. This changes the text in the Netscape status bar when the mouse is over the link, and displays the Alert dialog box when the link is actually clicked:

```
<A HREF="http://www.mcp.com/que" onClick="alert('You\'re leaving my
Web page. Goodbye')" onMouseOver="window.status='Visit the Que Web
page immediately, do not pass GO'; return true">Que Publishing Web
Page</A>
```

Note

As you may have deduced, you can also execute an alert, or other JavaScript command, when the mouse simply moves over a link, as in this case:

```
<A HREF="http://www.mcp.com/que" onMouseOver="alert('You\'re
leaving my Web page.  Goodbye')">Que Publishing Web Page</A>
```

Adding Buttons to Your Web Page

Although you can give actions to hypertext links, this method can sometimes be inconvenient. You may want to simply display information without linking to another page. Netscape allows you to add actual buttons to your Web pages, and you can define actions for them in JavaScript.

Buttons are actually defined as a standard form element. You probably remember the Submit and Reset buttons I talked about in Chapter 12, "Figuring Out Where Forms Fit In." You can also add your own customized buttons, and attach JavaScript commands to them. Although I didn't talk about adding customized buttons in Chapter 12, they're easy to use. Just add the <INPUT> tag and set the TYPE= keyword as a BUTTON and you're all set. You'll find yourself using buttons a lot as you start integrating JavaScript commands into your Web page.

The following is an example of a button that tells me when this HTML document's last change occurred:

```
<FORM>
<INPUT TYPE="BUTTON" NAME="ModifiedButton" VALUE="When
was this document last modified?" onClick="alert('This HTML page
was last modified on: ' + document.lastModified)">
</FORM>
```

Notice how I used the <FORM> and </FORM> tags. Without them, I couldn't have added a button to my Web page. This tag simply adds a button on my Web page that is labeled When was this document last modified? (see fig. 13.6). Once clicked, a small Alert box appears and gives the answer (see fig. 13.7).

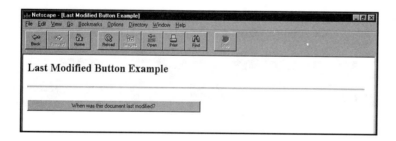

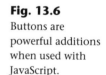

Fig. 13.6
Buttons are powerful additions when used with JavaScript.

Fig. 13.7
Here's the answer to my question.

Each HTML page has several variables set automatically, including the date it was last modified; the various colors for your text, backgrounds, and links; and more. You can then directly access this information in an Alert box like I did or on your actual page. See the JavaScript documentation at Netscape's home for a complete list of all the attributes of an HTML page that you can manipulate. Also, take a look at my background colors example in a few pages to see another way to manipulate these document attributes.

As you probably noticed, buttons are extremely useful elements. You can add all sorts of buttons to your Web pages that display information when clicked upon, or perform other, more advanced JavaScript commands.

Add Your Own Back Button to Your Web Page

Here's another way you can use a button on your Web page. One common JavaScript command is `history.back()`. This command sends visitors back to the last page they just visited—just like the Back button in the Netscape navigation bar:

```
<FORM>
<INPUT TYPE="BUTTON" NAME="GoBack" VALUE="Go Back"
onClick="history.back()">
</FORM>
```

Figure 13.8 shows this simple button on a Web page. When visitors click it, they are automatically brought back to the previous document loaded (I added a small heading to the top of the screen). There's also a `history.forward()` JavaScript command as well. These types of navigation buttons allow you to let users wander through your Web pages by adding buttons wherever you'd like. So, instead of making them rely on clicking the Back button for themselves, you can make your own navigation buttons. Larger Web sites with lots of pages to navigate will find this and related JavaScript commands extremely useful.

Fig. 13.8
Emulating the Back button is pretty easy with JavaScript.

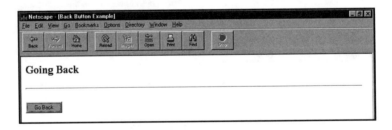

Confirm That Visitors Really Want To Leave

Instead of using the `alert` command to display information on the screen, you might want to consider using `confirm` instead. This JavaScript command displays a simple dialog box that let's you confirm your actions. For example, let's say you wanted to enhance the Back button you just created. Whenever a visitor clicks the Back button, you want to double-check that he or she really wanted to go backwards.

Instead of just arbitrarily issuing the `history.back()` command, you can add `confirm`:

```
<FORM>
<INPUT TYPE="BUTTON" NAME="GoBack" VALUE="Go Back"
onClick="if(confirm('Do you really want to go
back?'))history.back(); else alert('Good thing I double-checked')">
</FORM>
```

This snippet of JavaScript adds a button labeled Go Back on-screen (just like figure 13.8). When the button is clicked, Netscape brings up a box that asks whether the user really wants to go back (see fig. 13.9). If the users click OK, then Netscape brings them to their previous page. If the users click Cancel, then another dialog box appears and nothing else happens—the command is canceled (see fig. 13.10).

Fig. 13.9
I'm double-checking the Back button.

Fig. 13.10
Here's the alert box that appears when I hit Cancel.

The `confirm` command sends a simple dialog box to the screen. If the user clicks OK, then a TRUE value is saved, and the first part of the IF statement executes. The Cancel button sends back a FALSE to the IF statement.

Note

As you may have noticed, scrunching up all of these JavaScript commands into an HTML tag can sometimes be difficult and make your sequence of events unreadable. In these situations, you can create separate functions that store your sequence of JavaScript commands and can be called with a single phrase. That's where the <SCRIPT> tag mentioned earlier in the chapter comes into play. To simplify this example, here's how I'd create a function in JavaScript:

```
<SCRIPT LANGUAGE="JavaScript">
<!--
function checkback() {
if(confirm('Do you really want to go back?'))
history.back();
else
alert('Good thing I double-checked')
```

(continues)

```
(continued)

        }
//-->
</SCRIPT>
Then I'd change the definition of the Go Back button:
<FORM>
        <INPUT TYPE="BUTTON" NAME="GoBack" VALUE="Go Back"
onClick="checkback()">
</FORM>
```

Now when clicked, the Go Back button runs the JavaScript function named checkback. As you can see, checkback does the same thing as the old Go Back button did, only it's much more readable and understandable. Remember, when you create functions, they must be defined before they are called in a page of HTML, preferably in the document's <HEAD> and </HEAD> tags.

Change the Background Color On-The-Fly

With JavaScript, you can also dynamically change the background color of your pages. By clicking the appropriate button, visitors can customize the color scheme of a particular Web page according to the colors you provide.

The following JavaScript example is very simple, but it shows how you can interactively change information and the appearance of your Web page for visitors depending on which buttons they click or which links they select.

All I'm going to do is change the document.bgColor attribute with a button. This is another document attribute which you can control directly in JavaScript:

```
<FORM>
        <INPUT TYPE="BUTTON" NAME="Blue" VALUE="BackGround is
Blue" onClick="document.bgColor='blue'">
        </FORM>
```

This simple button looks like the other buttons you've created, but when it is clicked, the background color of your Web page changes to blue.

Use the following code to add several of these buttons to your Web page:

```
<FORM>
        <INPUT TYPE="BUTTON" NAME="Blue" VALUE="BackGround is
Blue" onClick="document.bgColor='blue'"> <BR>
        <INPUT TYPE="BUTTON" NAME="Red" VALUE="BackGround is Red"
onClick="document.bgColor='red'"> <BR>
        <INPUT TYPE="BUTTON" NAME="White" VALUE="BackGround is
White" onClick="document.bgColor='White'"> <BR>
        <INPUT TYPE="BUTTON" NAME="Maroon" VALUE="BackGround is
Maroon" onClick="document.bgColor='maroon'"> <BR>
        </FORM>
```

Figure 13.11 shows the results of this sample bit of HTML and JavaScript. Clicking each button changes the corresponding background color.

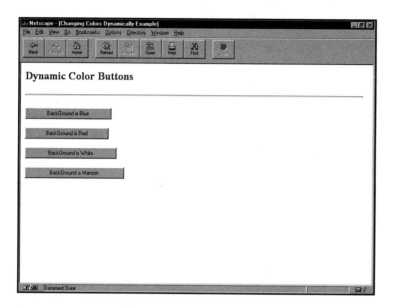

Fig. 13.11
Too bad this book's not in color—see the CD-ROM to use the buttons.

Note

Nearly half of all problems with JavaScript can be attributed to the weird case sensitivity. Figuring out the correct capitalization for `document.bgColor` took several tries—particularly since the debugging capabilities for JavaScript are practically nonexistent.

Display a Message When Your Web Page is Loaded

Now that you're familiar with using JavaScript functions, I'm going to show you another similar example. The main difference in this example is that Netscape runs your JavaScript commands immediately when your HTML file is loaded instead of waiting for a link or button to trigger the function. This is accomplished by adding a new tag to <BODY>, like the following:

```
<BODY onLoad="check()">
```

This example tells Netscape that after loading (the `onLoad` event) this HTML page, it should perform the function named `check`. You can only use `onLoad` in the <BODY> and <FRAMESET> tags to run a default JavaScript applet when a new page or frame is loaded.

The following is my `check` function:

```
<SCRIPT LANGUAGE="JavaScript">
<!--
function check() {
    if(confirm('Did anyone follow you here?'))
        {
        if(confirm('Are you absolutely sure?'))
            {
            alert('You\'re clean, continue.');
            }
        else
            {
            alert('Sorry, can\'t let you in my Web page');
            history.back();
            }
        }
    else
        {
        alert('Sorry, can\'t let you in my Web page');
        history.back();
        }
    }
//-->
</SCRIPT>
<BODY onLoad="check()">
```

This function has several `confirm` commands embedded within it. The first thing that happens is an initial dialog box appears (see fig. 13.12).

Fig. 13.12
This page is paranoid. I wonder why?

Depending on how you answer that question, a different message appears. By clicking OK, you see figure 13.13, which repeats the process.

Fig. 13.13
Look behind your shoulder before you answer this one.

Click OK again, and you made it through this rigorous checkpoint. If you clicked Cancel from either window, figure 13.14 appears and you are immediately taken back to your previous page.

Fig. 13.14
Too bad, you can't
visit this page!

IV

CGI Scripts, Forms, and Java

> **Note**
>
> Although this example is meant to be humorous, many sites that contain material
> inappropriate for children are beginning to use this and other similar methods on
> their Web pages. This ensures that visitors who stop by acknowledge that they are of
> appropriate age to legally visit this particular Web site. For more information on this
> and other related legal issues, see Chapter 4, "Important Details for Enhanced Sites."

In-Depth JavaScript Examples

Now that I've whetted your appetite with several simple JavaScript applets,
this section profiles three more advanced ways JavaScript can be used on your
Web pages.

Build a Simple Calculator

One of the powerful ways you can use JavaScript is to perform operations on
the various elements on a form. In fact, it seems like many of JavaScript's features are centered around verifying and manipulating information in text
fields, radio buttons, checkboxes, and more.

In this example, I've built a very simple calculator using form elements. It
takes two numbers that you type in and either adds, subtracts, multiples,
or divides them. It's not fancy and won't win any design prizes for best
JavaScript applet, but it is an excellent example of how you can manipulate
fields of information on a form.

My first step is creating a table on-screen. It's a simple table with four
columns of information—one for the first number, one for the numeric
operation, one for the second number, and one for the total. You create
this table by using the following code:

```
<FORM>
<TABLE BORDER=1>
<TR>
    <TD VALIGN=MIDDLE>
        <B>First Number</B><BR>
        <INPUT NAME="First" TYPE="TEXT" SIZE="10">
    </TD>
```

```
<TD VALIGN=MIDDLE>
    <B>Arithmetic Operations will go here.</B>
</TD>
<TD VALIGN=MIDDLE>
    <B> Second Number </B><BR>
    <INPUT NAME="Second" TYPE="TEXT" SIZE="10">
</TD>
<TD VALIGN=MIDDLE>
    <B>Total</B><BR>
    <INPUT NAME="Total" TYPE="TEXT" SIZE="10">
</TD>
</TABLE>
</FORM>
```

Figure 13.15 shows how this table appears in Netscape.

Fig. 13.15
My simple
calculator isn't
pretty, but it
works.

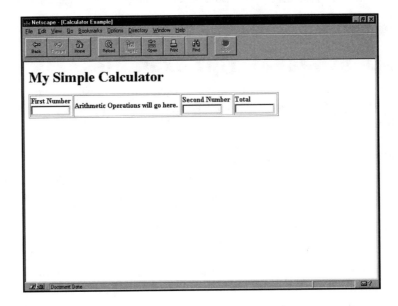

Notice how I named each text box in the table—either First, Second, or Total. Now, let's go back and add the appropriate arithmetic operations. I'm going to add four buttons to the second column of my table with the following code:

```
<INPUT TYPE="button" NAME="Add" Value="Add"
onClick="add(form)" ><BR>
        <INPUT TYPE="button" NAME="Subtract" Value="Subtract"
onClick="subtract(form)"><BR>
        <INPUT TYPE="button" NAME="Multiply" Value="Multiply"
```

```
onClick="multiply(form)"> <BR>
          <INPUT TYPE="button" NAME="Divide" Value="Divide"
onClick="divide(form)">
```

Each button calls a different function when clicked upon. I am passing the current form as a parameter to each of my functions. This allows my mathematical operations to know which fields I want to add, subtract, and so on.

Once the table is built, the next step is to build the JavaScript for the four mathematical functions. Each of them is extremely simple, but they show how JavaScript works with forms. Here's my add function:

```
function add(form)
{    form.Total.value = eval(form.First.value) +
eval(form.Second.value)}
```

This function tells Netscape to display the value of the boxes First and Second in the text box named Total. I used the built-in `eval` function to tell Netscape that it should evaluate the values it is working with as numbers instead of strings of text.

Caution

As I said before, this calculator is exceedingly simple—it can't handle letters and gives an error if both First and Second don't have numbers in them before clicking a mathematical operation.

As you can guess, the other three operations are similar:

```
function multiply(form)
{    form.Total.value = eval(form.First.value) *
eval(form.Second.value)}
```

```
function subtract(form)
{    form.Total.value = eval(form.First.value) -
eval(form.Second.value)}
```

```
function divide(form)
{    form.Total.value = eval(form.First.value) /
eval(form.Second.value)}
```

That's it, the whole calculator from start to finish. Figure 13.16 shows my calculator in action after all four operation buttons have been pushed.

Fig. 13.16
My calculator's working up a storm.

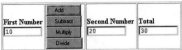

Here's the HTML for my entire calculator page so you can see how all the pieces fit together:

```
<HTML>
<HEAD>
<TITLE>Calculator Example</TITLE>
<SCRIPT LANGUAGE="JavaScript">
<!--
function multiply(form)
{   form.Total.value = eval(form.First.value) *
eval(form.Second.value)}
function subtract(form)
{   form.Total.value = eval(form.First.value) -
eval(form.Second.value)}
function divide(form)
{   form.Total.value = eval(form.First.value) /
eval(form.Second.value)}
function add(form)
{    form.Total.value = eval(form.First.value) +
eval(form.Second.value)}
//-->
</SCRIPT>
<BODY>
<H1>My Simple Calculator</H1>
<FORM>
<TABLE BORDER=1>
<TR>
    <TD VALIGN=MIDDLE>
        <B>First Number</B><BR>
        <INPUT NAME="First" TYPE="TEXT" SIZE="10">
    </TD>
    <TD VALIGN=MIDDLE>
        <INPUT TYPE="button" NAME="Add" Value="Add"
onClick="add(form)" SIZE="25"><BR>
        <INPUT TYPE="button" NAME="Subtract" Value="Subtract"
onClick="subtract(form)"><BR>
        <INPUT TYPE="button" NAME="Multiply" Value="Multiply"
onClick="multiply(form)"> <BR>
        <INPUT TYPE="button" NAME="Divide" Value="Divide"
onClick="divide(form)">
```

```
        </TD>
        <TD VALIGN=MIDDLE>
            <B> Second Number </B><BR>
            <INPUT NAME="Second" TYPE="TEXT" SIZE="10">
        </TD>
        <TD VALIGN=MIDDLE>
            <B>Total</B><BR>
            <INPUT NAME="Total" TYPE="TEXT" SIZE="10">
        </TD>
    </TABLE>
    </FORM>
    </BODY>
    </HTML>
```

Add a Scrolling Marquee to Netscape's Status Bar

This is my favorite JavaScript applet. This applet transforms your Netscape status bar into a simple marquee. You can specify several pieces of information that constantly scroll across the bottom of the Web page.

This JavaScript applet was developed by Chris Skinner (**http://www.websys.com**) and free for everyone. Many large sites use it constantly. To add it to your Web page, all you have to do is type in the text you want to marquee across the bottom of the screen—all of the other work is already done for you.

The following is the complete code for this JavaScript applet. You can find a copy on the CD-ROM in the back of this book ready to use, or study how it works by glancing at it here. Just change the values in the four variables at the top of the script to tell Netscape what text should appear in marquee fashion:

On the CD

```
<!-- Beginning of JavaScript Applet ------------------

function scrollit_r2l(seed)
{
        var m1  = "Type in your Marquee text here";
        var m2  = "and here";
        var m3  = "and here";
        var m4  = "and finally here";

        var msg=m1+m2+m3+m4;
        var out = " ";
        var c   = 1;

        if (seed > 100) {
                seed--;
                var cmd="scrollit_r2l(" + seed + ")";
                timerTwo=window.setTimeout(cmd,100);
```

```
                    }
                    else if (seed <= 100 && seed > 0) {
                            for (c=0 ; c < seed ; c++) {
                                    out+=" ";
                            }
                            out+=msg;
                            seed--;
                            var cmd="scrollit_r2l(" + seed + ")";
                                window.status=out;
                            timerTwo=window.setTimeout(cmd,100);
                    }
                    else if (seed <= 0) {
                            if (-seed < msg.length) {
                                    out+=msg.substring(-seed,msg.length);
                                    seed--;
                                    var cmd="scrollit_r2l(" + seed + ")";
                                    window.status=out;
                                    timerTwo=window.setTimeout(cmd,100);
                            }
                            else {
                                    window.status=" ";
                                    timerTwo=window.setTimeout("scrollit_r2l(100)",75);
                            }
                    }
            }
    }
    // -- End of JavaScript code ------------- -->
    </SCRIPT>
```

Once your JavaScript code is added, you need to modify your <BODY> tag to tell it to start the marquee script once the page is loaded:

```
<BODY
onLoad="timerONE=window.setTimeout('scrollit_r2l(100)',500);">
```

Tic-Tac-Toe JavaScript Style

On the CD

Remember the simple Tic-Tac-Toe game back in Chapter 6, "Framing Your Work"? Well now it's back, only powered by JavaScript. On the CD-ROM, is a complete version of Tic-Tac-Toe written in JavaScript—you versus the computer.

Figure 13.17 shows me in the middle of an action-packed game. Take a look at the source code if you get a moment. It's a true example of how JavaScript can be used as a complete programming language, not for simple tricks and features.

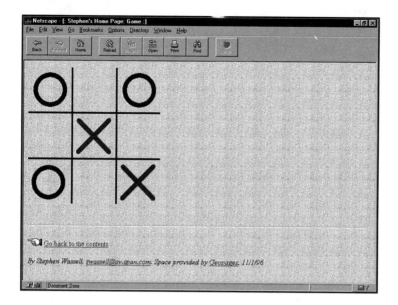

Fig. 13.17
I can never beat
the computer.

Where To Go for More JavaScript Information

Although you've seen many different examples of how you can use JavaScript in your Web page, this chapter is literally the tip of the iceberg. JavaScript is a fully functional, robust scripting language—as complex as many programming languages. Although it's easy to add a few JavaScript commands to your Web pages, being a JavaScript programmer takes time and patience.

This chapter merely introduces you to how JavaScript can be used to enhance your Web pages. For additional information, check out Que's *JavaScript by Example* or *The Complete Idiot's Guide to JavaScript*—both excellent books that take you through the entire scripting language.

Additionally, the WWW is a virtual hotbed of JavaScript information. The following are some of my favorite sites:

- JavaWorld:

     http://www.javaworld.com
- Verifying Form Input with JavaScript:

     http://gmccomb.com/valid.htm

- JavaScript Mailing List:

  http://www.obscure.org/javascript/

- JavaScript Resource Index:

  http://www.c2.org/~andreww/javascript/

- Gamelan Comprehensive JavaScript Index:

  http://www.gamelan.com/Gamelan.javascript.html

Fitting Java into the Netscape Puzzle

If you think JavaScript is powerful, wait until you get a closer look at regular Java! Simply put, Java is a new programming language recently developed by Sun Microsystems. Java was created to be a usable programming language that experienced C and C++ programmers would find familiar (because it is similar to those language's syntax) and run on virtually any computer platform imaginable. A sample Java applet, or program, will run on Windows, Macintosh, and UNIX computers without any changes being made to its structure. Figure 13.18 shows the Java home page at Sun Microsystems (**http://java.sun.com**).

Fig. 13.18

Not originating from the coffee bean, Java was ground out by Sun.

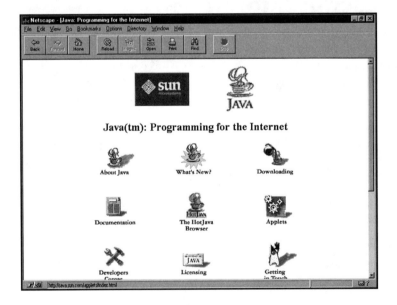

Here's how Java works. Java applets are linked to HTML pages. Whenever you visit a page attached to a Java applet, Netscape downloads the applet and then begins to run it on your personal computer. As you can see, it's the antithesis of CGI scripting—where all of the scripts/programs run on the WWW server.

This keeps your WWW server from running too many programs, and allows Java authors to take advantage of running on a personal platform. One other important element of Java is security. Java applets cannot write to your hard drive—they only reside in memory. So there's no worry of getting a virus or other security breaches when you run a Java applet with Netscape.

For a Java program to run, it needs to be compiled and executed by a separate program—on the WWW, that's Netscape. That means a single Java program will run on every computer that Netscape works on without any changes. These features—multi-platform, security, and performance—make Java an extremely powerful programming platform.

Building Java Applets

If you're interested in creating your own Java applets to run with Netscape, Sun distributes a Java Developers Kit (JDK) from the Java home page. This Developers Kit comes with thorough documentation of this new programming language, several examples and samples to build from, and important programming tools that make Java development easier and more manageable.

If you're interested in developing a Java application, visit **http:// java.sun.com/devcorner.html** to download your own free version of the Developer's Kit.

> ### Note
>
> As Java matures and is available on the WWW for a longer period of time, more and more tools become available to make it easy for Web developers to build and add Java applets to their Web pages without being an accomplished programmer.
>
> One of those such tools is Egor, a program which allows you to build Java-powered animations directly into your Web page. Created by Sausage Software (the same people who make HotDog), Egor lets you create a Java applet graphically, without even looking at a single Java-specific command (very nice). I talk about Egor in more depth in Chapter 9, "Working with Netscape Animation."
>
> Be on the lookout for Egor and other easy-to-use tools that let non-programmers create Java applets quickly and easily.

Getting More Information on Java

Because Java is a complete programming language, creating applets for it can be difficult and complex. In this book, I simply wanted to introduce you to Java and make sure you understood what it is and how it works.

There are several excellent resources available to would-be Java programmers. Your first stop should be the Java Developer's Kit that I mentioned in the previous section.

On the WWW, several valuable sites offer you tutorials and comprehensive examples:

- Gamelan's comprehensive Java listing:

     http://www.gamelan.com/

- Java Developers CyberSpace:

     http://www.hamline.edu/personal/matjohns/ webdev/java/

- Yahoo's Java listing:

     http://www.yahoo.com/Computers_and_Internet/ Languages/Java/

Additionally, check out Que's *Special Edition Using Java*, a comprehensive book about Java and Java programming. If you prefer a lesson-based tutorial style, Sams' *Teach Yourself Java Programming in 21 Days* is an excellent book for programmers and non-programmers alike. ❖

Appendixes

A   References Used in This Book

B   How To Register Your Own Domain Name

C   What's on the CD-ROM?

Appendix A

References Used in This Book

In this appendix, I've listed a comprehensive guide to all of the WWW pages that I mention and talk about throughout this entire book. I've spent some time organizing and optimizing this list to make it easier for you to use. You'll also find a version of this reference on the CD-ROM, in HTML format—meaning you can visit each site by clicking your mouse, instead of typing them in one by one. Enjoy!

The home page for this book

http://www.shafran.com/enhance

Sausage Software (home of HotDog and Egor)

http://www.sausage.com

Download Netscape Gold

http://home.netscape.com/comprod/mirror/index.html

WWW Browsers

Netscape home page (download Netscape 2.0 from here)

http://home.netscape.com

HotJava home page

http://java.sun.com

Microsoft Internet Explorer

http://www.microsoft.com/windows/ie/ie.htm

Spry's Mosaic 95

http://www.spry.com

General Internet and WWW Information

Graphic, Visualization, and Usability Center's (GVU) 4th WWW User Survey

http://www.cc.gatech.edu/gvu/user_surveys/survey-10-1995/

Web Consortium's home page

http://www.w3.org

InterNIC

http://www.internic.net

InterNIC Whois page (lookup Internet domain names)

http://rs.internic.net/cgi-bin/whois

Good Internet service and domain name registration provider

http://wworks.com

Electronic Freedom Foundation

http://www.eff.org

Links for Making Web Pages Exciting

When building and enhancing a Web page, the WWW is a fantastic resource (besides this book) for learning new techniques. In this section, I've listed many of the links that I used that will help add multimedia and images to your Web page.

Graphics and Image Information

Asymetrix's Web3D home page

http://web3d.asymetrix.com

The PNG graphic format information center

http://quest.jpl.nasa.gov/PNG/

Paint Shop Pro home page

http://www.jasc.com

Comprehensive list of colors available for your Web page

http://www.infi.net/wwwimages/colorindex.html

"User Interface Task Centered Design" by Lewis and Rieman

ftp://ftp.cs.colorado.edu/pub/cs/distribs/clewis/HCI-Design-Book/

Frequently Asked Questions about JPEG images

http://www.cis.ohio-state.edu/hypertext/faq/usenet/jpeg-faq/part2/faq.html

Multimedia and Animation for Your Web Page
Netscape's documentation for dynamic animation

http://home.netscape.com/assist/net_sites/pushpull.html

The Quicktime movie player (Apple Computer)

http://www.apple.com

Macromedia home page

http://www.macromedia.com

Shockwave download page

http://www.macromedia.com/Tools/Shockwave/sdc/Plugin/index.htm

The Macromedia gallery of cool Shockwave animations

http://www.macromedia.com/Tools/Shockwave/Gallery/index.html

Netscape Plug-Ins
Netscape's comprehensive list of plug-ins

http://home.netscape.com/comprod/products/navigator/version_2.0/plugins/index.html

Adobe Acrobat Amber plug-in

http://www.adobe.com/Amber/Index.html

Envoy rich document plug-in

http://www.twcorp.com

FIGleaf multiple image format plug-in

http://www.ct.ebt.com/

Real Audio Sound plug-in

http://www.realaudio.com/

Macromedia Shockwave

**http://www.macromedia.com/Tools/Shockwave/sdc/Plugin/
index.htm**

VDOLive integrated video plug-in

http://www.vdolive.com/newplug.htm

WebFx VRML plug-in

http://www.paperinc.com

Apple Quicktime Video plug-in

http://www.apple.com

Advanced Programming for Your Web Page

Much of this book is dedicated to showing you how to incorporate many different types of programs, scripts, and applets into your Web pages. You have already learned all about CGI, Java, and JavaScript. This section shows you several of the best places on the WWW to learn more about combining HTML and programs together under one roof.

Creating CGI Scripts

NCSA CGI scripting introduction

http://hoohoo.ncsa.uiuc.edu/docs/cgi/overview.html

Yahoo page on CGI scripts

**http://www.yahoo.com/Computers_and_Internet/Internet/
World_Wide_Web/CGI___Common_Gateway_Interface/**

CGI programmer's reference

http://www.best.com/~hedlund/cgi-faq/

CGI scripting tutorial

http://WWW.Stars.com/Seminars/

Perl scripting language home page

http://www.perl.com

Cmm scripting language home page

http://www.nombas.com

WWW security FAQ

http://www-genome.wi.mit.edu/WWW/faqs/www-security-faq.txt

CGI security FAQ

http://www.cerf.net/~paulp/cgi-security/

Matt's fantastic CGI script archive

http://worldwidemart.com/scripts/

Matt Kruse's CGI script archive for Perl scripts

http://web.sau.edu/~mkruse/www/scripts/index.html

Free Web visitor counter

http://www.digits.com

Selena Sol's Public Domain Script Archive

http://www.eff.org/~erict/Scripts

Shareware CGI scripts

http://128.172.69.106:8080/cgi-bin/cgis.html

CGI newsgroup

news:comp.infosystems.www.authoring.cgi

Important JavaScript Links

Netscape's JavaScript Web page

http://home.netscape.com/eng/mozilla/Gold/handbook/javascript/index.html

Collection of free JavaScript applets

http://www.websys.com

JavaWorld

http://www.javaworld.com

V

Appendixes

Verifying form input with JavaScript

http://gmccomb.com/valid.htm

JavaScript mailing list

http://www.obscure.org/javascript/

JavaScript resource index

http://www.c2.org/~andreww/javascript/

Gamelan comprehensive JavaScript index

http://www.gamelan.com/Gamelan.javascript.html

Good Java WWW Pages

Java home page at Sun Microsystems

http://java.sun.com

Gamelan's comprehensive Java listing

http://www.gamelan.com/

Java Developers CyberSpace

http://www.hamline.edu/personal/matjohns/webdev/java/

Yahoo's Java listing

http://www.yahoo.com/Computers_and_Internet/Languages/ Java/

Fun Stuff on the Web

As you've probably figured out, much of the WWW is about fun and games. Many Web pages are casually created and all about enjoying yourself in this new electronic world.

Besides having fun, you can learn a great deal from how other people and places build Web pages. This section shows you some of the fun and enjoyable examples that I've used throughout this book. I think you'll find them a blast to stop by and experience, and quite educational as well.

Games and Entertainment

Play Asteroids through Shockwave

http://www.macromedia.com/Gallery/Shockwave/Games/Stroids/index.html

Zoop—quite possibly the most addictive game besides Tetris

http://www.zoop.com

Dilbert home page

http://www.unitedmedia.com/comics/dilbert

Peanuts home page

http://www.unitedmedia.com/comics/peanuts

Winnie-the-Pooh home page

http://www.midtown.net/~olen/pooh

Rocky and Bullwinkle

http://mindlink.net/charles_ulrich/frostbite.html

The Case—a weekly mystery game

http://www.thecase.com/

Cool WWW Sites for Large Companies

Que's home page (the publisher of this book)

http://www.mcp.com/que

The Annex—a cool cyber site

http://www.pcworld.com/annex/

Asymetrix home page

http://www.asymetrix.com

General Motors

http://www.gm.com

Toyota

http://www.toyota.com

Magnavox

http://www.magnavox.com

Warner Brothers Online

http://www.warnerbros.com

The Disney home page

http://www.disney.com

CompuServe Incorporated (Shockwaved!)

http://www.compuserve.com

Cool Individual and Smaller Web Sites

Bill Gerrard's home page

http://ourworld.compuserve.com:80/homepages/DigitalDaze/

Clickable human skeleton

http://www.cs.brown.edu/people/art035/Bin/skeleton.html

The Columbus Pages—cool graphics

http://www.columbuspages.com

How To Register Your Own Domain Name

You're already extremely familiar with Internet domain names—even if you aren't aware of it. Internet domain names are the unique phrase that makes up every WWW and e-mail address such as **ibm.com** or **whitehouse.gov**. The Internet domain name is the "mailing" address of the Internet—the word or phrase that points to a particular site.

Throughout this entire book, I've shown you HTML examples from all over the Internet at many different domains. Now, in this appendix, it's time to show you how you can register your very own Internet domain name.

Specifically, in this appendix, you'll learn the following:

- More about domain names
- How much they cost to register
- Where to check if a particular domain name is available
- How you can register your own personal domain name
- What steps I took to register my own personal domain

What is a Domain Name?

One of the newest rages on the Internet is registering your own unique and individual Internet domain name. This trend has exploded in popularity with more and more companies and individuals registering unique domain names for themselves. Since each domain name is unique, every day fewer domain names are available for a business or individual to register and call their own.

Internet domain names are issued by InterNIC (**http://www. internic. net**), the international organization in charge of the technical backbone of the Internet (see fig. B.1). Each and every domain name must be registered through InterNIC and go through a standard application process. InterNIC also maintains a searchable database of every registered domain name so you can quickly see which domain names are available, and which have already been taken.

Fig. B.1
InterNIC is the domain name registration starting point.

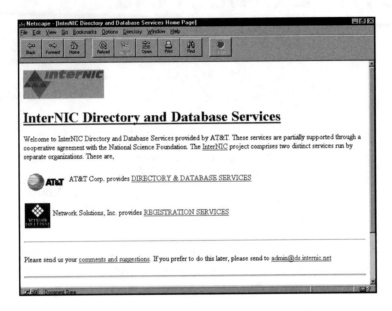

The following section will outline some of the associated issues that you might experience when you start thinking about registering your own domain name.

Why Should I Register One?

Many different companies and people register their own domain names for a variety of reasons. Following are some of the more popular reasons you might want to look into registering your own name:

- It's good publicity for a company to have its own unique Internet address.
- Visitors remember Internet domains much easier than a complicated mess of an address. It's easy to remember **www.ibm.com** in your mind, but no one will think of **www.somedomain.com/my/ company/page/here.html**.
- They're affordable and easy to register. For a reasonable startup cost (described in more detail later), you can be the proud owner of your very own domain.

■ Someone else might register your favorite domain name first. Domain names are being registered at an astronomical rate, and whoever registers a particular name first owns it forever (as long as they can pay the yearly maintenance charge and haven't registered someone else's registered trademark). Registering now is an investment many companies can't afford to miss.

Understanding the Costs

Basically, there are two costs associated with domain name registration. The first is the yearly charge that InterNIC levies for everyone across the Internet. It's $50 a year to maintain each domain name. This money goes to support the National Science Foundation's (NSF) grant to InterNIC and helps upgrade the hardware backbone of the Internet making for a faster and more reliable Internet worldwide.

The second cost is more significant. Registering a domain name means that you will actually hook up a computer to the Internet. Called an Internet or Web server, this machine must be dedicated solely to communicating with the Internet and requires a significant hardware and software investment (usually, many thousands of dollars as a minimum).

Alternatively, you can also pay someone else, an Internet Service Provider (ISP) to do basically the same thing. Instead of running your own Web server for your personal domain name, you end up paying an ISP to host your domain name on their computer. This method works wonderfully—especially for those reluctant to make a huge hardware, software, and training investment into the WWW and will run you about $15-$50 a month.

The Rash Explosion of Domain Names

Paralleling the gigantic explosion of the World Wide Web, new Internet domain names are being snapped up as fast as you can imagine. Over 20,000 new domain names are being registered each month—that's a huge number.

Because each domain name must be unique—there can only be one **cocacola.com**—soon available names may be few and far between. For most companies and individuals, the $50 yearly expense of registering each domain name is peanuts, so they register multiple domain names even if they don't plan on using them for awhile, to avoid someone else registering it instead.

Once you register a domain name, it's yours forever, as long as you can afford the $50 yearly maintenance fee. At that price, many individuals (including myself) are also registering domain names.

V

Appendixes

Check To See if Your Domain is Available

Once you've decided that you want to register your own domain name, the first step is to see if the domain you want to use is already registered. With over 200,000 existing domain names, there's a decent chance that the particular domain you want to register has already been spoken for.

To check domain name availability, InterNIC offers an online searchable database of each and every of the 200,000 existing domain names. Visit the InterNIC Whois page at **http://rs.internic.net/cgi-bin/whois** as shown in figure B.2.

Fig. B.2
Search for existing domain names here.

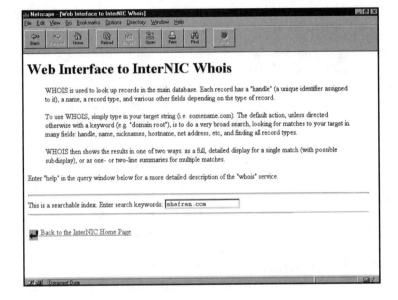

Type in the domain name you want to look up and hit the enter key. InterNIC looks at its listing of domain names and tells you whether or not the one you want has already been registered. Figure B.2 shows me looking up **shafran.com**, and figure B.3 shows the results of that search. Fortunately for me, the domain name I want to register is still available.

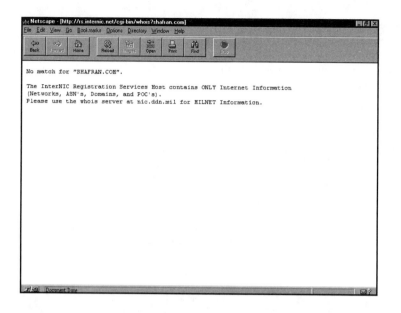

Fig. B.3
Wow, an available domain name—I better snap it up before it's gone.

Note

If the exact domain name you are looking for isn't available, try a similar word. For example, let's say you wanted to register **garden.com**. You'd quickly find out that this domain name is already registered, as is **gardens.com**, **gardener.com**, and even **gardeners.com**.

But if you have a little patience, you'd also find out that **garden1.com**, **greengarden.com**, and **lotsofgreenplants.com** are all available for you to register. Don't be discouraged if an exact domain name you want isn't available—most likely, something similar to it is.

Caution

Make sure you don't try to register a trademark as a domain name. For example, someone had registered **superbowl.com** several months before NBC and Microsoft realized that they could publicize SuperBowl XXX on the Web. As a result, the original domain name registrant was forced into giving up **superbowl.com** because he didn't own the rights to that trademarked phrase.

V

Appendixes

Registering One

Once you've found an available domain name, the next step is to start the registration process. I'm not going to step you through the entire process. Instead, I'll show you where you can fill out the application form and let you communicate directly with InterNIC for more information.

Read this section to learn how to fill out a domain name application for yourself, and how most people actually end up registering domain names.

Registering Yourself

Anyone, company or individual, can register a domain name for themselves.

To fill out the Internet domain name registration form online, visit **http:// rs.internic.net/cgi-bin/reg/new-domain** with your WWW browser, as shown in figure B.4.

Fig. B.4
I'm well on my way to my own domain name.

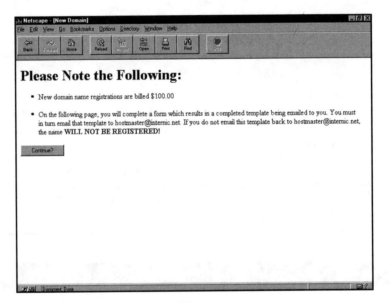

Click the Continue button to see the entire form on-screen. Follow the instructions listed there to complete your domain name registration. InterNIC will also e-mail you a blank copy of this form to fill out in your leisure and is available for assistance via e-mail at **questions@internic.net**.

> **Note**
>
> Notice how figure B.4 indicates that you've got to pay $100 to register a domain name. If you recall, a few pages ago, I said that you'll have to pay only $50 a year to maintain your particular domain name with InterNIC. This is true; however, when you register a new domain name, InterNIC requests the first two years of registration fees up front.

Paying Someone Else To Take Care of It

The other way to register a domain name is to pay someone else to do it for you. Usually the company you sign up as your Virtual Domain Host will take care of all the registration details for a minimal charge ($50-$100).

Most likely, it makes more sense to have them register your domain name anyway. Filling out the registration requires significant technical knowledge of how your Web server is set up and how it is connected and communicating with the rest of the Internet—knowledge people like you and me aren't likely to know.

How I Registered shafran.com

For this book, I investigated and registered **shafran.com** as my permanent domain name. I wanted to have my own unique address on the World Wide Web that would never change and always be around for people (like you) to visit for more information about myself and my books.

Not wanting to set up and install my own personal web server, I decided to hire another company to take care of all the details for me. I searched the InterNIC database and found out that **shafran.com** was available for registration. Armed with that knowledge, I contacted Web Works (**http://www.wworks.com**) and hired them to serve as my virtual domain host. A few weeks later, I received an e-mail message saying everything was completed and that **shafran.com** was ready to go—it was literally that easy.

Web Works charges $50 to register domain names and another $10 (that's right, I said $10) a month to host a site with one of their Internet connections. For the amount of effort required to register my own domain name, I consider it money well spent.

V

Appendixes

In case you're wondering about the **www** part of my personal URL (**http:// www.shafran.com**), that's something that is set up and customized by your virtual domain host. By default, most hosts will set it up for you auto-matically (like Web Works did for me). ❖

Appendix C
What's on the CD-ROM?

The CD-ROM bound in the back of this book has been carefully prepared and researched so you'll have a variety of tools and examples to assist you in enhancing your Web pages. The entire CD has been linked with HTML Web pages so it can be accessed via your favorite browser (there's even a browser included, in case you need one). You'll find the Web pages have links to the software programs on the disk, the graphics files and examples, and to actual Web sites on the World Wide Web (you'll need an Internet connection to use these).

Starting up the CD is simple. From within your browser, load the file LOADME.HTM. The first page will lead you to the next pages, whereupon you can choose what you'd like to see next. At the bottom of the page will always be a Back button to return you to the selections page.

Keep in mind that some of the programs you'll see on the CD are beta versions, meaning that they're a work in progress—functional, but not all of the bugs are worked out or all the features active yet. We offer them so you can sample what their technology has to offer; and if you're sufficiently tantalized, you can download the latest version from the Web. But first, cut your Internet connect charges by using the version on the CD.

> **Note**
>
> Many of the programs on the CD are shareware—offered free for a period of time so you may evaluate them and decide if you would like to use them. If so, you can register with the software company, pay a fee, and receive a fully working version and possibly other perks. Please respect the efforts of the software authors who have toiled over a hot monitor late into the night to bring you a quality program at a reasonable price.

I've highlighted many special programs and examples on the CD-ROM that I think you'll find particularly useful. At the end of the appendix, there is a complete list of all the files and programs you'll find on the CD-ROM.

This CD-ROM is virtually 100 percent full—that is, hundreds of megs of files, programs, and examples all designed around creating Web pages. Enjoy the collection; we've spent a lot of time making it the best it could be.

Programs and Examples Used in This Book

This collection—including programs, samples, and information—is the cream of the crop on this CD-ROM and you should take some time exploring them and looking in the relevant sections of the book.

HotDog HTML Editor

HotDog was mentioned throughout the book for one simple reason: it's one of the best and easiest tools for creating and managing Web pages. The program you'll find on the CD is the standard version which is upgradable to the Professional version (click the link to Sausage Software for more information). It's solid and reliable, and will serve you for years to come.

You can reach HotDog by clicking the Tools link from the main HTML page that references the entire CD-ROM. Its location on the CD-ROM is \TOOLS\HOTDOG\.

Paint Shop Pro

There are a lot of shareware programs available for manipulating graphics, but almost none for creating them from scratch. Paint Shop Pro is a fully featured paint program that also excels at image manipulation, making it the program of choice for creating your Web page graphics. On the CD-ROM, you'll find a 16-bit (Windows 3.1) and a 32-bit (Windows 95) version of Paint Shop Pro.

You can reach Paint Shop Pro by clicking the Tools link from the main HTML page that references the entire CD-ROM. Its location on the CD-ROM is \TOOLS\PSP\16 and \TOOLS\PSP\32.

MapThis!

Those lovely image maps you see on other Web pages can be difficult to create unless you have a program such as MapThis!. It's an excellent utility for setting up the links from different areas of your image. MapThis! is freeware and can be run directly from the CD-ROM.

You can reach MapThis! by clicking the Tools link from the main HTML page that references the entire CD-ROM. Its location on the CD-ROM is `\TOOLS\MAPTHIS\`.

Cmm Scripting Language

When I talked about CGI, I mentioned a new programming language that CGI developers will want to take a hearty look at—Cmm. Included on this CD-ROM, Cmm is a "lazy man's C" and has lots of tools, samples, and examples for budding CGI programmers.

You can reach Cmm by clicking the Tools link from the main HTML page that references the entire CD-ROM. Its location on the CD-ROM is `\TOOLS\CMM\`.

Egor Animator

Another product from Sausage Software, Egor allows you to build seamless Java animations without any programming. A shareware program, Egor must be registered before you can use animations on your Web pages.

You can reach Egor by clicking the Tools link from the main HTML page that references the entire CD-ROM. Its location on the CD-ROM is `\TOOLS\EGOR\`.

Netscape Plug-Ins

On the CD-ROM, you'll find a directory full of the latest Netscape plug-ins, many of which were mentioned earlier in this book. If you're going to set up your pages to use plug-in features, you'll need these to see if your page works for your visitors!

Some of the plug-ins that you can expect to find on the CD-ROM include the following and many more:

- Adobe Amber
- Macromedia Shockwave
- RealAudio
- Xing Video
- Inso Word Viewer

You can reach the list of Netscape plug-ins by clicking the Plug-ins link from the main HTML page that references the entire CD-ROM.

Collections of Images and Graphics

When creating Web pages, one of the most valuable tools in your arsenal is a robust collection of creative images, buttons, bars, and graphics. I've literally scoured all over the world to find impressive samples and collections of graphics that you can use on your Web page. All of the images found on this CD-ROM are royalty free and can be used and modifed however you like for your Web page.

In fact, I have so many different collections of graphics, I can't even name them all here. You can see all of them from the CD-ROM by clicking the Graphics link from the main HTML page that references the entire CD-ROM.

Sound Clips and Sample Backgrounds

Jawai Software is a multimedia company that specializes in creating cool special effects. We've included several sounds from them on the CD-ROM. You can experience the sounds by clicking the Sounds link from the main HTML page that references the entire CD-ROM. Its location on the CD-ROM is \JAWAI.

Video Clips

One of the crown jewels of this CD-ROM is over 90 megs of impressive video clips (in Windows AVI format) that you can use however you like. Put together by FourPalms Software, I have over 20 different video clips in two different resolutions.

You can watch and use these video clips directly from the CD by clicking the Video link from the main HTML page that references the entire CD-ROM. Its location on the CD-ROM is \VIDEO.

Example Files

Throughout this book, you have probably noticed the many practical and useful examples that I created when discussing a new topic. Whether it is working with frames or building JavaScript applets, I have included virtually all of my sample files on the CD-ROM.

Each chapter that has examples has its own index of examples. You can see how the examples look in Netscape for yourself, pick apart the HTML files, and look behind the scenes.

You can reach the example files by clicking the Examples link from the main HTML page that references the entire CD-ROM.

Sample Scripts

Besides all of the samples, I also put together a large collection of existing CGI scripts that can be used immediately on Web pages. These scripts are discussed in detail in the book.

You can find the CGI sample scripts on the CD-ROM by clicking the Samples link from the main HTML page that references the entire CD-ROM. Its location on the CD-ROM is \SCRIPTS.

References Used in This Book

Appendix A in this book is a useful collection of links that any Web developer, new or experienced, will find useful. It is a list of all the sites on the WWW that I mentioned somewhere in this book. I've converted it into HTML format so you can directly reference each of those sites while browsing in Netscape—that's so you don't have to type in a URL for every spot you want to visit.

Click the References link from the main HTML page to see the list of references online.

More Useful Tools for Web Developers

Besides the many tools mentioned in this book, there are even more available for you on this CD-ROM. Many of these tools are optimized specifically for Web developers and users. The following is a shortened list of some of my favorites that I didn't get to talk about in the book:

- **HTML Index**—Traces and reports files and links—great for managing and documenting a Web site without using HotDog Pro. Additionally, there are several other tools from the same author.

- **Katalog Master**—Another useful tool for managing and cataloging many Web pages and their embedded images and multimedia files.

- **WebForms**—The creation of a Web page form can be a daunting task without a program such as WebForms which makes it simple and easy. WebForms shows you how to make forms in a different way than I described in the book and is easy to use and manage—it's a must-see.

- **Color Machine**—A simple program, Color Machine lets you graphically pick colors from a complete listing and find the right hexadecimal combination for your Web page.

A Complete Listing of Software on the CD-ROM

For those of you who want to know what else is available, there's a lot of other software on the CD. You might find that you prefer some of them to the programs mentioned in this book. Many of them are useful WWW tools

V

Appendixes

and browsers, while you'll also find important file management and general Internet tools.

World Wide Web Browsers and Utilities

The following Web browsers and utilities are available on the attached CD-ROM:

- Microsoft Internet Explorer
- Microsoft Virtual Explorer
- Hot Java
- I-Comm
- Indexer
- Fountain
- HomeSpace Builder
- WebWatch

HTML Editors and Utilities

The following HTML editors and utilities are available on the attached CD-ROM:

- Color Wizard
- Color Manipulator
- EasyHelp
- HotDog
- HTML Assistant for Windows
- HTML Author
- HTML Easy Pro
- HTML Notepad
- HTML Writer
- HTMLed
- Kenn Nesbitt's WebEdit
- Live MarkUp
- Web Spinner
- Web Wizard: The Duke of URL
- Webber
- WebEdit

- WebForms
- WebWebMania

Multimedia Editors and Viewers

The following multimedia editors and viewers are available on the attached CD-ROM:

- Adobe's Acrobat Reader
- ACDSee
- CoolEdit
- Drag and View
- GraphX Viewer
- LView Pro for Windows 95
- MapThis!
- Midi Gate
- Mod4Win
- MPEGPLAY
- Paint Shop Pro
- PolyView
- QuickTime Player
- QuickTime VR Player
- Real Audio
- Streamworks
- VuePrint
- Web Image
- Wham
- WinJpeg
- WinECJ
- WPLANY

Internet Tools

The following general Internet tools are available on the CD-ROM:

- WS FTP
- NewsExpress
- WIRC
- FTP-IC95

V

Appendixes

Important File Management Tools

The following file management tools are available on the CD-ROM:

- WinZip
- UUCode
- WinCode
- BinHex

Index

video, 226-227
PreVu MPEG, 226-227
QuickTime, 226
VDOLive, 227
PNG (Portable Network Graphics)
graphics, 153
PNG file extension, 214
pornography, 79-80, 285
Portable Document Format extension, *see* **PDF**
PPM file extension, 214
presentation plug-ins, 216-220
previewing HTML code, 45-46
PreVu MPEG, 226-227
PreVu Web site, 226-227
programming language for CGI, 235-236
programs, CGI, *see* **CGI scripts**
progressive JPEG files, 151-152
Project Manager dialog box, 70
Project Name dialog box, 71
projects
closing, 72-73
creating, 69-71
opening, 72-73
reporting, 73
uploading, 74
publishing Web pages, 42-44

Q-R

Que home page, 18

radio buttons on forms, 260
RealAudio, 220-221
adding to Web pages, 222-223
downloading, 221-222
setting up WWW server, 222
RealAudio Encoder, 223
RealAudio Web site, 222-223
recursive frames, 126
references, CGI, 235
registering Internet domain names, 305-307, 310-311
reporting projects, 73
Reset button for forms, 264
resolution of screens, graphics display considerations, 133
resources
Java, 294
JavaScript, 291-292
CGI Scripts, 302-304

VRML, 228
Web sites
CGI Scripts, 300-301
JavaScript, 301-302
WWW/Internet, 298
right-clicking mouse button, backing up to previous frame, 112
rows, creating with frames, 115

S

Sausage Software, 293
Egor the Animator program, 194
home page, 8
Web site, 297
saving CGI scripts, 239
scanners for graphics, 146-147
screens and resolution, graphics display considerations, 133
<SCRIPT> tag, JavaScript commands, 275
scripting languages, CGI, 235-236
scroll bars for frames, 121
scrollable list boxes, 262
SCROLLING keyword, <FRAME> tag, 121
scrolling text across pages, <MARQUEE> tag, 100
secure transactions, 34
security and Java, 293
SELECT buttons on forms, 261-263
<SELECT> tag, 261
separating and organizing text on Web pages with boxes and lines, 53
Serial Line Input Protocol/ Point-to-Point Protocol, *see* **SLIP/PPP**
Server Push animation, 182-183
Server Push/Client Pull animation, 178
Server Side Includes, *see* **SSI**
server-side image maps, 158
servers, 180
see also WWW servers
Settings dialog box, 164
SHAPE keyword, <AREA> tag, maps, 169

shareware, 33
Shockwave program, 18, 220
animations, example construction, 191-194
interactive presentations with Director program, 193
Shockwave Web site, 220
simple lines with <HR> tag, 53
sites
clip art graphics, 138
Web
Andy Shafran's, 29
Enhancing Netscape Web Pages book site, 10
HotDog, 8
Java, 8
managing, 44
Macromedia, 18
Microsoft, 20
Netscape, 8
Warner Brothers, 15
see also home pages
six-character codes for colors, 96
sizes
fonts on Web pages, 90
headlines, 53
titles, 53
skeleton Web site, 160
Skinner, Chris, Web site, 289
sliding text, 101
SLIP/PPP (Serial Line Input Protocol/Point-to-Point Protocol), running HotFTP, 74
<SMALL> tag, smaller text, 88
sorting information with frames, 108
sounds
creating with Toolvox, 225-228
playing with Toolvox, 224
Web pages, 55-56
special characters in text, 98
splitting home pages into frames, 57
Spry home page, 21
square shaped boxes, 53
SRC keyword, <EMBED> tag, 205
SRC= keyword, <SCRIPT>tag, 275
SSI (Server Side Includes), 233
configuring WWW servers, 237-239
visitor counter scripts, 246

Y-Z

A V I A C O M SERVICE

The Information SuperLibrary™

Bookstore

Search

What's New

Reference

Software

Newsletter

Company Overviews

Yellow Pages

Internet Starter Kit

HTML Workshop

Win a Free T-Shirt!

Macmillan Computer Publishing

Site Map

Talk to Us

CHECK OUT THE BOOKS IN THIS LIBRARY.

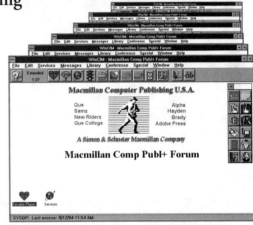

Complete and Return this Card
for a *FREE* Computer Book Catalog

Thank you for purchasing this book! You have purchased a superior computer book written expressly for your needs. To continue to provide the kind of up-to-date, pertinent coverage you've come to expect from us, we need to hear from you. Please take a minute to complete and return this self-addressed, postage-paid form. In return, we'll send you a free catalog of all our computer books on topics ranging from word processing to programming and the internet.

Mr. ☐   Mrs. ☐   Ms. ☐   Dr. ☐

Name (first) ☐☐☐☐☐☐☐☐☐☐☐☐   (M.I.) ☐   (last) ☐☐☐☐☐☐☐☐☐☐☐☐☐☐☐☐☐☐

Address ☐☐☐☐☐☐☐☐☐☐☐☐☐☐☐☐☐☐☐☐☐☐☐☐☐☐☐☐

City ☐☐☐☐☐☐☐☐☐☐☐☐☐☐☐   State ☐☐   Zip ☐☐☐☐☐ ☐☐☐☐

Phone ☐☐☐ ☐☐☐ ☐☐☐☐   Fax ☐☐☐ ☐☐☐ ☐☐☐☐

Company Name ☐☐☐☐☐☐☐☐☐☐☐☐☐☐☐☐☐☐☐☐☐☐☐☐☐☐

E-mail address ☐☐☐☐☐☐☐☐☐☐☐☐☐☐☐☐☐☐☐☐☐☐☐☐☐☐

1. Please check at least (3) influencing factors for purchasing this book.

Front or back cover information on book .... ☐
Special approach to the content .... ☐
Completeness of content .... ☐
Author's reputation .... ☐
Publisher's reputation .... ☐
Book cover design or layout .... ☐
Index or table of contents of book .... ☐
Price of book .... ☐
Special effects, graphics, illustrations .... ☐
Other (Please specify): _____ ☐

How did you first learn about this book?

Saw in Macmillan Computer Publishing catalog .... ☐
Recommended by store personnel .... ☐
Saw the book on bookshelf at store .... ☐
Recommended by a friend .... ☐
Received advertisement in the mail .... ☐
Saw an advertisement in: _____ ☐
Read book review in: _____ ☐
Other (Please specify): _____ ☐

How many computer books have you purchased in the last six months?

This book only .... ☐   3 to 5 books .... ☐
books .... ☐   More than 5 .... ☐

4. Where did you purchase this book?

Bookstore .... ☐
Computer Store .... ☐
Consumer Electronics Store .... ☐
Department Store .... ☐
Office Club .... ☐
Warehouse Club .... ☐
Mail Order .... ☐
Direct from Publisher .... ☐
Internet site .... ☐
Other (Please specify): _____ ☐

5. How long have you been using a computer?

☐ Less than 6 months   ☐ 6 months to a year
☐ 1 to 3 years   ☐ More than 3 years

6. What is your level of experience with personal computers and with the subject of this book?

	With PCs	With subject of book
New	☐	☐
Casual	☐	☐
Accomplished	☐	☐
Expert	☐	☐

Source Code ISBN: 0-7897-0790-x

7. Which of the following best describes your job title?

- Administrative Assistant .... ☐
- Coordinator .... ☐
- Manager/Supervisor .... ☐
- Director .... ☐
- Vice President .... ☐
- President/CEO/COO .... ☐
- Lawyer/Doctor/Medical Professional .... ☐
- Teacher/Educator/Trainer .... ☐
- Engineer/Technician .... ☐
- Consultant .... ☐
- Not employed/Student/Retired .... ☐
- Other (Please specify): _____ ☐

8. Which of the following best describes the area of the company your job title falls under?

- Accounting .... ☐
- Engineering .... ☐
- Manufacturing .... ☐
- Operations .... ☐
- Marketing .... ☐
- Sales .... ☐
- Other (Please specify): _____ ☐

9. What is your age?

- Under 20 .... ☐
- 21-29 .... ☐
- 30-39 .... ☐
- 40-49 .... ☐
- 50-59 .... ☐
- 60-over .... ☐

10. Are you:

- Male .... ☐
- Female .... ☐

11. Which computer publications do you read regularly? (Please list)

_____
_____
_____
_____
_____
_____
_____
_____
_____
_____

Comments: _____
_____
_____

Fold here and scotch-tape to mail.

Licensing Agreement

By opening this package, you are agreeing to be bound by the following:

This software product is copyrighted, and all rights are reserved by the publisher and author. You are licensed to use this software on a single computer. You may copy and/or modify the software as needed to facilitate your use of it on a single computer. Making copies of the software for any other purpose is a violation of the United States copyright laws.

This software is sold *as is* without warranty of any kind, either expressed or implied, including but not limited to the implied warranties of merchantability and fitness for a particular purpose. Neither the publisher nor its dealers or distributors assumes any liability for any alleged or actual damages arising from the use of this program. (Some states do not allow for the exclusion of implied warranties, so the exclusion may not apply to you.)